THE UNITED STATES AND THE KOREAN PENINSULA IN THE 21ST CENTURY

The United States and the Korean Peninsula in the 21st Century

Edited by

TAE-HWAN KWAK
*Eastern Kentucky University, USA
and Kyungnam University, Seoul, Korea*

and

SEUNG-HO JOO
University of Minnesota-Morris, USA

LONDON AND NEW YORK

First published 2006 by Ashgate Publishing

Reissued 2018 by Routledge
2 Park Square, Milton Park, Abingdon, Oxon, OX14 4RN
605 Third Avenue, New York, NY 10017

First issued in paperback 2021

Routledge is an imprint of the Taylor & Francis Group, an informa business

© Tae-Hwan Kwak and Seung-Ho Joo 2006

Tae-Hwan Kwak and Seung-Ho Joo have asserted their right under the Copyright, Designs and Patents Act, 1988, to be identified as the editors of this work.

All rights reserved. No part of this book may be reprinted or reproduced or utilised in any form or by any electronic, mechanical, or other means, now known or hereafter invented, including photocopying and recording, or in any information storage or retrieval system, without permission in writing from the publishers.

A Library of Congress record exists under LC control number: 2006003909

Notice:
Product or corporate names may be trademarks or registered trademarks, and are used only for identification and explanation without intent to infringe.

Publisher's Note
The publisher has gone to great lengths to ensure the quality of this reprint but points out that some imperfections in the original copies may be apparent.

Disclaimer
The publisher has made every effort to trace copyright holders and welcomes correspondence from those they have been unable to contact.

ISBN 13: 978-0-815-39831-8 (hbk)
ISBN 13: 978-1-351-14508-4 (ebk)
ISBN 13: 978-1-138-35763-1 (pbk)

DOI: 10.4324/9781351145084

Contents

List of Figures   *vi*
List of Tables   *vii*
Notes on Contributors   *ix*

Chapter 1	Introduction *Tae-Hwan Kwak and Seung-Ho Joo*	1
Chapter 2	The Six-Party Nuclear Talks and the Korean Peninsula Peace Regime Initiative: A Framework for Implementation *Tae-Hwan Kwak*	15
Chapter 3	US–ROK Relations: The Political–Diplomatic Dimension *Seung-Ho Joo*	39
Chapter 4	Korea, the US, China and Japan: The Rise of Asian Regionalism *Claude E. Barfield and Jason Bolton*	61
Chapter 5	The Realignment of USFK and the US–ROK Alliance in Transition *Seong-Ryoul Cho*	99
Chapter 6	Assessing the Present and Charting the Future of US–DPRK Relations: The Political–Diplomatic Dimension of the Nuclear Confrontation *Bruce E. Bechtol, Jr*	115
Chapter 7	US–DPRK Relations: The Nuclear Issue *Edward A. Olsen*	139
Chapter 8	Restraining the Hegemon: North Korea, the US and Asymmetrical Deterrence *Terence Roehrig*	163
Chapter 9	Stability with Uncertainties: US–China Relations and the Korean Peninsula *Fei-Ling Wang*	185

Index   *205*

List of Figures

Figure 4.1	Korea's total trade	64
Figure 4.2	Korea 1996–2004 imports: Nation or bloc source contribution	68
Figure 4.3	Korea 1996–2004 exports: Nation or bloc source contribution	70
Figure 4.4	China's production response to trade and FDI inflows: 1985–2004	76
Figure 4.5	Korea's trade with China: 1996–2004	78
Figure 4.6	Total regional (Asia) trade as percentage of total trade	90
Figure 4.7	ASEAN+4: Regional import and export percentage of total world import and export	91
Figure 4.8	Intraregional total trade (ASEAN+4) as percentage of East Asia's total world trade	91

List of Tables

Table 2.1	A comprehensive roadmap for the KPRI	18
Table 2.2	Contents of six-party joint statement (September 19, 2005)	24
Table 2.3	Three-phase roadmap for denuclearization on the Korean peninsula	27
Table 4.1	Progress of regionalism in East Asia	62
Table 4.2	Korea balance of trade, selected years: 1960–2004 (000s USD)	63
Table 4.3	Korea per annum total trade: 1996–2004 (000s USD)	64
Table 4.4	Korea per annum imports: 1996–2004, selected blocs and nations (000s USD)	65
Table 4.5	Percentage of total per annum import	65
Table 4.6	Korea per annum exports: 1996–2004, selected blocs and nations (000s USD)	66
Table 4.7	Percentage of total per annum export	66
Table 4.8	Nation/bloc source of Korea imports: 1980, 1990, 2000, 2004 (000s USD)	67
Table 4.9	Nation/bloc source of Korea exports: 1980, 1990, 2000, 2004 (000s USD)	69
Table 4.10	Korea's bilateral US trade relationship: 1980-2004 (000s USD)	71
Table 4.11	Republic of Korea exports to the US: 1996, 2000, 2004	73
Table 4.12	Republic of Korea imports from the US: 1996, 2000, 2004	75
Table 4.13	Republic of Korea exports to China: 1996, 2000, 2004	80
Table 4.14	Republic of Korea imports from China: 1996, 2000, 2004	81
Table 4.15	Republic of Korea exports to Japan: 1996, 2000, 2004	83
Table 4.16	Republic of Korea imports from Japan: 1996, 2000, 2004	85
Table 4.17	Republic of Korea exports to ASEAN: 1996, 2000, 2004	86
Table 4.18	Republic of Korea imports from ASEAN: 1996, 2000, 2004	88
Table 4.19	Total Asia trade and intraregional trade	89
Table 4.20	Effects of various Asian trade agreement formations on Korea and US welfare and trade	95
Table 5.1	Proportions of South Korea's trade with the US, China and Japan (%)	102
Table 5.2	Differences between the ROK and US in relation to the alliance	109

Notes on Contributors

Editors

Tae-Hwan Kwak is Professor Emeritus of International Relations, Eastern Kentucky University; former President of Korea Institute for National Unification (KINU); former Director of the Institute for Far Eastern Studies, Kyungnam University. Dr. Kwak, a specialist in East Asian affairs, international politics and foreign policy, and currently visiting professor at the Graduate School of North Korean Studies, Kyungnam University (Seoul, Korea), is the author of *In Search for Peace and Unification on the Korean Peninsula* (Seoul Press, 1986), and *The Korean Peninsula in World Politics* (Seoul Press, 1999, in Korean). He is the editor and co-editor of 24 books, including *The Korean Peace Process and the Four Powers* (Ashgate, 2003), *Korea in the 21st Century* (Nova Science, 2001), and *The Major Powers of Northeast Asia: Seeking Peace and Security* (Lynne Rienner, 1996). Dr. Kwak has contributed more than 60 book chapters and published more than 200 articles on Korean unification and four major powers' foreign policies toward the Korean peninsula. Dr. Kwak was editor-in-chief of the *International Journal of Korean Unification Studies* and *Asian Perspective*. He is a regular columnist for *Local Self-Government* (*Jibangjachi* in Korean) and freelance for Korean daily newspapers, monthly magazines, and the Internet.

Seung-Ho Joo is Associate Professor of Political Science, The University of Minnesota, Morris. He has held visiting positions at six universities in the US and Korea, including The Pennsylvania State University, Norwich University, and Yonsei University (Korea). His research interest areas include Russian foreign and security policy, Russo-Korean relations, and Korean foreign relations. Dr. Joo is the author of *Gorbachev's Foreign Policy Toward the Korean Peninsula, 1985-1991: Reform and Policy* (Edwin Mellen, 2000) and co-editor of *Korea in the 21st Century* (Nova Science, 2001) and *The Korean Peace Process and the Four Powers* (Ashgate, 2003). He has authored over 40 book chapters and journal articles, with the latter appearing in *Pacific Affairs*, *World Affairs*, *Journal of Northeast Asian Studies*, *American Asian Review*, *Comparative Strategy*, *Arms Control*, and *The Korean Journal of Defense Analysis*. He is currently completing a book manuscript on *Russia and Korea, 1992–2003*. He is Associate Editor for North America of *Pacific Focus* and was North American Editor of the *International Journal of Korean Unification Studies* (1999–2000) and a Distinguished Research Fellow, Korea Institute for National Unification (1999–2000).

Contributors

Claude E. Barfield is Director of Science and Technology Policy Studies of The American Enterprise Institute. A former consultant to the office of the United States Trade Representative, Claude Barfield researches international trade policy (including trade policy in China and East Asia), the World Trade Organization (WTO), intellectual property, science and technology policy. His many books include *Free Trade, Sovereignty, and Democracy: The Future of the World Trade Organization (AEI Press, 2001),* in which he identifies challenges to the WTO and to the future of trade liberalization. Among his other most recent publications is: *High-tech Protectionism: the Irrationality of antidumping Laws* (AEI Press, 2003).

Bruce E. Bechtol, Jr. is Associate Professor of International Relations at the Marine Corps Command and Staff College in Quantico, Virginia. Prior to joining the faculty at Quantico, he was Assistant Professor of National Security Studies at the Air Command and Staff College at Maxwell Air Force Base, Alabama, from 2003–05. He received his PhD in National Security Studies from the Union Institute, Cincinnati, Ohio. He also holds a Master of Arts in International Affairs from Catholic University in Washington, DC, and a Master of Military Studies from the US Marine Corps Command and Staff College (Distinguished Graduate) in Quantico, Virginia. Prior to joining the faculty of the Air Command and Staff College, Dr. Bechtol was employed by the Defense Intelligence Agency, serving as the Senior Analyst for Northeast Asia with the Directorate for Intelligence, Joint Chiefs of Staff in the Pentagon from 1997 to 2003. Dr. Bechtol is the author of *Avenging the General Sherman: The 1871 Battle of Kang Hwa Do* (Marine Corps University Foundation, 2002) and a contributing author of *Divided Korea: Longing for Reunification* (North Park University Press, 2004). His writing has also appeared in, among other publications, the *International Journal of Korean Studies*, the *Korea Observer*, *Korean Quarterly*, the *International Journal of Korean Unification Studies*, *Pacific Focus*, the *Air and Space Power Journal*, and *Occasional Papers, the Journal of the Korean American Historical Society*. He is the former editor of the *Defense Intelligence Journal* (2004–05) and sits on the Editorial Advisory Board of the *East Asian Review*.

Jason Bolton is currently a Trade and Industry Analyst at the United States Department of Commerce, Bureau of Industry and Security, Office of Strategic Industries and Economic Security. He holds a Master of Business Administration (MBA) from Case Western Reserve University in Cleveland, Ohio and a Master of International Management (MIM) from Thunderbird in Phoenix, Arizona. Jason is also currently enrolled in a part-time Master of Liberal Studies (MALS) program at Georgetown University, specializing in defense industrial base programs, international trade, and national security policy.

Seong-Ryoul Cho is Senior Research Fellow at the Research Institute for International Affairs, Seoul, Korea. Prior to joining RIIA, he was a researcher at the Institute for National Security (INSP) in Korea, a Visiting Fellow at Tokyo University, and a Visiting Fellow at Keio University in Japan. He holds a BS in Chemical Engineering from Seoul National University and an MA and a PhD in political science from Sungkyunkwan University, Korea. He has contributed numerous articles and chapters on contemporary military and international issues in Northeast Asia, including *US Forces Korea: Retrospect and Prospect* (in Korean, Hanul Publishing, 2003).

Edward A. Olsen is Professor of National Security Affairs at the Naval Postgraduate School (NPS), Monterey California. Prior to joining the NPS faculty in 1980, he was a political analyst on Korea and Japan at the US Department of State, Bureau of Intelligence & Research (INR). His most recent books are: *US National Defense for the Twenty-First Century; The Grand Exit Strategy* (Frank Cass, 2002), *Toward Normalizing US–Korea Relations: In Due Course?* (Lynne Rienner, 2002), the latter's expanded Korean translation *Hanmi kwangae ui sae jipyung* (New Horizons of US–Korea Relations), (Ingansarang, 2003); and *Korea, A Divided Nation* (Praeger Security International, 2005).

Terence Roehrig is Associate Professor in the National Security Decision Making Department, Naval War College, Newport, Rhode Island. He received his PhD from the University of Wisconsin-Madison and is the author of two books, *From Deterrence to Engagement: The U.S. Defense Commitment to South Korea* (Lexington Books, 2006) and *The Prosecution of Former Military Leaders in Newly Democratic Nations: The Cases of Argentina, Greece, and South Korea* (McFarland Press, 2002). He has also published articles and book chapters on North Korea's nuclear weapons program, Korean security issues, human rights, and transitional justice.

Fei-Ling Wang is a professor at The Sam Nunn School of International Affairs, Georgia Institute of Technology, Atlanta, Georgia. He taught at the US Military Academy (West Point), guest-lectured at 15 other universities in several countries, and held visiting and adjunct positions in three universities in Singapore and China. In 2005–06, he is an International Affairs Fellow of the Council on Foreign Relations. Wang is the author of four books: *Organizing through Division and Exclusion: China's Hukou System* (Stanford University Press, 2005), *Zoujin Xidian Junxiao* (US Military Academy at West Point) Chinese Youth Press, 2004), *Institutions and Institutional Change in China: Premodernity and Modernization* (Macmillan & St. Martin's, 1998) and *From Family to Market: Labor Allocation in Contemporary China* (Rowman & Littlefield, 1998). He has co-edited two books, authored two monographs and published over 50 book chapters and journal articles in several languages and many countries. Some of his articles have been published in journals such as *The China Quarterly*, *The Journal of Contemporary China*, *Harvard*

International Review, International Politics, Problems of Post-Communism, The Washington Quarterly, and *Pacific Affairs* (Canada).

Chapter 1
Introduction

Tae-Hwan Kwak and Seung-Ho Joo

In the post-Cold War era, US relations with the two Korean states – the Republic of Korea (ROK or South Korea) and the Democratic People's Republic of Korea (DPRK or North Korea) – are undergoing drastic and profound changes. The 9/11 terrorist attacks on American cities were a watershed in US–Korea relations. President George W. Bush's grand strategy of the global war on terrorism and non-proliferation of the weapons of mass destruction (WMD) had immediate and critical repercussions on US policy toward the Korean peninsula. The Bush doctrine of preemptive war, the second North Korean nuclear crisis, the future of the US–ROK alliance and US forces in Korea (USFK), the rise of anti-American sentiments in South Korea, deepening economic and cultural ties between the US and the ROK, continuing inter-Korean cooperation and exchanges all intermingled and intersected, impacting and reshaping US relations with the two Koreas. US–ROK relations in political, security, and economic spheres are now in flux. Old ties are becoming outdated or inadequate; new ties have not yet firmed up. What are the issues, problems, and future prospects of US relations with the two Korean states? These are the questions the chapters in this volume will address.

Even in the post-Cold War era, the Korean peninsula remains an area of crucial importance in overall US geo-strategic and geo-economic calculations. As ROK's close ally, the US still maintains 37,500 troops in Korea to deter North Korea's aggression. North–South Korean relations have improved remarkably since the first inter-Korean summit meeting in June 2000. the North Korean nuclear issue, however, poses a grave threat to lasting peace and security in the Korean peninsula and Northeast Asia. The DPRK, a communist state based on *juche* (self-reliance) ideology, officially declared in February 2005 that it already owned nuclear weapons and it would suspend its participation in the six-party talks on the North Korean nuclear issue. The six-party nuclear talks were held four times in 2003–05 to resolve the North Korean nuclear issue, but at the time of writing had not led to any breakthroughs. The US now must deal with nuclear armed North Korea. US–ROK relations in recent years have been peppered with frictions and tension. The US and ROK governments no longer see eye-to-eye, and disagree on the North Korean nuclear issue and the US plan to restructure its forces in Korea.

A Brief Historical Overview

The Korean peninsula was divided into the two Koreas by the US and the Soviet Union in 1945, when Korea became independent after 36 years of Japanese colonial rule. In 1948, two separate Korean states were created – the ROK in the south under the auspices of the US and the DPRK in the north with the Soviet Red Army's support. During the Korean War (1950–53), South Korea was saved from invading North Korea with a massive military intervention by the US. After the Korean War, the US–ROK mutual defense treaty was signed in October 1953 and US troops remained on Korean soil. Since then, the US–ROK alliance and US military presence in Korea served as the deterrent against North Korea's aggression and guarantor of peace and security in Northeast Asia. The US also provided generous economic aid to the ROK and served as the largest market for Korean exports, which undoubtedly contributed to ROK's rapid economic growth in the 1960s–1980s.

During the Cold War, US–ROK relations remained stable and predictable despite periodic frictions over human rights, democracy, and trade issues. US–ROK relations have long been a model alliance. As long as North Korea's military threat was genuine and US commitment to ROK's security was credible, South Korean governments were willing to accept US leadership. The ROK considered its ties with the US central to its external relations and pivotal to its own survival. The US also needed the ROK as an ally in the global crusade against Soviet expansionism and in the regional strategy for peace and stability in Northeast Asia. The two countries' national interests, however, were not identical. Since 1945, the US and the ROK periodically experienced political frictions, but their differences were downplayed and hidden from public view.

The collapse of the Soviet empire, South Korea's economic development and democratization, North Korea's nuclear threat, the rise of new political elites, and changing public perceptions and attitudes all provided the backdrop against which US–ROK political relations underwent rapid, qualitative changes in the 1990s–2000s. The ascendancy of G.W. Bush and neo-conservatives in the US and the rise of Roh Moo-Hyun and the so-called '386-generation' in South Korea further contributed to mutual distrust and tensions. In the past, frictions between the US and ROK governments were manageable, infrequent, and invisible to the public; now they are deep, frequent, and open. US–ROK political relations are now in flux. One of the peculiar changes is that nowadays neither side even pretends to hide or downplay their differences. Bilateral political discords became pronounced after G.W. Bush came to power in January 2001.

At the heart of current US–ROK frictions and distrust is the North Korean nuclear issue. In the late 1980s and early 1990s, North Korea became increasingly isolated and debilitated. The Soviet Union established formal diplomatic ties with South Korea in 1990 despite North Korea's fierce objections, and its successor state, Russia, discontinued economic and military assistance to the DPRK and renounced the 1961 Moscow–Pyongyang alliance. China remained North Korea's sole remaining ally, but it established diplomatic relations with South Korea in 1992.

Since then, Seoul–Beijing economic cooperation has risen by leaps and bounds and their cooperative political, military, and cultural ties have been forged. China–DPRK economic cooperation is now maintained on a commercial basis and China's military intervention in case of a Korean war is not guaranteed. North Korea's economic hardships combined with the disappearance of its traditional sources of aid, especially the Soviet Union, progressively reduced DPRK's conventional military capability. By the early 1990s, North Korea's nuclear weapons capability, instead of its conventional military capability, emerged as the main threat to peace and security in and around the Korean peninsula. President Kim Dae-Jung's 'sunshine policy' of flexible engagement with North Korea and the historic inter-Korean summit meeting in June 2000 substantially reduced tensions between the two Korean states, but North Korea's nuclear threat did not dissipate. Improved inter-Korean relations and the unresolved North Korean nuclear issue created the milieu in which US–ROK and US–DPRK relations evolved in the 2000s.

Presidents R. Reagan and G.H. Bush engaged North Korea in a very limited manner, which came to be known as 'smile diplomacy.' The Clinton Administration adapted to Kim Dae-Jung's sunshine policy and accommodated South Korea's engagement initiatives vis-à-vis North Korea. Before Clinton, the US rarely allowed South Korea to take a leading role on Korean issues. US relations with the two Koreas entered into a new phase with the inauguration of President G.W. Bush in January 2001. Bush did not hide his intense hatred and contempt for DPRK leader Kim Jong-Il and was bent on undoing Clinton's engagement policy vis-à-vis North Korea. In contrast to his predecessor, Bush took a hardline policy toward North Korea, and refused to accept President Clinton's approach to North Korea. He also disagreed with President Kim Dae-Jung's sunshine policy. Kim's sunshine policy and Bush's hardline policy toward North Korea collided, creating tensions and friction in US–ROK relations.

The first US–ROK summit meeting between Bush and Kim held in Washington, DC in March 2001 turned out to be a disaster. Instead of endorsing Kim's sunshine policy, Bush lectured Kim Dae-Jung about Kim Jong-Il's untrustworthiness. Bush's disrespectful treatment and open disagreement offended many South Koreans and hurt Kim Dae-Jung's ego. Subsequently, Presidents Bush and Kim 'never established much of a connection, and relations between the nations, longtime allies, have only grown worse.'[1]

The 9/11 terrorist attacks in the US further hardened Bush's stance toward North Korea. Shortly after the attacks, President Bush declared a global war on terrorism on September 20, 2001. In his January 2002 State of the Union address, Bush elaborated on the war on terrorism. He stated that the war had two great objectives, i.e. to defeat terrorism and to prevent the 'terrorists and regimes who seek chemical, biological, or nuclear weapons from threatening the United States and the world.' Bush then lumped three states – North Korea, Iran and Iraq – together as the 'axis of

---

1 Howard W. French, 'Korean Diplomacy Enters a New Era', *The New York Times*, April 20, 2003.

evil.'[2] By including North Korea in that category, he indicated that the US intended to destroy North Korea or force it to change its behavior.

During his visit to South Korea in February 2002, Bush revealed his hostile attitudes toward North Korea when he stated that he would not let the world's 'most dangerous regimes' acquire its 'most dangerous weapons.'[3] He also expressed his skepticism of North Korea's reforms. Bush, however, tried to assuage South Koreans' anxiety over a possible war when he stated that the US had no intention of attacking North Korea. Kim Dae-Jung, in contrast, reaffirmed his commitment to the sunshine policy of engaging North Korea. Kim thanked Bush for 'clarifying' any misunderstanding created by his State of the Union speech, in which he included North Korea as part of an 'axis of evil.' The two governments still maintained diplomatic decorum, but their diverging approaches to North Korea and resultant frictions were clearly visible.[4]

The Bush administration adopted a new doctrine of preemptive war in the National Security Strategy issued on September 20, 2002.[5] The new doctrine included the preemptive war (the use of force in the face of an imminent attack) as well as the preventive war (the use of force before a serious threat to the US gathers or grows over time). The preventive nature of the doctrine is well manifested in President Bush's cover letter to the September 2002 National Security Strategy, which stated: '… as a matter of common sense and self-defense, America will act against [such] emerging threats before they are fully formed.'[6]

The war on terrorism, the inclusion of North Korea in the axis of evil, and the doctrine of preemptive war raised serious concerns in the ROK government since US sanctions or military strikes on North Korea could easily lead to an all-out war in Korea, which would certainly spell unspeakable disasters for the Korean people. Bush's hardline policy toward North Korea and DPRK's inflexibility resulted in the freezing of US–North Korean relations and the suspension of the inter-Korean peace process that had been set in motion following the June 2000 inter-Korean summit.

The Bush administration was frustrated with Kim's sunshine policy toward North Korea and would have preferred the victory of a cooperative, conservative political figure in the December 2002 presidential election of South Korea. The US rooted for

---

2   David E. Sanger, 'The State of the Union Address: The Overview', *The New York Times*, January 30, 2002.

3   Elisabeth Bumiller, 'Bush Says US and China Want to See Koreas Unified', *The New York Times*, February 21, 2002; 'With Due Respect, Mr. President', *Economist*, February 23, 2002.

4   Ihlwan Moon, 'How Bush is Pushing South Koreans Apart', *Business Week*, February 25, 2002.

5   President Bush first mentioned the concept of preemptive war in his June 22, 2002 speech at West Point.

6   For the full text of the National Security Strategy, go to the website at <http://www.whitehouse.gov/nsc/nss.html>. See also Michael E. O'Hanlon, Susan E. Rice, and James B. Steinberg, 'The New National Security Strategy and Preemption', *The Brookings Institution Policy Brief*, December 2002.

the conservative, pro-American Lee Hoe-Chang of the opposition Grand National Party over the progressive, independent-minded Roh Moo-Hyun of the ruling New Millenium Party.

Roh Moo-Hyun's election as South Korea's President in December 2002 did not augur well for US–ROK relations. Roh came to power riding the tide of anti-American sentiment that was spreading across South Korea at the time and vowing an independent, nationalistic foreign policy as well as sweeping domestic reforms. Before assuming presidency, he had very limited experience in government and no experience in foreign affairs.[7] He promised to continue President Kim's sunshine policy vis-à-vis North Korea.[8]

Roh came to power at a critical time. The second crisis over the North Korean nuclear issue erupted in October 2002 when Assistant Secretary of State for East Asia and the Pacific, James Kelly, visited Pyongyang and allegedly got a confession from a senior North Korea official to a secret nuclear weapons program based on highly enriched uranium. By early 2003, the North Korean nuclear issue topped the agenda in US–ROK relations. By the time of Roh's inauguration in February 2003, the US invasion of Iraq was imminent and there was a widespread concern among South Koreans that North Korea would be the next target for US attack.

In late 2002, anti-American sentiment was spreading rapidly in South Korea. The Status of Forces Agreement (SOFA) between the US and the ROK, which stipulates the legal rights of US soldiers in Korea, is woefully lopsided when compared with similar US agreements with other countries, such as Japan and Germany. South Koreans' perception of the unfair SOFA, Bush's hardline policy toward North Korea, and US insensitivity to South Korean feelings and interests all added fuel to persistent anti-American protests.

Roh has consistently and unequivocally opposed Bush's hardline policy toward North Korea and advocated an engagement policy with North Korea. At the outset, the Roh government decided to attempt resolving the North Korean nuclear issue while continuing inter-Korean exchanges and cooperation.[9] This policy line was in direct conflict with Bush's hardline policy, which called for isolating and pressuring North Korea into abandoning its nuclear program before providing any rewards. The Bush administration is divided between the hardliners who advocate North Korea's regime change and prefer forceful means to change North Korea's behavior and

---

7   Roh had served as a National Assembly (ROK's national legislature) member for six years and as a ROK's Maritime and Fisheries Minister for six months. Born into a poor peasant family, he became a human-rights lawyer and political activists in the 1980s. He is a leftist in ideological orientation. His father-in-law died after 18 years in prison for communist activities during the Korean War. See Ihlwan Moon and Mark L. Clifford, 'The Politics of Peril: South Korea's Untested Roh Moo Hyun Faces a Bizarre and Dangerous Foreign Policy Crisis. Is He Up to It?' *Business Week*, February 24, 2003.

8   Oh Young-jin, 'Roh Takes Nation's Highest Office', *Korea Times*, February 25, 2003; and Shin Jong-rok, 'Roh Promises "Peace and Prosperity"', *Chosun Ilbo*, February 25, 2003.

9   Se-Hyun Jeong, 'Inter-Korean Relations under Policy for Peace and Prosperity', *Korea and World Affairs*, vol. 28, no. 1 (spring 2004), p. 6.

the moderates who are skeptical of Kim Jong-Il regime's immediate collapse and favor a negotiated solution to the nuclear issue. This division resulted in the lack of consistency and comprehensive strategy in the Bush administration's North Korea policy.

Frictions between the Roh and Bush governments over the North Korean nuclear issue were clearly discernable from the very beginning. Like his predecessor, President Roh initially urged direct talks between the US and the DPRK, but accepted the US position for a multilateral framework for discussing the North Korean nuclear issue. With the issue of redeployment or even withdrawal of US troops becoming increasingly salient, Roh in his inaugural address underlined the importance of the US–ROK alliance and expressed his intention to maintain an equal relationship with the US.[10]

The Bush–Roh summit in May 2003 in Washington, DC failed to narrow their differences over North Korea's nuclear crisis. At a Beijing meeting in April, North Korea declared that it already possessed nuclear weapons and that it had turned 8,000 spent nuclear fuel rods into bomb-grade plutonium. The US and South Korea shared the goal of nuclear-free North Korea, but differed on strategy. The ROK insisted that all peaceful means should be exhausted first before any sanctions or the use of force should be applied against North Korea. In contrast, the US wanted to consider all options, including economic embargo and the use of military force. Roh was elected as president, taking advantage of widespread anti-American sentiment. In the past he had even advocated the withdrawal of American troops, but as president he realized that the US–ROK alliance and US troops in Korea were essential for Korea's security and economy.

Roh's independent foreign policy with anti-American and pro-North Korean tones continued to cause tensions and friction with the Bush administration. This policy was highly divisive and controversial inside South Korea as well. ROK's National Security Council, comprising mostly leftist, former political activists who shared President Roh's ideological orientation and political agenda was the stronghold for 'independent' (or anti-American) foreign policy. ROK's Ministry of Defense and Ministry of Foreign Affairs and Trade (MOFAT) were mostly staffed with conservative, pro-American individuals. The confrontation came to a head in January 2004, when Foreign Minister Yoon Young-Kwan was fired because he was held responsible for a scandal in which some MOFAT officials criticized Roh's independent foreign policy posture (the Blue House was tipped off about these critical remarks by an informant). Pro-American officials in MOFAT criticized the Roh government for jeopardizing traditional US–ROK friendly ties. Roh fired Yoon, blaming him 'for not being able to handle and manage the ministry.' In addition, the Blue House carried out personnel changes in MOFAT on the grounds that 'some Foreign Ministry bureaucrats could not leave behind the dependent foreign policy

---

10 Inaugural Address of President Roh Moo Hyun, February 25, 2003, available at <http://www.ciaonet.org/wps/app01/app01a.pdf>.

of the past and could not fully understand the direction of the basic spirit of the new independent foreign policy.'[11]

With reelection in the November 2004 presidential election, George W. Bush will be in the White House until January 2009, and Roh Moo-Hyun will be in the Blue House until February 2008. Roh and Bush will have to deal with each other for the next two years. Bush will continue his hardline policy toward North Korea, believing that his bellicose unilateralism was vindicated with his reelection. He is now surrounded by hardliners more than ever. Colin Powell was a voice of reason in Bush's foreign policy. With his replacement as Secretary of State by Condoleezza Rice we can expect 'a squeeze on North Korea' and 'a collision with Iran.'[12] Rice's referring to North Korea as one of the 'outposts of tyranny' at her Senate confirmation hearing[13] did not bode well for US–DPRK talks and US–ROK relations. Vice President Cheney will continue to press for anything short of military invasion and Defense Secretary Rumsfeld will keep pushing for hardline measures. Continuity in national security personnel in the Bush Administration term is remarkable. North Korea is not going to be given a priority in Bush's foreign policy. He is now preoccupied with domestic issues such as social security reform and external conflicts in Iraq and Afghanistan. There are no East Asia specialists in the top leadership of the State Department. Secretary of State Rice is a Russia specialist and has limited experience with East Asia. Deputy Secretary of State Bob Zoellick has expertise in trade issues. Undersecretary for Political Affairs Nicholas Burns served as ambassador to NATO and Ambassador to Greece. Chris Hill, Assistant Secretary of State for East Asia, served most of his diplomatic career in Europe before he was recently appointed as Ambassador to Korea.[14]

President Roh is now at the height of his political power. His staunch supporters are positioned in top government positions and his ruling party is in control of the legislature. Besides, ROK's national trade union, teachers' union and courts are controlled by, or under strong influence of, Roh's supporters, who were political activists in the 1980s.[15] After Bush's reelection, senior government officials in South Korea expressed concern about US hardline policy toward North Korea.

President Roh in a Los Angeles speech in November 2004, shortly before he held summit talks with US President G.W. Bush at the Chile Asia-Pacific Economic Cooperation (APEC) summit meeting, sounded a warning against the

---

11 Anthony Faiola, 'S. Korean Foreign Minister Resigns After Dispute Over US Ties', *The Washington Post*, January 15, 2004.

12 Nicholas D. Kristof, 'The Bush Revolution', *The New York Times*, November 17, 2004.

13 Rice said: 'To be sure, in our world there remain outposts of tyranny, and America stands with oppressed people on every continent: in Cuba and Burma and North Korea and Iran and Belarus and Zimbabwe.' Pablo Bachelet, 'Rice: Cuba an "outpost of tyranny", Venezuela a "negative force"', *The Miami Herald*, January 19, 2005.

14 James B. Steinberg 'Condoleeza Rice and US Foreign Policy during the Second Term', *Chosun Ilbo*, January 18, 2005.

15 *Chosun Ilbo*, January 18, 2005.

Bush administration's hardline policy toward North Korea.[16] Roh also stated that North Korea's main concern is security and its nuclear program is for defensive purposes: 'After all, the North's nuclear issue boils down to whether we can give it security guarantees and lead it out of its current plight through reform and openness.' Washington did not hide its disagreement with Roh's speech when the State Department issued a statement: 'There are elements in President Roh's speech that we hope to have an opportunity to discuss with senior ROK officials in the near future.'[17] The North Korean nuclear issue continues to divide the US and the ROK, and will remain the main source of friction and distrust between the two allies.

North Korea's Nuclear Dilemma: What is to be Done?

The future of the six-party nuclear talks depends largely on how North Korea perceives President Bush's next move after it declared its possession of nuclear weapons. The North's nuclear weapons have to be verified. Nevertheless, the US should deal with North Korea who possesses nuclear weapons.

In his 2005 State of the Union address, President Bush avoided offensive language aimed directly at the Kim Jong-Il regime. Three years ago, he called North Korea as 'an axis of evil', along with Iran and Iraq, but this time he used more conciliatory language about North Korea: 'We are working closely with governments in Asia to convince North Korea to abandon its nuclear ambitions.'[18] Bush's remarks were still soft after reports on North Korea's alleged export of UF6 (uranium hexafluoride) to Libya were released in the *New York Times* and *Washington Post*.[19] The articles suggested North Korea had provided Libya in 2001 with nearly 2 tons of UF6 material that can be enriched to weapon-grade level. North Korea denied the charge.

The Bush administration appeared to be inducing North Korea to the stalled six-party talks. President Bush's speech reflected his will to resolve the North Korean nuclear issue in a peaceful and diplomatic way. Many predicted that North Korea would be unlikely to come to the six-party talks soon because of President Bush's harsh words about North Korea. North Korea appeared to be disappointed with the second-term Bush administration's specific responses to North Korea's preconditions for the resumption of the six-party talks.

---

16 Sim Chae-yun and Ryu Chin 'Roh Makes Efforts "To Advert" "Unfavorable" Shift in US Policy on DPRK', *The Korea Times*, November 15, 2004.

17 'US Wants Talks on Roh's Controversial Remarks on North Korea', *Yonhap*, November 18, 2004.

18 For full text, see *New York Times*, February 21, 2005.

19 David E. Sanger and William J. Broad, 'Tests Said to Tie Deal on Uranium to North Korea', *New York Times*, February 2, 2005; Glenn Kessler, 'North Korea May Have Sent Libya Nuclear Material, US Tells Allies', *Washington Post*, February 2, 2005; Glenn Kessler and Dafna Linzer, 'Nuclear Evidence Could Point To Pakistan', *Washington Post*, February 3, 2005.

In a statement issued on February 10, 2005, the DPRK Foreign Ministry announced its decision to suspend participation in the six-party talks for an indefinite period and officially declared its production of nuclear weapons to be complete.[20] This statement came as a big shock to the six parties and the world. The DPRK said that the Bush administration had clear 'intention to antagonize the DPRK and isolate and stifle it at any cost.' The DPRK urged the US to renounce its hostile policy toward North Korea and switch to a policy of peaceful coexistence. The DPRK stated that it closely watched for a policy change in President Bush's inaugural and State of the Union addresses and Secretary of State Rice's testimonies at the Senate confirmation hearing but observed that the Bush administration had not dropped its hostile policy toward North Korea. According to North Korea's commentaries, the US continued to treat North Korea as an enemy, calling it an 'outpost of tyranny.' Under the circumstances, the DPRK stated, it could not justify its participation in the negotiations of the six-party talks since it did not want to waste another four years in the same way as the past four years.

The DPRK also expressed its anger toward Japan over the Japanese abduction issue. The DPRK said that Japan persistently pursued its hostile policy toward the DPRK and it 'fabricated the issue of false remains over the "abduction issue" that had already been settled in a bid to nullify the DPRK–Japan Pyongyang Declaration and stop any process to normalize diplomatic relations with the DPRK.' The DPRK asked, 'how can we sit at the negotiating table with such a party?' The DPRK then refused to sit together with Japan at the six-party talks.

The DPRK justified its possession of nuclear weapons in terms of self-defense and as a reaction to the Bush administration's 'evermore undisguised policy to isolate and stifle the DPRK.' The DPRK emphasized that its 'principled stand to solve the issue through dialogue and negotiations and its ultimate goal to denuclearize the Korean Peninsula remains unchanged.' The DPRK clearly stated that it would be willing to come to the stalled six-party talks if the conditions for the talks were met.

The DPRK officially declared that it had produced nuclear weapons. However, its possession of nuclear weapons needs to be verified. Why, then, did the DPRK made the declaration at the time? North Korea could have been bluffing to get a better deal with the US. The DPRK has maintained that it will dismantle its nuclear programs in exchange for US security guarantees and economic assistance. If the US is willing to provide the right inducements, the DPRK will come to the six-party talks and it may bargain away its nuclear programs, including the existing nuclear weapons.

The six-party talks process is not dead yet, and it will continue. The US needs to be prepared for defining its roadmap for multilateral security guarantees and economic incentives to North Korea in exchange for North Korea's nuclear freeze to dismantle its nuclear programs. The US and the DPRK could resolve this nuclear

---

20 For full text, see 'DPRK FM on Its Stand to Suspend Its Participation in Six-party Talks for Indefinite Period', available at <http://www.kcna.co.jp/index-e.htm>, February 11, 2005.

dilemma through direct bilateral bargaining within the framework of the six-party talks. Therefore, the Bush administration should not delay making a compromise with, and concessions to, North Korea. Bilateral talks between the US and the DPRK are essential to the resolution of North Korea's nuclear standoff both from the perspective of peace and of diplomacy. Both need to engage in direct negotiations without preconditions within the framework of the six-party talks process. Both the US and North Korea's hardline policies cannot solve the nuclear issue peacefully. Therefore, both sides need to be flexible and should have a political will to compromise.

The authors would like to make policy recommendations for productive six-party talks. First of all, North Korea and the US have to remove preconditions for resolving the nuclear issue. North Korea's commitment to a Complete, Verifiable, Irreversible Dismantlement (CVID) formula, US commitment to written security guarantees and economic incentives to North Korea among other issues should be simultaneously discussed in good faith without preconditions. It is desirable that the six participants adopt a six-party agreement; tentatively entitled a 'six-party peace declaration' in which five participants will make commitments to guarantee North Korea's security and the DPRK will also commit to dismantle its nuclear programs. It should also include the following agreements on humanitarian food supply and re-supply of heavy fuel oil provided by five participants in return for North Korea's return to the Non-Proliferation Treaty (NPT), and the dismantlement of its highly enriched uranium program verified by International Atomic Energy Agency's (IAEA's) inspection team or a five-party special inspection team.

The DPRK should renounce its highly enriched uranium program in the future and freeze all its nuclear programs. Simultaneously, the international community should resume suspended heavy fuel oil supply to North Korea. With the renewal of the suspended fuel oil shipment, the DPRK should rejoin the NPT and accept IAEA's special inspections of its nuclear programs. These actions should take place simultaneously, without preconditions. The Korean Peninsula Energy Development Organization (KEDO) may resume its nuclear reactor construction in North Korea, and South Korea may consider supplying electricity to North Korea. If the next round of the six-party talks adopts a six-party agreement as suggested above, subsequent steps will proceed smoothly to dismantle North Korea's nuclear program gradually and sequentially, as discussed in Chapter 2, eventually leading to the realization of nuclear-free Korean peninsula.

Contributions to the Book

New developments in US–Korea relations and their implications for inter-Korean relations, US–ROK relations, US–DPRK relations, and Northeast Asian peace and security deserve careful scrutiny and analysis. This volume consists of nine chapters, which examine the dynamics of US–ROK and US–DPRK relations, focusing on salient issues and reflecting divergent viewpoints. The issues to be covered in this volume include US policy on the Korean peace regime building, US policy toward the ROK, US–ROK alliance in transition, US–ROK economic relations, US policy on the North Korean nuclear issue, and US–DPRK political relations. To help the reader better grasp the essence of the chapters, a brief summary of each chapter is provided here.

Chapter 2, by Tae-Hwan Kwak, 'The Six-Party Nuclear Talks and the Korean Peninsula Peace Regime Initiative: A Framework for Implementation,' proposes a long-term, comprehensive roadmap for the Korean peninsula peace regime initiative, which is designed to replace the 1953 Korean armistice agreement with a Korean peninsula peace treaty. The two approaches to Korean peninsula peace regime building are examined in detail at the inter-Korean and international levels. The two Koreas at the inter-Korean level, and the six parties involving the two Koreas, the US, China, Japan, and Russia at the international level may concurrently make efforts to build a peace regime by replacing the 1953 Korean armistice agreement with a peace treaty through confidence-building measures, national reconciliation and international cooperation. A peace regime can be institutionalized by implementing the inter-Korean basic agreement (1991) through inter-Korean cooperation and by concluding a Korean peninsula peace treaty through the four-party peace talks involving the US, China, and the two Koreas. However, the current North Korea nuclear issue has been a key obstacle to the peace regime building process. Three major arguments are presented. First, the two Koreas and the four major powers need to agree on a comprehensive roadmap for the Korean peace regime. Second, in the short-term, the North Korea nuclear issue should be resolved peacefully and diplomatically through the six-party process. Third, the two Koreas need to abandon their respective positions: the Seoul proposal for an inter-Korean peace treaty and the Pyongyang proposal for a DPRK–US peace treaty to replace the 1953 Korean armistice agreement. The author of Chapter 2 proposes that a Korean peninsula peace treaty among the four parties involving the ROK, the DPRK, the US and China should be an alternative, and the proposal needs to be seriously considered.

Chapter 3, by Seung-Ho Joo, 'US–ROK Relations: The Political–Diplomatic Dimension,' examines the nature and sources of US–ROK political frictions in recent years. It begins with a brief discussion of the evolution of US–ROK relations, focusing on the Roh Moo-Hyon regime and G.W. Bush presidency. It then discusses the salient issues and examines the sources of tensions and distrust in US–ROK relations. Finally, it concludes with an assessment of US–ROK relations. Diverging approaches to the North Korean nuclear issue, Roh's assertive and independent postures, anti-American sentiment in South Korea, and Bush's abrasive and self-centered behavior have all led to frictions, distrust, and awkwardness in US–ROK relations. Frictions in US–ROK relations are also ascribable to emotionalism and simplistic approaches on both sides. The ROK needs to assert itself, defending its own national interest vis-à-vis the US, but should not confuse aspirations (equality) with political reality. The Bush administration should realize that 'soft power' is often more persuasive and effective than hard power and that even the global superpower cannot manage international affairs alone without cooperation and support from interested states. The North Korean nuclear issue will test the US–ROK alliance. It would be prudent for the US and the ROK to get their acts together on North Korea and coordinate their policies at the six-party negotiation table. The US still remains ROK's most important friend as a political interlocutor, military ally, and economic partner. The US and the ROK relations are now undergoing a transitional period, and it will take a lot of imagination, patience, and efforts on both sides to sustain friendship and the alliance.

Chapter 4, by Claude E. Barfield and Jason Bolton, 'Korea, the US, China and Japan: The Rise of Asian Regionalism,' analyzes evolving trade and investment patterns between Korea, the US and China against the background of rising East Asian regionalism. The chapter also suggests optimal responses for Korea and the US to these new trends and policy shifts. The chapter is organized as follows. After the Introduction, the second section describes the growth of Korea as a trading nation. The third section analyzes in more detail the bilateral trade relationships between Korea and its four largest trading partners: the US, Japan, China, and the Association of Southeast Asian Nations (ASEAN) nations. The fourth and final section traces the growth of Asian regional trading patterns and the evolution of institutional arrangements that accompany these tightening trade relations. It analyzes negotiated and proposed bilateral, subregional and regional free trade agreements (FTAs). The chapter concludes with recommendations regarding the optimal responses for Korea and the US to these new realities of Asian trade and regionalism. The authors argue that for both the region as a whole and for individual nations, APEC-wide liberalization yields the most significant economic welfare gains.

Chapter 5, by Seong-Ryoul Cho, 'The Realignment of USFK and the US–ROK Alliance in Transition,' examines the main issues in the US–ROK alliance and makes projections for its future development. The author argues that the readjustment of the US Forces Korea (USFK) will definitely make a profound impact on the overall nature of the alliance between the two allies. The US and the ROK disagree on guarantees of strategic flexibility of USFK, formation of the ROK–US Quick Response Force (QRF) and the regional coalition of the US, Korea, Japan and Australia. These will be the main topics of the current Security Policy Initiative (SPI) conferences between two countries. The factors influencing the future of the ROK–US alliance are US security policy toward East Asia and South Korea's national security strategy. South Korea no longer regards North Korea as its main enemy, and South Korea cannot participate in containing China given the fact that ROK needs China's goodwill and cooperation for economic benefits and security. Although the mid- and long-term national interests of the ROK and the US coincide, their short-term interests are not identical. The future of the ROK-US alliance will depend on whether both allies can share a strategic harmony based on common interests and shared responsibility.

Chapter 6, by Bruce E. Bechtol, Jr, 'Assessing the Present and Charting the Future of US–DPRK Relations: The Political–Diplomatic Dimension of the Nuclear Confrontation,' focuses on the rocky relationship that has existed between the US and North Korea since bi-lateral relations between Pyongyang and Washington broke down as a result of the October 3, 2002 talks held between negotiators from these two nations. Because North Korea's nuclear program is the primary reason for the impasse in the relationship, the author first discusses the reasons for tensions leading up to the events that occurred during the fall of 2002. He next addresses the two-fold problem that has existed with North Korea since late 2002: (1) the freeze versus dismantle debate; and (2) the argument over the validity of Washington's assertion that Pyongyang has an active highly enriched uranium (HEU) weaponization program. While the debate over a 'freeze' of North Korea's nuclear program versus 'dismantlement' (CVID) was a political one, the author asserts that the evidence is clear regarding the existence of an HEU weaponization program, and thus should be viewed as an item that must be discussed at the bargaining table during any future talks resolving North Korea's nuclear programs, no matter what political perspective the nuclear confrontation is viewed from. Other issues that are also important with regard to the present and future relationship between North Korea and the US include recent attempts by Pyongyang at involvement in both Washington's and Seoul's internal affairs – particularly comments made during elections of 2004 in both countries by Kim Chong-il's state-run press, and the recently surfaced North Korean stability issues that came to the world's attention during the fall of 2004. These two issues have had an effect on the how the US is able to deal with North Korea diplomatically, but perhaps even more importantly, differences in perspectives on how to contain North Korea within the ROK–US Alliance have had, and will continue to have, an impact on the US–DPRK relationship. It is clear from ongoing developments that Washington continues to be concerned about the threat North Korea poses to regional stability, and the proliferation threat that Pyongyang continues to pose to regions outside of East Asia. As breakthroughs in the six-party talks during the fall of 2005 emerged, the author is hopeful that North Korea will not only dismantle its nuclear programs, but will take other important steps in state behavior that will lead to security and stability on the Korean peninsula and in the region.

Chapter 7, by Edward A. Olsen, 'US–DPRK Relations: The Nuclear Issue,' examines the changes and continuity in US North Korea policy during G.W. Bush's second term. This chapter specifically discusses the following questions: How has US policy toward the DPRK's nuclear policies (energy and weapons) evolved to date? What policy options does the US possess? What are the prospects of the US resolving its concerns about North Korea's nuclear capabilities? The US and North Korea have had a troubled relationship since the creation of the DPRK in 1948. For the US, the DPRK was one of many strategic adversaries, but a particularly nasty one. For North Korea, in principle the US epitomized an imperial threat to everything the DPRK represented and in practice posed a tangible military threat to the DPRK's very existence.

Chapter 8, by Terence Roehrig, 'Restraining the Hegemon: North Korea, the US and Asymmetrical Deterrence,' examines North Korean efforts to implement a deterrence policy in the post-Cold War world. In addition, this chapter addresses the implications for asymmetrical deterrence as smaller states seek to deter larger powers, particularly through the development of a nuclear capability. Since the Korean War, deterrence has been the dominant theoretical framework guiding security relations in Korea. The US and South Korea have maintained an alliance with the goal of deterring another attack from the north. Indeed, most of the literature on Korean security focuses on deterrence and US–South Korean security policy. Yet, deterrence has also been a part of North Korean security planning, particularly with the end of the Cold War. In the early 1990s, North Korea saw its security situation gravely shaken as both of its traditional allies, China and Russia, distanced themselves and sought a relationship with the economically vibrant south. Not coincidently, this became a time of increased North Korean efforts to acquire a nuclear capability. During the 1990s, the North Korean economy also began its descent with the loss of trading partners and preferential deals from the Communist bloc that made it increasingly difficult to match South Korea's defense spending. As a result, North Korea assumed a defense posture that increasingly resembled that of deterrence, a task even more difficult given it needed to deter the US in an asymmetrical relationship.

Chapter 9, by Fei-Ling Wang, 'Stability with Uncertainties: US–China Relations and the Korean Peninsula,' describes the US–China relations and its impact on the Korean peninsula. It outlines the key motivations behind the making of Chinese foreign policy and then reports on the current stability and uncertainties between Beijing and Washington. As a result of its overall objectives in diplomacy, Beijing is seeking a shared strategic interest with the US on the Korean issue. The People's Republic of China (PRC) prefers the continued survival of the DPRK regime and develops ever-closer relations with the ROK; it's basic policy towards the Korean peninsula remains pro-status quo and anti-nuclearization. However, the uncertainties and complications of the Sino-American relations profoundly affect China's strategic calculation about the Korean peninsula and indicate changes and problems in the Chinese Korea policy.

Chapter 2

The Six-Party Nuclear Talks and the Korean Peninsula Peace Regime Initiative: A Framework for Implementation

Tae-Hwan Kwak

A legal and institutional arrangement for building a peace regime on the Korean peninsula has not been established yet, over a half century since the conclusion of the Korean armistice agreement of 1953. The Korean peninsula is still technically at war, despite the fact that the two Koreas have established a framework for de facto peaceful coexistence since the June 15, 2000 joint declaration. The joint statement signed by six nations at the fourth round of the six-party talks on September 19, 2005 stated, 'The directly related parties will negotiate a permanent peace regime on the Korean Peninsula at an appropriate separate forum.' It is expected that the directly related parties involving the US, China, and two Koreas will soon engage in the four-party talks over the Korean peninsula peace regime building.

The Kim Dae-Jung government's sunshine policy toward the Democratic People's Republic of Korea (DPRK or North Korea) contributed to the inter-Korean first-ever summit meeting held in Pyongyang on June 13–15, 2000. The historic summit produced the joint declaration of June 15, 2000, which provided a framework for institutionalizing de facto peaceful coexistence between the two Korean states. The inter-Korean summit meeting showed that Chairman Kim Jong-Il changed his strategic policy vis-à-vis the Republic of Korea (ROK or South Korea).

The inter-Korean peace process went on smoothly, but North Korea's alleged admission of a highly enriched uranium (HEU) program in October 2002 sparked the second nuclear crisis. The DPRK was accused of violating international agreements, including the 1968 Non-Proliferation Treaty (NPT), the International Atomic Energy Agency's (IAEA) safeguards agreement, Inter-Korean Joint Declaration on Denuclearization on the Korean Peninsula (1992), and the 1994 Geneva Agreed Framework. The six-party talks (US, China, Russia, Japan, and the two Koreas) were held to resolve the North Korean nuclear issue by peaceful means. Without first resolving the nuclear issue, the building of the Korean peace regime may not be achieved. The second North Korean nuclear crisis has thus been a key obstacle to the Korean peace regime building process.

The Korean peace regime building process may be defined as the process by which the two Korean states at the inter-Korean level, and the two Koreas and concerned powers – the US, China, Japan, and Russia – at the international level cooperate to establish a peace regime on the Korean peninsula through confidence-building measures, tension reduction, national reconciliation and international cooperation, and the replacement of the 1953 Korean armistice agreement with a Korean peninsula peace treaty. The process is one of essential conditions for building a Korean peninsula peace regime and for eventually achieving a peaceful unification of the Korean peninsula. A peace regime can be institutionalized by implementing the Inter-Korean Basic Agreement (1991) through inter-Korean cooperation and by concluding a Korean peninsula peace treaty through the four-party peace talks involving the US, China, and the two Koreas.

The objectives of this chapter are: (1) to propose a comprehensive, long-term roadmap for the building of the Korean peninsula peace regime; (2) to examine an inter-Korean approach to peace regime building; and (3) to examine an international cooperation approach to peace regime building. Three major arguments are presented. First, the two Koreas and the four major powers need to agree on a comprehensive roadmap for the building of the Korean peninsula peace regime, as suggested here. The inter-Korean and international approaches to peace regime building should be considered in parallel to establish a permanent peace in Korea. Second, the North Korean nuclear issue should be resolved peacefully through the six-party talks. Third, the two Koreas need to work together to find an alternative to the South's proposal for an inter-Korean peace treaty and the North's proposal for a DPRK–US peace treaty to replace the 1953 Korean armistice agreement. The author proposes a Korean peninsula peace treaty among the ROK, the DPRK, the US and China as an alternative. Let us first take a look at the proposed Korean peninsula peace regime initiative.

A Comprehensive Roadmap for the Korean Peninsula Peace Regime Initiative

It is desirable for the four parties directly related (the two Koreas, the US and China) to agree on a comprehensive roadmap for the Korean Peninsula Peace Regime Initiative (KPRI), which will be implemented through a step-by-step sequence. The proposed KPRI is based on several assumptions: (1) the North Korean nuclear issue should be resolved through peaceful, diplomatic means; (2) North Korea's system should not collapse and will be sustained through social-economic changes and reform; (3) the inter-Korean reconciliation, cooperation and peace process will continue; (4) the US will not launch a preemptive strike against North Korea; and (5) a US–China cooperation will be maintained, the PRC-Taiwan relations will be stable, the DPRK and the US will cooperate to achieve the verifiable denuclearization of the

Korean peninsula, and North Korea will neither test nuclear weapons nor transfer weapons of mass destruction (WMD) to a third party.

Based on these assumptions, the author would like to propose a roadmap for a peace regime in Korea. In the short term, the North Korean nuclear issue should be first resolved by peaceful means. Without resolving the issue, the other issues relating to peace regime building on the Korean peninsula cannot even be discussed in the medium and long terms. After resolving the nuclear issue, the second stage will begin with the resumption of the stalled four-party talks separately or four-party talks within the framework of the six-party talks. This stage will prepare for military confidence building measures and a legal, institutional mechanism for building a peace regime. Finally, a legal and institutional arrangement for replacing the Korean armistice agreement with a permanent Korean peninsula peace treaty will be signed by the four parties (the US, China, and two Koreas) and guaranteed by the six parties (four plus Russia and Japan).

Let us now outline the three-stage roadmap for building a peace regime on the Korean peninsula (see Table 2.1).

Short-term stage

The North Korean nuclear issue is one of major obstacles to the Korean peace process. The issue needs to be peacefully resolved through diplomatic negotiations at the six-party talks in the short term. It is important to set basic principles for resolving the North Korean nuclear issue.[1] The author suggests the following principles. First, the US and the DPRK need to resume direct dialogue and negotiations without preconditions. The peaceful resolution requires bilateral direct dialogue and negotiations over the nuclear issue. Both US and North Korean hardline policies cannot resolve the nuclear issue peacefully. Second, the US and North Korea need to make mutual concessions to implement the 9.19 joint statement adopted by the fourth round of the six-party talks. Third, international cooperation is also necessary for a peaceful resolution of the North Korean nuclear issue. South Korea, Japan, China, Russia, the EU and other concerned countries should play active roles in resolving the nuclear issue. Finally, the US and the DPRK need to engage in mutual confidence-building measures to build mutual trust.

The author would like to make policy recommendations for productive six-party talks. First of all, the six parties must prepare a roadmap for implementing the principles and objectives of the 9.19 nuclear agreement, which will be discussed in detail in the third section of this chapter. It should also include the following agreements on humanitarian food supply and re-supply of heavy fuel oil provided by five participants in return for North Korea's return to the NPT, and the dismantlement

---

[1] Tae-Hwan Kwak, 'What Is To Be Done to Resolve North Korea's Nuclear Weapons Development Issue', *Vantage Point*, vol. 26, no. 1 (January, 2003), pp. 42–53.

Table 2.1 A comprehensive roadmap for the KPRI

Objectives and Goals of Different Stages	Concerned Parties	North Korea (NK)	International Community (5 Parties +)
Short-term Stage: Three-phase roadmap for verifiable denuclearization of Korean peninsula	Phase 1: Preparation	• Abandoning of all nuclear weapons/existing nuclear programs • Discontinuance of, and freeze on, all nuclear facilities • Return to NPT/ IAEA inspections • Renunciation of HEU	• Fuel oil supply to NK (5 parties) • Economic aid to NK discussed • South Korea's supply of electricity to NK discussed • Light-water reactor (LWR) provision discussed • Verification procedures agreed
	Phase 2: NK's dismantlement of nuclear weapons and facilities	• Implementation of nuclear dismantlement • IAEA inspections of nuclear facilities • NK's agreement on IAEA inspections on its past nuclear activities	• Resumption of suspended LWR or new construction of LWR • Written security guarantees by 5 Parties • NK–US, NK–Japan normalization talks began
	Phase 3: Completion of NK's dismantlement/ conclusion of six-party Guarantee Agreement on Korean peninsula denuclearization	• Completion of nuclear dismantlement • Conclusion of a non-nuclear guarantee agreement among the six parties • 2nd Inter-Korean Summit meeting prepared	• LWR nuclear reactor construction begins • Promise of grand economic assistance program to NK • US–NK, Japan–NK normalization agreement signed • Joint Korean peninsula denuclearization agreement registered at UN Secretariat
Mid-term stage: Implementation of Inter-Korean Basic Agreement / Resumption of Four Party Talks	Reactivation of the Four Party Talks/Preparatory Stage for Legal / Institutional Mechanism	• 2nd Inter-Korean Summit meeting • Revision of Inter-Korean Basic Agreement and declaration on nuclear-free Korean peninsula • Cessation of missile and WMD exports	• US-NK and Japan-NK Normalization • Resumption of Four-party talks • Financial compensation for cessation of WMD exports /dismantlement • USFK readjustment/ UNC dissolution
Long-term Stage: Korean Peninsula Peace Regime	Conclusion of a Korean Peninsula Peace Treaty	• Conclusion of Korean Peninsula Peace Treaty (inter-Korean peace agreement; US–NK peace agreement; PRC–ROK peace agreement) • Completion of legal, institutional mechanism of peace regime • Grand economic assistance to NK • Institutionalization of Northeast Asian security/economic cooperation	

of its HEU program verified by the IAEA's special team or the five party special inspection team.²

The DPRK needs to first renounce its enriched uranium program even if it does not have such a program, and freeze its nuclear programs, and simultaneously the international community needs to resume suspended heavy fuel oil supply to North Korea. With the renewal of the suspended fuel oil shipment, the DPRK should again join the NPT and accept the IAEA's special inspections of the nuclear programs in North Korea. These actions should be simultaneously taken without preconditions. In the future, the Korean Peninsula Energy Development Organization (KEDO) may resume its nuclear reactor construction in North Korea, and South Korea may supply electricity to North Korea. If the fifth round of the six-party talks adopts a proposed roadmap for achieving denuclearization of the Korean peninsula, a nuclear-free Korean peninsula will be achieved.³

Mid-term stage

After resolving North Korea's nuclear issue, the next stage should be taken to discuss the issue of WMDs in the context of arms control, tension-reduction, and the peace regime process between the two Koreas. For legal arrangements prior to the conclusion of a multilateral peace treaty, it would be desirable for the four parties (the US, China, and two Koreas) to resume the now-stalled four-party talks.

A second ROK–DPRK summit meeting may be arranged to discuss peace and unification issues. It may produce another historic document entitled a 'Joint Declaration on Peace and Unification on the Korean Peninsula.' The joint declaration must include a revision and/or reconfirmation of the historic two documents signed by the two Koreas – the Inter-Korean Basic Agreement (1991) and the Joint Declaration on the Korean Peninsula Denuclearization (1992). Chapter 2 ('South–North Non-Aggression') of the Inter-Korean Basic Agreement spelled out inter-Korean non-aggression provisions from Articles 9 to 14. Both sides must implement these provisions. If they are implemented in good faith, there may be no need to conclude a peace treaty between the two Koreas, which the ROK has officially maintained. Needless-to-say, the two Koreas must agree to specify mutual verification measures in the joint document. The two Koreas also must agree to stop North Korea's long-

---

2 For an earlier version by the author, see Tae-Hwan Kwak, 'Resolving the North Korean Nuclear Issue Through the Six-Party Talks', *Vantage Point*, vol. 26, no. 12 (December 2003), pp. 28–32.

3 For details, see the author's original proposal for a creative, three-stage formula for a comprehensive packaged solution to the North Korean nuclear crisis: Tae-Hwan Kwak, 'The Korean Peninsula Peace Regime Building Through the Four-Party Peace Talks: Re-evaluation and Policy Recommendations', *Journal of East Asian Affairs*, vol. 17, no. 1 (Spring/Summer 2003), pp. 1–32. For the problems of the Korean peace building process, see Tae-Hwan Kwak and Seung-Ho Joo, eds. *The Korean Peace Process and the Four Powers* (Hampshire, England: Ashgate Publishing, 2003), especially Chapter 2, 'The Korean Peace Process: Problems and Prospects' (Tae-Hwan Kwak).

range missile development and exports. It would be desirable for the international community to compensate for North Korea's loss of its exports of missiles and other WMDs.

Along with these measures taken by North Korea in good faith, US–DPRK and DPRK–Japan diplomatic relations should be established. An inter-Korean cooperation approach to peace regime building will be discussed in detail below.

Long-term stage

In the long term, the stalled four-party talks should be resumed and should discuss a Korean peninsula peace treaty to replace the Korean armistice agreement of 1953. Perhaps four-party talks within the framework of the six-party talks can also discuss this. A Korean peninsula peace treaty must be a multilateral one. It should not be a bilateral treaty between the two Koreas guaranteed by the US and China. The US, China, and two Koreas should sign a Korean peninsula peace treaty, which would be much more binding than a bilateral treaty between the two Koreas.

The Korean armistice agreement is a multilateral one, and thus it is desirable to replace it with a multilateral treaty among the four parties. The treaty should include verification measures and transparency. It could essentially be a collective security agreement for the Korean peninsula. The treaty should be reported to the United Nations (UN) Security Council and registered at the UN Secretariat. By so doing, the Korean peace regime will be firmly legally established on the Korean peninsula. The ROK government must support a multilateral Korean peninsula peace treaty instead of an inter-Korean bilateral peace treaty. The treaty will be a foundation of peace and stability in the Northeast Asian region. An international approach to peace regime building will be discussed in detail below. Let us now turn to the short-term stage to resolve North Korea's nuclear issue peacefully.

Short-Term Stage: Peaceful Resolution of North Korea's Nuclear Issue/A Proposed Roadmap for Denuclearization on the Korean Peninsula

The six nations signed the 9.19 joint statement of principles to guide future negotiations over North Korea's nuclear issue at the fourth round of the six-party talks. The peaceful resolution of the nuclear issue is a *sine qua non* for building a peace regime on the Korean peninsula.[4] Thus, it is significant to understand the key issues discussed at the fourth round of the six-party talks to resolve North Korea's nuclear issue.

---

4 For an assessment of the first three rounds of the six-party nuclear talks, see Tae-Hwan Kwak, 'The Six-Party Nuclear Talks: An Evaluation and Policy Recommendations', *Pacific Focus*, vol. 19, no. 2 (Fall 2004), pp. 7–55.

The first phase of the fourth six-party talks

The first phase of the fourth six-party nuclear talks held in Beijing on July 26 to August 7, 2005 went into recess on August 7 after the six nations engaged in intensive negotiations. The US and the DPRK actively engaged in direct bilateral negotiations for 13 days, but could not reach an agreement on the core issue of North Korea's right to peaceful nuclear activities.[5] This issue became a stumbling block to the consensus on a joint statement of principles by the six participants involving the US, China, Russia, Japan, the DPRK and the ROK.

DPRK's position: The right to peaceful use of nuclear energy Chief DPRK negotiator and Vice Foreign Minister Kim Kye-Gwan demanded that the DPRK be allowed to retain its right to pursue peaceful nuclear activities. 'We are for denuclearizing, but we also want to possess the right to peaceful nuclear activities,' Kim said. 'As you know, only one country is opposing that,' said Kim, referring to the US, and, 'Every country in the world has the right to peaceful nuclear activities.'

The DPRK expressed resentment with the US opposing its peaceful use of nuclear power. In the face of concerted diplomatic pressures at the talks, the DPRK consistently insisted on its right to a nuclear program for peaceful purposes. Pyongyang demanded the right to peaceful use of nuclear energy under the conditions that it would abandon all nuclear weapons development programs, including existing nuclear reprocessing and enriched uranium facilities in the future. However, North Korea wanted to restore the suspended KEDO light-water nuclear reactor project. Both Seoul and Washington opposed Pyongyang's demand. The DPRK's demand created complicated problems for the ROK government. Seoul's offer to supply 2 million kilowatts of electricity to Pyongyang was based on the premise that the KEDO project be scrapped and Seoul's financial contributions to the KEDO be redirected to the electricity supply project.

US position: North Korea should not have nuclear power plants The US argued North Korea should not even be allowed to maintain nuclear reactors for civilian use because it had turned research facilities at Yongbyon into a production center for weapons-grade plutonium after the collapse of the 1994 Geneva agreement. LWRs are considered less likely to produce weapons-grade plutonium than graphite-type nuclear reactors do, but the US still has nuclear proliferation concerns with such installations. Further, President Bush endorsed South Korea's offer of electricity to the North as another reason why Pyongyang doesn't need any kind of nuclear program even for power generation.

ROK's position: Conditional support for North Korea's position Unification Minister Chung Dong-young said in an interview on August 11, 2005, 'North Korea

---

5 For details, see Tae-Hwan Kwak, 'North Korea's Right to Peaceful Nuclear Activities', *Vantage Point*, vol. 28, no. 9 (September 2005), pp. 15–19.

has a general right to peaceful use of nuclear energy for agricultural, medical and power-generating purposes.' He also said, 'In this, our position differs from that of Washington.' Chung's initial statement did not attach conditional support, but later President Roh attached conditional support for DPRK's right to use nuclear energy peacefully. ROK Foreign Minister Ban Ki-moon also echoed Roh's position saying that South Korea supported the North's right to peaceful uses of nuclear energy if it rejoined the NPT and allowed inspections by the IAEA. Ban reiterated there was no major difference in principle between the US and South Korean views on the DPRK's possible future use of nuclear energy. Ban also said, 'The ROK government believes that if the North dismantles all nuclear programs, returns to the NPT and complies with IAEA safeguard measures, it will come to earn trust, and in that case the door to its peaceful nuclear use may open.'

Minister Chung made it clear that the ROK would not supply 2 million kilowatts of electricity to North Korea and fund the KEDO project to construct two LWRs at the same time. He said the ROK's electricity aid plan for North Korea was based on the premise that the DPRK would abandon its nuclear weapons programs and the KEDO project. His remarks were intended to make it clear that the ROK would not endorse the DPRK's demand for restoring the suspended KEDO project if the North would accept Seoul's offer of electricity. Chung reaffirmed ROK's conditional support for DPRK's right to peaceful use of nuclear energy.

No compromise over this issue would mean the failure of the fourth round of the six-party talks. Even if the second phase of the fourth-round talks resumed it would be difficult to bridge the wide gap between Pyongyang and Washington. Since both sides insisted on their respective positions on this issue, they could not find a solution.

The second phase of the fourth six-party talks

The second phase of the fourth six-party talks was held in Beijing from September 13 to 19, 2005, when the six nations finally signed a joint agreement of principles to guide a detailed roadmap for achieving the denuclearization of the Korean peninsula. The DPRK again declared on September 13 that it would not relinquish peaceful nuclear energy and its demand for a LWR to produce electricity was also the main sticking point at the second phase. The North Korean position remained unchanged. The key issue at the fourth six-party talks was North Korea's demand for a LWR to produce electricity as part of any deal to give up its nuclear weapons programs. In the meantime, the Bush administration remained adamant that the DPRK must abandon its nuclear weapons programs and forgo nuclear energy production. The US refused to consider a light-water nuclear reactor for North Korea.

The ROK has proposed supplying electricity to North Korea as part of the nuclear disarmament agreement, which chief US negotiator Christopher Hill suggested was a more practical way to meet North Korea's energy needs if that was the issue.[6] On September 14, 2005, North Korea again demanded that the US and other nations give it money to build a new light-water nuclear reactor before it would end its nuclear weapons programs. 'Neither the United States nor any other participant is prepared to fund a light-water reactor,' said Hill. A light-water reactor would cost $2 billion to $3 billion and take about a decade to build. The five participants in the talk agreed that North Korea's condition that it received a LWR before ending its arms programs was unacceptable. However, the US signaled a softening of its position, saying it would be willing to leave aside the issue of civilian uses of nuclear technology for now to clear the way for a general agreement on ending North Korea's nuclear weapons programs.[7]

Contents of the 9.19 Agreement signed by six participants The six-party joint statement was signed on the seventh day of the second phase of the fourth six-party talks, which had been deadlocked and appeared to be heading into another standoff. Although the accord included only general terms, it marked the first specific agreement among the six parties since the six-party talks began in August 2003. It was designed to serve as the basis for further talks on the timing of the North Korea's dismantlement of its nuclear weapons programs and the corresponding provision of economic aid and diplomatic relations and other incentives for the DPRK[8] (see Table 2.2).

The joint statement was a diplomatic victory for China as a host country and mediator. The agreement was based on a compromise proposal by China to bridge differences between Washington and Pyongyang over the issue of a LWR. The compromise was achieved: the DPRK would be accorded the right to peaceful nuclear energy in principle, but only after dismantling its nuclear weapons programs and rejoining the UN nuclear inspection regime and the NPT. The Chinese compromise proposal was introduced after it became apparent that North Korea would not accept an earlier draft agreement with no mention of its demand for LWR as part of any accord on abandoning its nuclear weapons programs.

The agreement said, 'The DPRK stated that it has the right to peaceful uses of nuclear energy. The other parties expressed their respect and agreed to discuss at an appropriate time the subject of the provision of a light-water reactor to the DPRK.' Those terms of the agreement represented a concession by the United States and the DPRK. Let us now turn to US and North Korean concessions.

---

6 Edward Cody, 'N. Korea Holds to Its Demands at Nuclear Talks', *Washington Post*, September 15, 2005; Joseph Kahn, 'North Koreans Insist on Demand for New Reactor in Nuclear Talks', *New York Times*, September 16, 2005.

7 Joseph Kahn, 'North Korea Sets New Demand for Ending Arms Program: Money to Buy a Civilian Reactor', *New York Times*, September 15, 2005.

8 For details, see 'Text of Joint Statement from Nuclear Talks', *New York Times*, September 19, 2005.

Table 2.2 Contents of six-party joint statement (September 19, 2005)

	Items	Content
1	Principles for verifiable denuclearization of the Korean peninsula	• North Korea's abandoning of all nuclear weapons and all existing nuclear programs/its return to NPT and IAEA safeguards • Reconfirmation of non-presence of nuclear weapons in South Korea • Respect for and implementation of Joint Declaration on Denuclearization of the Korean Peninsula (1992)
	Five-party promises to North Korea (NK)	• Respect for NK right to peaceful uses of nuclear energy • Discussion on the subject of provision of LWRs at appropriate time • Confirmation of no-use of force against NK by US
2	Behavioral norms in International relations	• Observation and respect for norms, objectives and principles in the UN Charter
	Commitments to peaceful relations in bilateral US–NK/NK–Japan relations	• Normalization of US-NK relations • Normalization of NK-Japan relations
3	Six-party commitments to economic aid to NK	• Promotion of bilateral/multilateral economic cooperation in energy, trade and investment • Five-party energy assistance to NK • Reaffirmation of SK proposal for 2 million kW of electricity to NK
4	Commitments to peace and security in Northeast Asia	• Korean peninsula peace regime building forum by directly related parties • Search for multilateral security cooperation system in Northeast Asia
5	Principles for implementing the joint agreement	• Coordinated steps in a phased manner in line with the principle of 'commitment for commitment, action for action'
6	Fifth six-party talks set	• Fifth six-party talks in Beijing to be held in early November 2005

DPRK concessions The agreement stated, 'The DPRK committed abandoning all nuclear weapons and existing nuclear programs and returning at an early date to the treaty on the non-proliferation of nuclear weapons (NPT) and to IAEA safeguards,' referring to the NPT and the IAEA. However, the agreement was vague at best, and did not specify anything about when or under what conditions the DPRK would dismantle all of its nuclear programs, re-enter the NPT and allow IAEA inspections.

There was no mention about HEU. The agreement does not explicitly address the issue of North Korea's uranium program. North Korea still denies having one, despite growing evidence that it at least tried to develop bomb fuel using HEU with Pakistan's assistance. However, the HEU issue was covered by the pledge to dismantle 'all nuclear weapons and existing nuclear programs' and by a separate reference to a 1992 inter-Korean joint declaration on the denuclearization of Korea, which prohibited uranium enrichment. But the accord did not require North Korea to confess the existence of the program, meaning that unless the North admits to the program in a declaration of all its nuclear facilities, inspectors would have to work to uncover the uranium program in an adversarial way down the road. This issue will be potentially explosive.

Moreover, the agreement says nothing about a verification process. Regarding the timing of the provision of LWR to North Korea, Secretary Rice argued that the wording of the agreement implied that North Korea would disarm first. 'At an appropriate time we are prepared to discuss – discuss the idea of building a nuclear reactor,' she said. She said several times that the discussion would not even begin until North Korea dismantled its weapons program.[9]

US concessions After four years of bitter arguments over whether to negotiate with the DPRK or try to engineer its collapse, the 9.19 Beijing agreement President Bush finally approved provided the bare minimum – an agreement in principle that the DPRK would abandon a five-decade pursuit of nuclear weapons programs. Part of the reason Bush signed the agreement was that he had to close the breach among his negotiating partners: China, Russia, Japan and the ROK. Hardliners in the Bush administration blocked negotiations for the first few years of Bush's presidency, but in the end, both President Bush and Secretary Rice were persuaded that if a confrontation ever occurred with North Korea, they had to be prepared to show that they had made every effort to reach a diplomatic solution. According to Ambassador Hill, the US was 'prepared to address the DPRK's energy needs.' This statement represented a change of position from the third round of the six-party talks in June 2004, when the US declined to provide energy assistance to North Korea. The US committed itself to providing energy assistance to the DPRK.

The Bush administration finally dropped its opposition to the DPRK receiving a LWR in the future, showing a softening of its hardline position. President Bush cautiously welcomed the agreement, but warned, 'We expect a verifiable process.' So verification will be a major issue at the upcoming fifth round of the six-party talks. Chief US negotiator Hill said that the administration didn't want to see any mention of providing North Korea with LWR in the joint statement, but the Chinese included it. The US also balked at the use of the vague term 'appropriate' to describe the timing. South Korea, Russia and China were happy to accept this language, because it left open the question of when the DPRK would receive the nuclear reactor. To break the impasse, Secretary Rice suggested that each country would issue separate statements describing their understanding of the deal with a specificity that is not in the agreement itself. The ROK and Japan went along with the idea, although Seoul

---

9   David E. Sanger, 'Yes, Parallel Tracks to North, but Parallel Tracks Don't Meet', *New York Times*, September 20, 2005.

complained that it would 'sour the atmosphere.' Russia and China issued vague statements that left unclear the sequence of events.[10]

An assessment Overall, both President Bush and Chairman Kim Jong-Il benefited by finally approving the 9.19 joint agreement. The DPRK took a major step toward securing international acceptance. It will allow Chairman Kim to hang on to power for the foreseeable future and will gradually open North Korea to foreign investment and avoid its sudden collapse. One long-term incentive in the joint statement was the call for the US and Japan to take steps to normalize relations with North Korea if the DPRK dismantles its weapons programs. Such a historic rapprochement could mean billions of dollars worth of economic assistance from Japan alone in belated World War II-era reparations. For President Bush, the agreement was welcome at a time when the war in Iraq had lost considerable support at home and negotiations with Iran over its nuclear programs had gone astray. In addition, the president's approval ratings were low in the wake of his administration's slow response to Hurricane Katrina.

Forthcoming talks

Several controversial issues will need to be resolved at the forthcoming six-party talks. First, the United States wants North Korea to issue a declaration of its nuclear weapons, materials, and facilities so that proper verification procedures can be devised. This request can be controversial because the US wants the declaration to include Pyongyang's uranium-enrichment program. Second, the US and the DPRK will likely disagree with the proper sequencing for issues in the joint statement. The US wants North Korea to fulfill its denuclearization commitments before providing any benefits. By contrast, the DPRK maintained that all issues 'should be resolved on the basis of simultaneous actions.' Third, the six nations should agree to verification procedures and the timing of LWR.

What the six parties should do at the fifth round of the six-party talks is to draw a roadmap for implementing the goals and principles contained in the 9.19 joint statement. Thus, the author would like to propose a three-phase roadmap for achieving verifiable denuclearization on the Korean peninsula (see Table 2.3).

Phase 1: Preparation for dismantlement of North Korea's nuclear programs The DPRK should make a complete declaration about all nuclear programs and freeze all nuclear activities in order to make preparations for dismantling all nuclear weapons and existing nuclear programs. It is reasonable for the DPRK to first renounce its enriched uranium program since it has denied the existence of its enriched uranium program. Thus, North Korea can declare that it will not have its enriched uranium

---

10 Joseph Kahn and David E. Sanger, 'US–Korean Deal on Arms Leaves Key Points Open', *New York Times*, September 20, 2005; Glenn Kessler and Edward Cody, 'N. Korea, US Gave Ground to Make Deal', *Washington Post*, September 20, 2005.

Table 2.3 Three-phase roadmap for denuclearization on the Korean peninsula

Objectives and Goals	Concerned Parties	North Korea (NK)	International Community (5 Parties +)
Three-phase roadmap for verifiable denuclearization of Korean peninsula	Phase 1: Preparation	• Abandoning of all nuclear weapons/existing nuclear programs • Discontinuance of and freeze on all nuclear facilities • Return to NPT/IAEA inspections • Renunciation of HEU	• Fuel oil supply to NK (5 parties) • Economic aid to NK discussed • South Korea's supply of electricity to NK discussed • LWR provision discussed • Verification procedures agreed
	Phase 2: NK's dismantlement of nuclear weapons and facilities	• Implementation of nuclear dismantlement • IAEA inspections of nuclear facilities • NK's agreement on IAEA inspections on its past nuclear activities	• Resumption of suspended LWR or new construction of LWR • Written security guarantees by 5 Parties • NK–US, NK–Japan normalization talks begin
	Phase 3: Completion of NK's dismantlement/ conclusion of six-party Guarantee Agreement on Korean peninsula denuclearization	• Completion of nuclear dismantlement • Conclusion of a non-nuclear guarantee agreement among the six parties • 2nd Inter-Korean Summit meeting prepared	• LWR nuclear reactor construction began • Promise of grand economic assistance program to NK • US–NK, Japan–NK normalization agreement signed • Joint Korean peninsula denuclearization agreement registered at UN Secretariat

program in the future. If North Korea simply renounces its enriched uranium in a verifiable manner, five nations would supply heavy fuel oil shipment to North Korea. With the supply of the fuel oil shipment, the DPRK would again join the NPT and invite the IAEA's special inspections of the nuclear programs in North Korea. Five nations should discuss their economic assistance to the DPRK and the LWR issue with North Korea. The ROK should discuss its supply of electricity to the DPRK. The six parties should also discuss and agree to verification procedures. These measures should be simultaneously taken.

Phase 2: Actual dismantlement of nuclear weapons and facilities The DPRK should implement the agreement on dismantlement of nuclear weapons and nuclear facilities in a phased manner. The IAEA should inspect and verify nuclear dismantlement and North Korea's past nuclear activities.

The five nations and the DPRK must agree on a new construction of LWR or resumption of the suspended KEDO project at Sinpo under the new arrangement.

Five parties should provide written security guarantees to the DPRK. At the same time, US–DPRK normalization and DPRK–Japan normalization talks should proceed.

Phase 3: The completion of nuclear dismantlement/conclusion of the six-party Korean Peninsula Denuclearization Guarantee Agreement At the third phase, there will be the end of nuclear dismantlement in North Korea, and the six parties should conclude a six-party non-nuclear guarantee agreement in which institutional and legal arrangements for enforcement measures of the denuclearization on the Korean peninsula should be contained. The six participants must draw up a multilateral nuclear agreement in which North Korea would completely dismantle its nuclear programs in exchange for multilateral security guarantees and economic cooperation. This agreement should be registered at the UN Secretariat. The construction of LWR should be under way, massive economic assistance to North Korea will be given, and US–DPRK and Japan–DPRK normalization agreements will be signed at this phase.

In the final analysis, there will be a long and rough road ahead to the peaceful resolution of North Korea's nuclear issue. The US and the DPRK should continue to cooperate through compromise and concessions to achieve the verifiable denuclearization of the Korean peninsula as shown in the fourth round of the six-party talks. The Bush administration now plans to ask North Korea to begin disclosing the extent and locations of its secret nuclear development programs to test the sincerity of DPRK's commitment to abandon its nuclear ambitions.[11] The US wants the DPRK to make a complete declaration about its nuclear programs, including HEU and nuclear weapons.

The 9.19 Beijing agreement seemed a major breakthrough after two years of deadlock, but it left much open to different interpretation. The DPRK reiterated that North Korea would not rejoin the NPT or allow international nuclear inspections until it received a light-water nuclear reactor from the US, while Washington equally insisted that all nuclear weapons and related programs should be first dismantled. This disagreement could be once again a key obstacle to the fifth round of the six-party talks.

Mid-Term Stage: Implementation of the Inter-Korean Basic Agreement/ Resumption of the Four-party Talks

Inter-Korean cooperation as an approach to peace regime building is key to the Korean peace process because the ROK and the DPRK are main actors in the peace regime-building process. The first inter-Korean summit between President Kim Dae-Jung and Chairman Kim Jong-Il held in Pyongyang on June 13–15, 2000 produced the historic inter-Korean joint declaration of June 15, 2000. This landmark declaration

---

11 Peter Baker and Glenn Kessler, 'US to Push Koreans on Nuclear Program', *Washington Post*, October 5, 2005.

provided a framework for de facto peaceful coexistence between the two Korean states. Chairman Kim's decision to accept the June summit meeting symbolized a strategic change in his policy toward the South. With the inauguration of President Kim Dae-Jung in February 1998, the Kim government adopted a new policy toward North Korea known as the 'sunshine policy.'[12] The basic objective of this new policy was to improve inter-Korean relations by promoting reconciliation, cooperation, and peace. Two specific goals of the sunshine policy were: (1) peaceful management of the national division; and (2) promotion of a favorable environment for North Korea to change and open itself without fear.[13]

The Kim government consistently implemented its engagement policy towards North Korea since February 1998. This policy produced some tangible results. First and foremost, the South's engagement policy contributed to a peaceful and stable environment in which North Korea could resolve difficult problems relating to its nuclear freeze and long-range missile testing.[14] Second, the engagement policy contributed to tension-reduction on the Korean peninsula and a favorable environment for improving inter-Korean relations. Thus, inter-Korean economic cooperation and exchanges on a non-governmental level substantially expanded.

President Kim-Chairman Kim's historic summit meeting[15] confirmed that they had no intention of invading the other side and they would refrain from any acts threatening the other side. President Kim quoted Chairman Kim as saying, 'It is desirable that the American troops continue to stay on the Korean peninsula and that he sent a high-level envoy to the United States to deliver this position to the American side.'[16] In short, this landmark declaration provided a framework for building a peace regime on the Korean peninsula. The two leaders shared the view that war should never recur on the Korean peninsula. But it is regrettable that they failed to agree on the specific provisions relating to the building of a peace regime on the Korean peninsula.

---

12 For further details, see the Inaugural Address by President Kim Dae-jung of the Republic of Korea entitled 'The Government of the People: Reconciliation and a New Leap Forward' (Seoul, February 25, 1998) in *Korea and World Affairs*, vol. 22, no. 1 (Spring 1998), pp. 93–99.

13 For an official policy, see *Policy Toward North Korea for Peace, Reconciliation and Cooperation* (Seoul, Korea: Ministry of Unification, ROK, 1999).

14 For North Korea's nuclear issues, see Leon V. Sigal, *Disarming Strangers: Nuclear Diplomacy with North Korea* (Princeton, NJ: Princeton University Press, 1998); Young Whan Kihl and Peter Hayes, eds., *Peace and Security in Northeast Asia: The Nuclear Crisis and the Korean Peninsula* (Armonk, NY: M.E. Sharpe, 1997).

15 For the South Korean government's official account of the summit, see *Together as One, the Inter-Korean Summit Talks: Opening a New Era in the History of Korea* (Seoul, Korea: Ministry of Unification, ROK, July 2000).

16 Doug Struck, 'South Korean Says North Wants US Troops to Stay: Summit Declaration Called "a Great Relief"', *Washington Post*, August 30, 2000. For details, see Tae-Hwan Kwak, 'Kim Jong-il's Stand on Presence of USFK', *Vantage Point*, vol. 24, no. 9 (September 2001), pp. 15–19.

The ROK and the DPRK held their first defense ministers' talks in September 2000 and agreed to eliminate the threat of war, cooperate militarily to carry out the terms of the June 15th joint declaration, and discuss tension reduction on the Korean peninsula. In the course of five working-level military talks, agreement was reached on a set of ground rules for the peaceful use of the Demilitarized Zone (DMZ) and the installation of 'South-North Joint Control Areas.'

The need to implement the Inter-Korean Basic Agreement

The ROK and the DPRK signed the historic accord on North–South reconciliation, non-aggression, cooperation and exchanges known as the 'Inter-Korean Basic Agreement,' and the joint declaration for a non-nuclear Korean peninsula in December 1991 and both documents went effective in February 1992. It is essential for the two Koreas to comply with and implement the provisions of the two historic agreements in good faith, thus creating favorable conditions for building a peace regime on the Korean peninsula. The author argued that the two Korean states must, first of all, comply with and implement the South–North non-aggression agreement and the joint declaration for a non-nuclear Korean peninsula in good faith. The author also argued that separating the North's nuclear issue from inter-Korean economic exchanges and cooperation is necessary and desirable, and that inter-Korean mutual cooperation and common interests will eventually induce North Korea to abandon its nuclear development programs.[17]

The two Koreas signed the historic Inter-Korean Basic Agreement on December 13, 1991. It included the following provisions regarding peace and security issues: (1) the two Koreas agreed to respect each other's political and social systems, end slander and vilification, and pledged not to sabotage or subvert the other; (2) they agreed to work toward a peace system to replace the 1953 armistice agreement; (3) a South–North liaison office would be established at Panmunjom, on the border, within three months; (4) they agreed to resolve disputes through dialogue; (5) a joint military committee and a telephone hot line would be established. They also agreed to exchange military information, give prior notification of major troop movements and work toward arms reduction, including weapons of mass destruction.

Article 5 of the Basic Agreement provided an important provision for establishing a peace system in Korea. It reads:

> The two sides shall endeavor together to transform the present state of armistice into a solid state of peace between the South and the North and shall abide by the present Military Armistice Agreement (of July 27, 1953) until such a state of peace has been realized.[18]

---

17 For details, see Tae-Hwan Kwak, 'Inter-Korean Military Confidence Building: A Creative Implementation Formula', *Korea Observer*, vol. 24, no. 3 (Autumn 1993), pp. 367–394.

18 For the full text in English translated by the South side, see *An Era of Reconciliation and Cooperation Begins* (Seoul, Korea: National Unification Board, ROK, 1992), pp. 35–43.

The two Koreas agreed to work together toward replacing the present armistice with a peace system. Until then, they agreed to observe the 1953 Korean armistice agreement. The question remains how to implement this provision. In order to implement this provision, international cooperation is desirable, i.e. the UN can play an important role in converting the armistice system into a peace system. The 'real' parties to the Korean armistice agreement are undoubtedly South and North Korea, the US, and China. Since the Korean armistice agreement of 1953 was signed under UN auspices, the four parties need to participate in converting the present armistice system into a peace system. Hence, the author has argued elsewhere that the stalled four-party talks should be reactivated and be resumed to conclude a peace treaty to replace the Korean armistice agreement.[19]

Chapter 2, 'South–North Non-aggression' (Article 9 through 14) of the Basic Agreement contains detailed provisions for achieving an inter-Korean non-aggression. Major contents related to non-aggression in the Inter-Korean Basic Agreement are: (1) no use of force and no armed aggression against the other side (Article 9); (2) peaceful settlement of differences and disputes through dialogue and negotiation (Article 10); (3) designation of the Military Demarcation Line in the 1953 Armistice Agreement as the demarcation line and zone of non-aggression (Article 11); (4) establishment and operation of a South–North Joint Military Commission to implement and guarantee non-aggression along with confidence-building matters to be dealt with by the committee (Article 12); (5) installation of a telephone hotline between the military authorities of both sides (Article 13); and (6) formation of a South–North Military Commission to discuss concrete measures for the implementation and observance of the agreement on non-aggression and the removal of military confrontation between the two (Article 14).

In accordance with Article 12, the South–North Joint Military Commission needs to implement provisions relating to military confidence-building and arms reduction (or disarmament), including: (1) the mutual notification and control of large scale movements of military units and major military exercises; (2) the peaceful use of the DMZ: (3) exchanges of military personnel and information; (4) the realization of phased arms reductions, including the elimination of WMDs (nuclear, chemical, and biological weapons) and attack capabilities, and verifications thereof.

The two Koreas agreed to establish and operate the South–North Joint Military Commission in May 1992 in Pyongyang. Article 2 of the agreement spelled out its detailed functions: The joint military commission as an implementation body of Chapter 2, South–North Non-aggression provisions of the Basic Agreement, shall discuss and act on the following matters: (1) concrete and practical measures to implement the non-aggression provisions; (2) preparation and implementation of an agreement to achieve, abide by and guarantee non-aggression; (3) implementation of agreed measures to dissolve military confrontation; and (4) supervision and verifi-

---

19 For details, see Tae-Hwan Kwak, 'The Korean Peninsula Peace Regime Building Through the Four-Party Peace Talks: Re-evaluation and Policy Recommendations', *Journal of East Asian Affairs*, vol. 17, no.1 (Spring/Summer 2003) pp. 1–32.

cation of the implementation of measures. Both sides also agreed to establish South–North Liaison Offices.[20]

The two Koreas signed and effectuated an Auxiliary Agreement for the Implementation of and Compliance with Chapter 2, South–North Non-aggression, in September 1992 in Pyongyang. The South–North Joint Military Commission was also established in September 1992, but did not perform its functions to implement any provisions of the non-aggression agreement in the Basic Agreement, primarily due to the North's nuclear weapons development issue in 1992–94.

Since the two Koreas agreed to implement the inter-Korean non-aggression agreement in good faith, they first need to implement less difficult military measures such as the installation and operation of direct telephone hotlines between the military authorities of both sides to prevent the outbreak of accidental armed conflicts. Even less difficult issues could include the use of the DMZ for peaceful purposes and the mutual exchange of military personnel. In short, the two Koreas need to implement these provisions to establish a peace system in Korea.

The Joint Declaration on the Denuclearization of the Korean Peninsula: A creative implementation wanted

Let us now take a brief look at problems of implementing the Joint Declaration on the Denuclearization of the Korean Peninsula, which came into effect on February 19, 1992. In accordance with the joint declaration, South and North Korean delegates met seven times from February 19 to March 14, 1992 to discuss and conclude the draft agreement on the formation and operation of North–South Joint Nuclear Control Commission (JNCC). The South–North joint communiqué of March 14, 1992 stated:

> The north and the south reached an agreement on making joint efforts to adopt a document needed for verifying the denuclearization of the Korean peninsula within about two months after the first meeting of the North–South Nuclear Control Joint Committee and starting inspection within 20 days after the adoption of the document.[21]

On March 19, 1992, the JNCC began to implement the denuclearization of the Korean peninsula. The issue of the North's suspected nuclear weapons development program was an obstacle to the peace process in Korea. It was a real threat to the security of the Korean peninsula as well as the Northeast Asian region. It was widely reported that North Korea had at least two nuclear reactors in operation, and it would produce enough plutonium to make a nuclear bomb in two to three years. North Korea officially denied having the intention and capability of producing nuclear

---

20 For further details, see *South–North Dialogue in Korea*, no. 55 (July 1992), pp. 28–36.

21 For details, see 'The South-North Joint Communique of March 14, 1992', *The Pyongyang Times*, March 21, 1992.

arms. Nevertheless, the international community believed that North Korea was embarking on the production of nuclear weapons.

Because of mounting international pressures on North Korea not to produce nuclear weapons, it finally ratified the safeguards agreement with the IAEA in April 1992. Then the IAEA conducted six international inspections of nuclear facilities in North Korea and did not find that the North was making nuclear weapons. However, in February 1993, North Korea rebuffed the IAEA's request for inspecting two sites, which were believed to store nuclear waste from plutonium production. Earlier tests of samples given to the IAEA proved that the plutonium and the waste did not match. In fact, North Korea had a bigger reprocessing program. North Korea produced the 7 to 10 kilograms of plutonium needed to make a bomb.[22]

In the meantime, the IAEA requested North Korea to open the two suspected sites for its inspection by March 25, 1993. In response to the IAEA's request, North Korea decided to withdraw from the NPT treaty and its safeguard agreement with the IAEA on March 12, 1993. The North's decision produced profound negative effects on inter-Korean relations and its relations with the US, Japan, and other UN member states.[23] The two Koreas negotiated a bilateral inspection regime at the JNCC meetings for a more than a year, but they failed to agree on an inspection regime.

In short, it is essential for the two Koreas to reactivate the JNCC meeting in order to implement an inter-Korean agreement on the denuclearization on the Korean peninsula. The two Koreas may resolve the current nuclear issue by abandoning the North's nuclear programs.

The Role of US Forces Korea (USFK) in the Korean Peace Process

As inter-Korean relations will be normalized, the presence of USFK may hardly be justified. Thus, it is desirable that USFK will gradually be reduced in the Korean peace process, and it is also desirable that the UN Command (UNC) will be dissolved in due course.

The US Department of Defense announced on October 6, 2004, that the US and the ROK reached final agreement regarding the June 2004 US proposal to re-deploy 12,500 US troops from Korea.[24] This agreement also includes the transfer of certain missions from US forces to ROK forces, such as ROK forces taking over security at the joint security area in the DMZ, and the transfer of responsibility for rear area chemical decontamination to a special ROK unit. Specifically, the US and the ROK agreed to the redeployment of 12,500 US troops in three phases that will last until

---

22 Tim Zimmermann, 'Marching toward a showdown in Asia', *US News & World Report*, February 22, 1993; David E. Sanger, 'Atom Agency Said to Issue Demand to North Korea', *New York Times*, February 11, 1993.

23 For further details, see Tae-Hwan Kwak/Seung-Ho Joo, 'The Denuclearization of the Korean Peninsula: Problems and Prospects', *Arms Control: Contemporary Security Policy*, vol. 14, no. 2 (August 1993), pp. 65–92.

24 See the website at <http://www.defenselink.mil/releases/2004/nr20041006-1356.html> (June 10, 2005).

2008. The first phase was implemented in 2004 and included the 2nd Brigade Combat Team that was sent to Iraq in August 2004, and associated units. The redeployment in 2004 totaled about 5,000 troops.

During the second phase, 2005 to 2006, the US will redeploy a total of 5,000 troops (3,000 in 2005, 2,000 in 2006), comprising combat units, combat support and combat service support units, units associated with mission transfer areas, and other support personnel. In the third and final phase, 2007 to 2008, the US will redeploy 2,500 troops consisting primarily of support units and personnel. The US will continue the $11 billion investment in enhancing its capabilities on the Korean peninsula and in the region to strengthen its mutual deterrent with South Korea. Additionally, the transformation of US Army units in Korea will continue and will lead to a significant overall increase in combat capability.

The planned withdrawal would be the first major troop cut on the Korean peninsula since the early 1990s, when 7,000 US troops were taken out as part of the most significant realignment of USFK in half a century. The withdrawal underscores a broader move by the Department of Defense to transform troops stationed at traditional, fixed bases into more mobile forces for rapid global deployments.

Long-Term Stage: Korean Peninsula Peace Regime Building through Conclusion of a Korean Peninsula Peace Treaty

An international cooperation as an approach to peace regime building is also essential to a solution to the Korean issue. Thus, the 1953 Korean armistice agreement needs to be replaced by a multilateral peace treaty for guaranteeing a peace regime on the Korean peninsula. A Korean peninsula peace treaty among the four parties (the US, PRC, and two Koreas) at the four-party peace talks is the best option for establishing a peace regime on the Korean peninsula. However, the four-party peace talks have been deadlocked since August 1999, when the sixth round of the four-party talks ended without even setting an agenda, because North Korea refused to come to the negotiation table. As discussed below, the four-party peace talks had six plenary sessions where North Korea repeatedly maintained that the four-party peace talks should deal with two issues: US troop withdrawal from the South and the conclusion of a peace treaty between the US and North Korea. Thus, the four parties failed to set an agenda to be discussed at the four-party talks. The author evaluated in detail the four-party peace talks in 1996–99.[25]

The ROK and the US jointly proposed the four-party peace talks involving the two Koreas, China and the US to replace the 1953 Korean armistice agreement with

---

25 For further analysis of the four-party talks, see Tae-Hwan Kwak, 'The Korean Peninsula Peace Regime Building Through the Four-Party Peace Talks: Re-evaluation and Policy Recommendations', *Journal of East Asian Affairs*, vol. 17, no. 1 (Spring/Summer 2003) pp. 1–32.

a peace treaty.²⁶ The four-party talks had six plenary sessions where North Korea repeatedly maintained that the four-party peace talks deal with the two issues of US troop withdrawal and the conclusion of a peace treaty between the US and North Korea. While South Korea maintained that it wanted to discuss those issues that were easily resolved, North Korea tenaciously insisted that the two issues – the withdrawal of US troops and a Washington–Pyongyang peace treaty – be resolved first. Hence, the four-party talks made little tangible progress. Only two subcommittees were established: a peace regime building committee and a tension reduction committee.

After the June 2000 inter-Korean historic summit meeting, President Kim Dae-Jung said in August 2000, 'Through the four-party talks, attended by the two Koreas, the United States and China, there should emerge a complete consensus on establishing a permanent peace system on the Korean peninsula,'²⁷ and he stressed that a peace regime on the Korean peninsula must be established at the four-party talks. It was significant that President Kim wanted to reactivate the deadlocked four-party peace talks. International support for a solution of the divided Korean problem is crucial for the successful four-party peace talks in the future. UN Secretary-General Kofi Annan called for an 'international support structure' to bolster the current Korean peace process, which was on track after the historic June 2000 inter-Korean summit. UN Secretary-General Annan himself pledged his full support to the current efforts by the two Koreas to end the animosity that lasted half a century.²⁸

US Assistant Secretary of State James Kelly in an exclusive interview with *The Korea Times* at his office in the State Department on December 13, 2004, said that North Korea could expect the current armistice agreement on the Korean peninsula to be replaced with a multi-party peace treaty and eventually hope for the normalization of relations, if the North agreed to dismantle all of its nuclear programs.²⁹

Proposals for six agenda items at the four-party talks

The author has argued that the deadlocked four-party talks need to be reactivated and the issue of the establishment of a peace regime on the Korean peninsula be discussed at the four-party talks. It is a formidable task to create a peace formula acceptable to the two Koreas, China and the US What has been proposed is a creative formula for establishing a peace regime on the Korean peninsula.³⁰ In order to implement

---

26 For details, see Tae-Hwan Kwak and Seung-Ho Joo, 'The Four-Party Peace Talks: Inter-Korean Bilateral Agenda', *Pacific Focus*, vol. 12, no. 1 (Spring 1997), pp. 5–24.

27 Lee Chang-sup, 'Kim Proposes Inter-Korean Peace Accord', *Korea Times*, August 25, 2000.

28 Son Key-young, 'UN Chief Annan Calls for "Int'l Support Structure" on Korean Peace Process', *Korea Times*, September 3, 2000.

29 Oh Young-jin, 'Kim Jong-il Can Transform North Korea, Kelly Says', *Korea Times*, December 14, 2004.

30 The author maintained a four-party peace formula in the mid-1980s, see Tae-Hwan Kwak, *In Search of Peace and Unification on the Korean Peninsula* (Seoul, Korea: Seoul Computer Press, 1986). For the author's proposal for the four-party peace formula prior to

the proposed peace treaty formula, a political will is required. No matter how good the formula may be, if there is a lack of political will to implement it, it remains unrealistic. Therefore, this author firmly believes it is necessary and desirable for the US, China, DPRK and ROK governments to reactivate the deadlocked four-party talks as soon as possible. The author has proposed six agenda items to be discussed at the four-party talks. First, a peace agreement between South and North Korea may be considered on the agenda. The two Koreas should reconfirm the implementation of Article 5 of the Basic Agreement and Article 19 of the Protocol on the Compliance with and Implementation of Chapter 1, 'South–North Reconciliation of the Basic Agreement', in order to transform the armistice regime into a peace regime on the Korean peninsula. In addition, Chapter 2, 'South–North Non-aggression' (Articles 9 through 14) of the Basic Agreement and its protocol need to be implemented in good faith by South and North Korea. If the two Koreas sincerely implement the non-aggression provisions in the inter-Korean Basic Agreement, it is not necessary to separately conclude a peace treaty between the two Koreas. Thus, it is argued that the ROK government needs to revise a proposal for a peace treaty between Seoul and Pyongyang.

Second, a US–North Korea non-aggression agreement may be placed on agenda. Since 1974, North Korea has insisted on a US–North Korea peace treaty. The North's demand for concluding a non-aggression agreement between the US and North Korea may be discussed within a multilateral framework of the four-party peace talks. The DPRK appeared to have abandoned a long-standing bilateral peace treaty between the US and North Korea. In May 2004, DPRK deputy representative to the UN Han Song Ryol suggested that the best way to resolve its nuclear standoff with the US would be to replace the Korean armistice with a trilateral peace treaty ending the Korean War, to be signed by the two Koreas and the US.[31] It is significant that North Korea is also interested in conclude a multilateral peace treaty.

Third, a peace agreement between South Korea and China may be added to the agenda. The ROK established its diplomatic relations with China in 1992, but there is no legal document signed by the two to formally terminate the Korean War. In my view, it is necessary for the two countries to sign a peace agreement to do this.

Fourth, a peace agreement between China and the US can also be placed on the agenda. China and the US were also belligerent powers during the Korean War, and yet the two powers have not concluded a peace agreement to formally end the war. It

---

the joint US–ROK proposal for the four-party talks, see Tae-Hwan Kwak, 'Building a Peace Regime on the Korean Peninsula', *Diplomacy*, vol. 22, no. 4 (May 1996), pp. 28–29. For detailed analysis of the four-party peace talks, see Tae-Hwan Kwak, 'The Four-Party Peace Treaty: A Creative Formula for Building a Peace Regime on the Korean Peninsula', *Korea Institute for Defense Analyses*, vol. 9, no. 2 (Winter, 1997), pp. 117–135. See Tae-Hwan Kwak, 'The Korean Peninsula Peace Regime Building Through the Four-Party Peace Talks: Re-evaluation and Policy Recommendations', *Journal of East Asian Affairs*, vol. 17, no. 1 (Spring/Summer 2003) pp. 1–32.

31 Barbara Slavin, 'North Korea suggests peace treaty to settle nuclear dispute', *USA Today*, May 13, 2004.

is argued that there is need to conclude a peace agreement between the two in view of conflicting security interests of the two powers in the Asia-Pacific region. In this context, a US–China peace agreement can be considered at the four-party talks.

Fifth, political and military confidence-building measures (CBMs) between the two Koreas should be placed on the agenda. The South–North Joint Military Commission needs to be re-activated to implement provisions of the non-aggression agreement as spelled out in the Chapter 2 of the Basic Agreement. The Commission should also discuss relevant issues relating to inter-Korean arms control, CBMs, the reduction of offensive weapons systems, chemical and biological weapons, long-range missiles and a verification regime.

Sixth, the establishment of an international peace observation body should be an agenda. This international body must enforce a Korean peninsula peace treaty and oversee the implementation of agreements to be concluded by the four parties concerned.

The six items as suggested above could be placed on the agenda for the future meeting of the four-party peace talks. At least four agreements among the four parties may be agreed upon: (1) a South-North Korean peace agreement; (2) a North Korea–US peace agreement; (3) a South Korea–China peace agreement; and (4) a US–China peace agreement. These four agreements will legally terminate the Korean War (1950–53). No party will demand war guilt, reparations, or the persecution of war criminals as usually demanded in a peace treaty.

Needless-to-say, the two Koreas should play key roles in transforming the armistice agreement into a peace treaty at the four-party peace talks. Since the 1953 Korean armistice agreement is a multilateral treaty, in my view, a peace treaty to replace the armistice agreement in the future should also be a multilateral one. As an alternative to the 'two-plus-two' formula, the leaders of the four nations at the summit meeting could sign a Korean peninsula peace treaty, which might be called, a 'Joint Declaration on a Comprehensive Peace on the Korean Peninsula.' The joint peace declaration is in effect equivalent to a four-party peace treaty and a system of collective security, whereby a unification-oriented peace regime on the Korean peninsula will be firmly established.

The four parties, Russia and Japan (all members of the six-party talks) will jointly guarantee this peace plan. The UN Security Council should endorse a resolution to guarantee this plan. The next stage would be to develop a multilateral security consultative body including Russia and Japan. In this way, there will be a durable, unification-oriented peace regime on the Korean peninsula and in Northeast Asia. In my view, the four-party peace talks as an international approach to a peace regime on the Korean peninsula provide the best option because it would legally replace the 1953 Korean armistice agreement with an internationally guaranteed Korean peninsula peace treaty.

Concluding Remarks

The long, rough journey toward a peace regime on the Korean peninsula has already begun. The North Korean nuclear issue needs to be resolved peacefully and diplomatically through the six-party talks in the short-term. Without resolving the nuclear issue, a peace regime initiative as argued here is nothing but a dream. Thus, the six-party nuclear talks and a peace regime initiative in Korea are closely related. As discussed above, inter-Korean and international cooperation approaches to a peace regime are essential requirements for building a peace regime on the Korean peninsula.

The inter-Korean June 15 joint declaration provided a framework for establishing de facto peaceful coexistence between the two Koreas. Unless the two Koreas demonstrate their desire to cooperate through sincere deeds and are willing to make concessions by working together for establishing a peace regime in Korea, there is little chance of achieving this goal. Thus, in my view, Seoul and Pyongyang need to take an initiative to reactivate the stalled South–North Korean Joint Military Commission as operated under the Inter-Korean Basic Agreement effective in 1992, to discuss a Korean peace system at the inter-Korean level.

On the international level, as discussed above, the ROK and the US need to take an initiative to reactivate the stalled four-party talks among the US, China, South and North Korea to build a peace regime on the Korean peninsula. The ROK government must continue pursuing the new engagement policy of 'peace and prosperity' toward North Korea. The ROK needs to play a leading role in peacefully resolving North Korea's nuclear issue to avoid a possible military confrontation between the US and North Korea if the nuclear issue cannot be resolved by a peaceful means. President Roh's new engagement policy and President Bush's hardline policy toward North Korea were occasionally in conflict in dealing with the nuclear issue. The Bush administration appears softening its hardline policy toward North Korea, and North Korea has made its strategic decision to abandon its nuclear programs. Chairman Kim's political will to resolve its nuclear issue is evidenced in the 9.19 joint statement.

Finally, the future of inter-Korean relations and multiple interactions among members in Northeast Asia will be important variables affecting a Korean peace regime initiative discussed here. The structure and political process of the Northeast Asian system will have a profound impact on the establishment of a peace system on the Korean peninsula. For instance, the future of US–ROK military, economic and political relations, US–DPRK relations, US–PRC relations, China-Japan relations, inter-Korean relations, US–Japan–ROK trilateral relations vs. China–Russia–North Korea trilateral relations and other multilateral patterns of interactions will have either a positive or negative impact on the peace regime building on the Korean peninsula.

Chapter 3

US–ROK Relations:
The Political–Diplomatic Dimension

Seung-Ho Joo

Traditionally the US has been the closest friend and ally of Korea. In the late 19th century, Korea (*Chosun dynasty*) expected the US to serve as a benign protector. Surrounded by major powers – China, Japan, and Russia – and unable to ensure its own survival and independence from their imperial designs, Korea sought protection from the US. The US had its own imperial designs on East Asia, and in the secret Taft-Katsura agreement of 1905, the US recognized Japan's sphere of influence over Korea in exchange for its dominant influence in the Philippines. After 36 years of Japanese colonial rule, Korea gained independence in August 1945, but was divided into two occupation zones by a US–Soviet agreement. In 1948, two separate Korean states were created – the Republic of Korea (ROK or South Korea) in the south under the auspices of the US and the Democratic People's Republic of Korea (DPRK or North Korea) in the north with the Soviet Red Army's support. During the Korean War (1950–53), South Korea was saved from invading North Korea with a massive military intervention of the US.

After the Korean War, the US–ROK mutual defense treaty was signed in October 1953 and US troops remained on Korean soil. Since then, the US–ROK alliance and US military presence in Korea has served as deterrent against North Korea's aggression and guarantor of peace and security in Northeast Asia. The US also provided generous economic aid to the ROK and served as the largest market for Korean exports, which undoubtedly contributed to the ROK's rapid economic growth in the 1960s to 1980s.

During the Cold War, US–ROK diplomatic relations remained stable and predictable, despite periodic frictions. The ROK considered its ties with the US central to its external relations and pivotal to its own survival. The US also needed the ROK as an ally for its global and regional strategic designs. The two countries' national interests, however, were not identical:

> Korea naturally perceived its interests in terms of the Korean Peninsula, its relations with North Korea being paramount …. The United States, however, views policies related to

security first as multifaceted ... then regional in Northeast Asia ... and only then focused on the Korean Peninsula.[1]

Since 1945, the US and the ROK periodically experienced political frictions, but their differences were downplayed and hidden from public view. There was a 'ritualized, official public relations gavotte that each side seems to regard as necessary and that each is reluctant to end.'[2]

US–ROK political relations were undergoing qualitative changes in the 1990s to 2000s. The ascendancy of George W. Bush and the neo-conservatives in the US and the rise of Roh Moo-Hyun and the so-called '386-generation' in South Korea deepened mutual tensions and distrust. In the past, frictions and tensions between the two allies were manageable, infrequent, and invisible to the public; now they are unmistakable, frequent, and open. US–ROK political relations are now in flux. One of the peculiar changes is that nowadays neither side even pretends to hide or downplay their differences.

This chapter examines US–ROK political relations in the 2000s, which are characterized by tensions, distrust and conflicting interests. It begins with a discussion of the rapidly deteriorating political relationship between Seoul and Washington after George W. Bush came to power. This is followed by an examination of salient issues dividing the two allies. The chapter then analyzes the sources of tensions and distrust in US–ROK relations. Finally, it concludes with an assessment of the current US–ROK relations.

Widening Distance and Rising Tension

The political-diplomatic relations between Seoul and Washington experienced rapid deterioration soon after George W. Bush was sworn in as US President in January 2001. In fact, US–ROK relations entered into a new phase in the 2000s. North Korea was the most divisive issue separating the two allies. President Bush harbored intense hatred and contempt for North Korean leader Kim Jong-Il. Departing from his predecessor's engagement policy, Bush took a hardline policy toward North Korea. Upon inauguration, Bush refused to resume Clinton's efforts at missile negotiations and normalizing relations with the North. He also disagreed with ROK President Kim Dae-Jung's 'sunshine policy' (conciliatory engagement policy) toward the DPRK. Consequently, Bush and Kim Dae-Jung collided over North Korea and US–ROK relations turned sour.

The first summit meeting in Washington, DC between Bush and Kim Dae-Jung in March 2001 turned out to be a disaster. Instead of endorsing Kim Dae-Jung's engagement policy, Bush lectured Kim Dae-Jung about Kim Jong-Il's

---

[1] David I. Steinberg, 'Building on the ROK: Reflections on the Korean-American Relationship', in Bae Ho Han and Chae-Jin Lee, eds., *The Korean Peninsula and the Major Powers* (Seoul: The Sejong Institute, 1998), p. 4.

[2] Ibid., p. 1.

untrustworthiness. Bush's disrespectful treatment and open disagreement offended many South Koreans and hurt Kim Dae-Jung's ego. Subsequently, US–ROK relations deteriorated.[3]

The 9/11 terrorist attacks in the US further hardened Bush's stance toward North Korea. In his 2002 State of the Union address, Bush lumped three states – North Korea, Iran and Iraq – together as an 'axis of evil.'[4] By including North Korea in that category, he indicated that the US intended to destroy North Korea or force it to change its behavior. During his visit to South Korea in February 2002, Bush reconfirmed his hostile attitudes toward North Korea when he stated that he would not let the world's 'most dangerous regimes' acquire its 'most dangerous weapons.'[5] He also expressed his skepticism of North Korea's reforms. Bush tried to assuage South Koreans' anxiety over a possible war when he stated that the US had no intention of attacking North Korea. Kim Dae-Jung, in contrast, reaffirmed his commitment to the sunshine policy of engaging North Korea. Kim thanked Bush for 'clarifying' any misunderstanding created by his State of the Union speech, in which he included North Korea as part of an 'axis of evil.' The two governments still maintained diplomatic decorum, but their diverging approaches to North Korea and resultant frictions were clearly visible.[6]

The Bush administration adopted a new doctrine of preemptive war as enshrined in the National Security Strategy issued on September 20, 2002.[7] The new US doctrine of preemption included preemptive attack (the use of force in the face of an imminent attack) as well as preventive attack (the use of force before a serious threat to the US gathers or grows over time). The preventive aspect of the doctrine is well manifested in President Bush's cover letter to the September 2002 National Security Strategy, which stated: '… as a matter of common sense and self-defense, America will act against [such] emerging threats before they are fully formed.'[8]

The global war on terrorism, the 'axis of evil' speech, and the doctrine of preemptive attack raised serious concerns on the part of the ROK government since US sanctions or military strikes on North Korea could easily lead to an all-out war

---

3 Howard W. French, 'Korean Diplomacy Enters a New Era', *The New York Times* April 20, 2003.

4 David E. Sanger, 'The State of the Union Address: The Overview', *The New York Times*, January 30, 2002.

5 Elisabeth Bumiller, 'Bush Says US and China Want to See Koreas Unified', *The New York Times*, February 21, 2002; 'With Due Respect, Mr. President', *Economist*, February 23, 2002.

6 Ihlwan Moon, 'How Bush is Pushing South Koreans Apart', *Business Week*, February 25, 2002.

7 President Bush first mentioned the concept of preemptive war in his June 22, 2002 speech at West Point.

8 For the full text of the National Security Strategy, go to <http://www.whitehouse.gov/nsc/nss.html>. See also Michael E. O'Hanlon, Susan E. Rice, and James B. Steinberg', The New National Security Strategy and Preemption', *The Brookings Institution Policy Brief* (December 2002).

in Korea, which would certainly spell unspeakable disasters for the Korean people. Bush's hardline policy toward North Korea and the DPRK's inflexible attitudes resulted in the freezing of US–North Korean relations and the suspension of the inter-Korean peace process that had been set in motion following the June 2000 inter-Korean summit.

The Bush administration was frustrated with Kim Dae-Jung government's engagement policy vis-à-vis North Korea and preferred the victory of a cooperative, conservative political figure in the December 2002 presidential election of South Korea. The US rooted for the conservative, pro-American Lee Hoe-Chang of the opposition Grand National Party over the progressive, independent-minded Roh Moo-Hyun of the ruling New Millenium Party. Bush's support for Lee was clear when his administration welcomed Lee Hoi-chang's visit to Washington earlier in 2002.

Roh Moo-Hyun's election as South Korea's President in December 2002 did not augur well for US–ROK relations. Roh came to power riding the tide of anti-American sentiment that was spreading across South Korea at the time and vowing for an independent, nationalistic foreign policy as well as sweeping domestic reforms. Before assuming presidency, he had very limited experience in government and no experience in foreign affairs.[9] As a presidential candidate, Roh vowed that if elected he would not 'kow-tow' to Washington and that he would mediate between the US and North Korea to prevent a war in Korea. He promised to continue President Kim's sunshine policy vis-à-vis North Korea.[10]

Roh came to power at a critical time. The second crisis over the North Korean nuclear issue erupted in October 2002 when Assistant Secretary of State for East Asia and the Pacific, James Kelly, visited Pyongyang and allegedly got a confession from a senior North Korea official to secret nuclear weapons based on highly enriched uranium (HEU). By early 2003, the North Korean nuclear issue topped the agenda in US–ROK relations. By the time of Roh's inauguration in February 2003, a US invasion of Iraq was imminent and there was a widespread concern among South Koreans that North Korea would be the next target for US attack. In March 2003, Japan announced that it would launch a preemptive attack on North Korea if there was evidence that North Korea's missile attack was imminent. In defiance of the US, North Korea resumed its nuclear weapons program and withdrew from the Nuclear Nonproliferation (NPT) treaty.

---

9   Roh served as a National Assembly (ROK's national legislature) member for six years and as a ROK's Maritime and Fisheries Minister for six months. Born into a poor peasant family, he became a human-rights lawyer and political activist in the 1980s. He is a leftist in ideological orientation. His father-in-law died after 18 years in prison for Communist activities during the Korean War. See Moon Ihlwan and Mark L. Clifford, 'The Politics of Peril: South Korea's Untested Roh Moo Hyun Faces a Bizarre and Dangerous Foreign Policy Crisis. Is he Up to It?' *Business Week*, February 24, 2003.

10 Oh Young-jin, 'Roh Takes Nation's Highest Office, President Declares "Age of Peace and Prosperity"', *Korea Times*, February 25, 2003; and Shin Jong-rok, 'Roh Promises "Peace and Prosperity"', *Chosun Ilbo*, February 25, 2003.

In late 2002, anti-American sentiment was spreading rapidly in South Korea. The immediate cause was the crushing death of two Korean middle school girls in June by an armored personnel carrier driven by American soldiers in a military exercise. The trial and acquittal of the two soldiers responsible for the accident by a US military court sparked massive anti-American protests in which tens of thousands of South Koreans took to the street and held candlelight vigils night after night. The Status of Forces Agreement (SOFA) between the US and the ROK, which stipulates the legal rights of US soldiers in Korea, is woefully lopsided when compared to similar US agreements with other countries, such as Japan and Germany. South Koreans' perception of the unfair SOFA, Bush's hardline policy toward North Korea, and US insensitivity to South Korean feelings and interests all added fuel to persistent anti-American protests.

Roh has consistently and unequivocally opposed Bush's hardline policy toward North Korea and advocated an engagement policy with North Korea. At the outset, the Roh government decided to attempt resolving the North Korean nuclear issue while continuing inter-Korean exchanges and cooperation.[11] This policy line was in direct conflict with Bush's hardline policy, which called for isolating and pressuring North Korea into abandoning its nuclear program before providing any rewards.

The Bush administration has been divided between the hardliners, who advocate North Korea's regime change and prefer forceful means to change North Korea's behavior, and the moderates, who are skeptical of Kim Jong-Il regime's immediate collapse and favor a negotiated solution to the nuclear issue. The hardliners consisted of 'the offices of the Secretary of Defense and the Vice President, and non-proliferation specialists in the State Department and the National Security Council [NSC],' and the moderates were found 'mainly in the State Department and NSC, [which] was composed of officials with experience on East Asian and Korean issues.'[12] This division resulted in the lack of consistency and comprehensive strategy in the Bush administration's North Korea policy.

Roh and Bush got off to a bad start. According to Bruce Cumings's testimony, Roh's brief meeting on February 26 with 13 Americans, intended as a festive gathering, turned out to be an unpleasant confrontation:

> The next day I [Cumings] met with President Roh along with twelve other Americans for what was supposed to be a brief congratulatory get-together. Instead, three prominent Americans gathered across the table from Roh and began to lecture him on what was wrong with just about everything he had said about his position vis-à-vis the North. One of them, a former ambassador to Japan, hulked menacingly over the table, his face red and seemingly angered, telling Roh that Americans would never understand his statement that

---

11 Se-Hyun Jeong, 'Inter-Korean Relations under Policy for Peace and Prosperity', *Korea and World Affairs*, vol. 28, no. 1 (spring 2004), p. 6.

12 Mark E. Manyin, Emma Chanlett-Avery, and Helene Marchart, 'North Korea: A Chronology of Events, October 2002–December 2004', CRS Report for Congress, Order Code RL32743 (January 24, 2005), p. 4.

he would 'guarantee the security and survival of the North', since the American people found that regime 'detestable.'[13]

In response to a US–North Korean military confrontation on March 1, 2003, in which four North Korean MiG fighters came within 50 feet of a US RC-135 reconnaissance airplane and tried to intercept it over international waters in the East Sea, Roh refused to condemn North Korea's military provocation. Instead, he urged the US 'not to go too far' and stated that 'it was a very predictable chance of events' because of increased aerial surveillance by the US over North Korea's nuclear facilities.[14] This response from a long-time ally certainly angered US policy-makers.

The Bush-Roh summit in May 2003 in Washington, DC failed to narrow their differences over the North Korean nuclear crisis. At a Beijing meeting in April, North Korea declared that it already possessed weapons and had turned 8,000 spent nuclear fuel rods into bomb-grade plutonium. The US and South Korea shared the goal of nuclear-free North Korea, but differed on strategy. The ROK insisted that all peaceful means should be exhausted first before any sanctions or the use of force should be applied against North Korea. In contrast, the US wanted to consider all options, including economic embargo and the use of military force. By using vague diplomatic statements, the two allies 'stepped around serious differences.' The joint statement issued by Bush and Roh was deliberately vague on the question of when and how pressure could be increased on North Korea. The statement said: 'While noting that increased threats to peace and stability on the peninsula would require consideration of further steps [Bush and Mr. Roh] expressed confidence that a peaceful resolution can be achieved.' In the statement, Roh conceded that 'future inter-Korean exchanges and cooperation will be conducted in light of developments on the North Korean nuclear issue.'[15]

Following the May summit meeting, the ROK and the US further smoothed over some of the pending issues and recovered the appearance of cooperation. Roh in the past even advocated the withdrawal of American troops. But as president he realized that the US–ROK alliance and US troops in Korea were essential for Korea's security and economy. Roh now wanted to postpone the Pentagon's plans to reduce or redeploy US troops in Korea until after the North Korean nuclear crisis was resolved. He stated that such Pentagon's moves might send a wrong signal to the North. In an effort to bolster the US–ROK alliance and win US support for his

---

13 Bruce Cumings, 'Rising Danger in Korea', *Nation*, vol. 276, no. 11 (March 23, 2003), p. 10.

14 Roh's Interview with *The Times* (London) (March 3, 2003), cited from Byung Chul Koh, 'Inter-Korean Relations under Roh Moo-Hyun', *Korea and World Affairs* (Spring 2003), pp. 10–11.

15 David E. Sanger, 'Aftereffects: Nuclear Standoff: Bush and New President of South Korea Are Vague On North Korea Strategy', *The New York Times*, May 15, 2003.

engagement policy vis-à-vis North Korea, Roh gave a strong support for the US war in Iraq in March 2003 and agreed to send non-combat troops to Iraq there.[16]

Nevertheless, Roh's independent foreign policy with Anti-American and pro-North Korean tones continued to cause tensions and friction with the Bush administration. This policy was highly divisive and controversial inside South Korea as well. ROK's National Security Council, manned mostly with leftist, former political activists who shared President Roh's ideological orientation and political agenda was the stronghold for 'independent' (or anti-American) foreign policy. ROK's Ministry of Defense and Ministry of Foreign Affairs and Trade (MOFAT) were mostly staffed with liberal, pro-American individuals. The confrontation came to a head in January 2004, when Foreign Minister Yoon Young Kwan was fired when he was held responsible for a scandal in which some MOFAT officials criticized Roh's independent foreign policy posture (the Blue House was tipped off about these critical remarks by an informant). Pro-American officials in MOFAT criticized the Roh government for jeopardizing traditional US–ROK friendly ties. One official reportedly likened Roh's supporters to pro-North Korean activists. Roh fired Yoon, blaming him 'for not being able to handle and manage the ministry.' In addition, the Blue House carried out personnel changes in MOFAT on the grounds that 'some Foreign Ministry bureaucrats could not leave behind the dependent foreign policy of the past and could not fully understand the direction of the basic spirit of the new independent foreign policy.'[17]

Roh's independent foreign policy vis-à-vis the US and conciliatory postures toward North Korea met with strong resistance from many segments of South Korean society. The Roh government lacked widespread support from South Koreans and the ruling party was in a minority in the National Assembly. Roh's imprudent words and deeds plus his violation of election laws led to an impeachment motion in the National Assembly early in 2004. His presidency was saved by a Constitutional Court's ruling to dismiss the National Assembly's impeachment move. This episode turned out to be a blessing in disguise for Roh. In accordance with the Court ruling, his presidential powers were fully restored in May 2004. The impeachment effort backfired, conservative parties lost and the ruling Uri Party won gaining a slim majority in the National Assembly in a general election held the following month.[18] The general election also brought about generational changes in the legislature. Younger and more progressive candidates, who did not have personal memories of the Korean War, gained seats there en masse. The outcome of all this was that both the legislative and executive branches comprised the youngest, most progressive and ideological, least experienced, and least pro-American government in South

---

16 David H. Hackworth, 'Air Power Just Won't Work', *Newsweek*, May 17, 1993.

17 Anthony Faiola, 'S. Korean Foreign Minister Resigns After Dispute Over US Ties', *The Washington Post*, January 15, 2004.

18 The ruling Uri Party won 152 seats, a majority in the 300-seat Assembly and the leftist Democratic Labour Party gained ten seats. The conservative Grand National Party (GNP) dropped from 138 seats to 121.

Korea's history. In polls, majorities of Uri Party legislators classified themselves as 'progressives', and considered South Korea's relations with China more important than those with the US.[19] Nearly half of all legislators are under 50, only 13 per cent over 60. In August 2004, *Joongang Ilbo* classified 45 per cent of the current National Assembly as progressives and only 20 per cent as conservatives, with the rest being moderates.[20]

G.W. Bush will stay in power until January 2009 and Roh Moo-Hyun will remain ROK's President until February 2008. Roh and Bush will have to deal with each other until early 2008. Bush is now surrounded by hardliners more than ever. Colin Powell was a voice of reason in Bush's foreign policy. With his replacement as Secretary of State by Condoleezza Rice we can expect 'a squeeze on North Korea' and 'a collision with Iran.'[21] Rice's referring to North Korea as one of the 'outposts of tyranny' at her Senate confirmation hearing[22] did not augur well for US–DPRK talks and US–ROK relations.

US Presidential advisers have been talking of repairing ties and acting within alliances when they can. It is not because the US changed its goals, strategy, or priorities. It is because the US now has limited options dealing with North Korea because it is bogged down in Iraq. '... Iraq has made it harder to be hawkish in this White House, not because desires to act have changed, but because it has tied down American combat troops and magnified the need to juggle scarce military resources.' The US is now over-stretched militarily, constrained economically, and has alienated many of its allies and friends. The Bush Administration seems to recognize the need to cultivate friendly ties with states through public diplomacy.[23]

After Bush's reelection, senior government officials of South Korea expressed concern about US hardline policy toward North Korea. President Roh in a Los Angeles speech in November 2004, shortly before he held summit talks with US President G.W. Bush at the Chile APEC summit meeting, sounded a warning against the Bush administration's hardline policy toward North Korea: 'This [peaceful resolution to the nuclear crisis] is our strong wish for the people of the US, the only ally of South Korea, and will be the most important factor in strengthening

---

19 James Brooke, 'Constitutional Court Reinstates South Korea's Impeached President', *The New York Times*, May 14, 2004.

20 'Progressives 44.5 per cent, Conservatives 20 per cent', *Joongang Ilbo*, August 31, 2004.

21 Nicholas D. Kristof, 'The Bush Revolution', *The New York Times*, November 17, 2004.

22 Rice said: 'To be sure, in our world there remain outposts of tyranny, and America stands with oppressed people on every continent: in Cuba and Burma and North Korea and Iran and Belarus and Zimbabwe.' See Pablo Bachelet, 'Rice: Cuba an "outpost of tyranny", Venezuela a "negative force"', *The Miami Herald*, January 19, 2005.

23 David E. Sanger, 'Hawk Sightings Could Be Premature', *New York Times*, November 21, 2004.

our friendship.'[24] Roh also stated that North Korea's main concern is security and its nuclear program is for defensive purposes: 'After all, the North's nuclear issue boils down to whether we can give it security guarantees and lead it out of its current plight through reform and openness.' Washington did not hide its disagreement with Roh's speech when the State Department issued a statement: 'There are elements in President Roh's speech that we hope to have an opportunity to discuss with senior ROK officials in the near future.'[25] The North Korean nuclear issue continues to divide the US and the ROK, and will remain the main source of friction and distrust between the two allies.

The Sources of Distrust and Tension

Seoul and Washington often state that the ROK–US friendship is intact and the bilateral alliance remains firm. But beneath the rhetorical surface lies the reality of tensions, friction, and mutual distrust. US–ROK political relations have been undergoing qualitative changes since 2001. What then led to the current uncomfortable state of the relationship? We will now look at the sources of the changing relationship, focusing on: (1) foreign policy goals and national interests; (2) perception and attitudes; and (3) the North Korean nuclear issue.

Foreign policy goals and national interests

In the Cold War years, the US pursued a goal of containing the global Communist threat and relied on superior military capability to achieve the goal. In the post-Cold War era (especially after 9/11), the US has pursued the twin goals of the destruction of terrorist networks and the prevention of nuclear proliferation by using superior military capability. Unilateralism, the preemptive doctrine and the militarization of foreign policy characterize G.W. Bush's foreign policy.

The 9/11 terrorist attacks were a turning point. After 9/11, President Bush's ideas about national security radicalized. The influence of neo-conservatives (neo-cons)[26] over Bush and his foreign policy increased dramatically after the terrorist attacks. Neo-cons aim to perpetuate US hegemony in a unipolar system. They see the world in terms of good and evil, and advocate the use of superior military power to defeat the forces of evil. They support spreading democracy to autocratic regimes. Neo-

---

24 Sim Chae-yun and Ryu Chin, 'Roh Makes Efforts "To Avert" "Unfavorable" Shift in US Policy on DPRK', *The Korea Times*, November 15, 2004.

25 'US Wants Talks on Roh's Controversial Remarks on North Korea', *Yonhap*, November 18, 2004.

26 Neo-cons include former professors such as Paul Wolfowitz (Under Secretary of Defense) and Steve Cambone (at the Pentagon), lawyers such as Doug Feith, Scooter Libby (Dick Cheney's former chief of staff), John Bolton (Deputy Secretary of State), and Richard Perle. Dick Cheney and Donald Rumsfeld (both former CEOs) became the neo-cons' most powerful supporters.

cons prefer 'moral clarity to diplomatic finesse, and confrontation to the pursuit of incremental advantage.' They are 'skeptical of multilateral institutions that limit American power and effectiveness; they prefer to focus on new threats and opportunities, rather than old alliances.'[27] The preemption doctrine contained in the 2002 'National Security Strategy of the United States' derived from neo-cons. It comprised neo-cons' ideas combined with Bush's sense of self-righteousness and certainty. In historian Robert Dallek's words: 'What you have ... is sort of secular evangelism: "I know I'm right. I know what to do."'[28] Bush's certainty and heavy-handedness alienated much of the world, including former friends and allies.

The US is preoccupied with global issues, most notably the global war on terrorism and nuclear nonproliferation. US relations with the DPRK and the ROK are circumscribed by its global concerns. As a result, 'much of the US response was less shaped solely by North Korea's role on the peninsula or the region than by US perceptions of North Korea as part of a far larger global problem identified with proliferation, rogue states, and supporters of terrorism.'[29] Nowadays, functional experts in counter-proliferation and counter-terrorism rather than area specialists on Korea formulate US Korea policy. This tendency of focusing on nuclear nonproliferation and overlooking the unique circumstances and interests of the ROK is a source of US–ROK frictions:

> North Korea's nuclear weapons program has assured continued American interest in the Korean Peninsula, but the functional nature of that interest has led to friction in the alliance because American global priorities have taken precedence over regional considerations in shaping US responses to the North Korean problem and have begun to supersede alliance cooperation with South Korea as the primary referent for managing policy toward North Korea.[30]

In the same context, the Pentagon's reconfiguring of the US global military basing structure known as the Global Posture Review (GPR) caused frictions with South Korea. In accordance with the GPR, the US announced its plan to reduce US troops in Korea by one-third by the end of 2005 and raised the possibility of transforming the security role of the US–ROK alliance to include regional security matters.

The restructuring of US troops in Korea and the future of US–ROK alliance has also emerged as a central issue in US–ROK relations. US Secretary of Defense Donald Rumsfeld stated early in 2003 that US troops would not stay where they were not welcome. In mid-March, a senior Pentagon official said the trip wire function of

---

27 'The Shadow Men', *The Economist*, April 26, 2003.
28 Kenneth T. Walsh, 'Command Presence', *US News & World Report*, March 31, 2003.
29 Edward A. Olsen, 'Trilateral (US, ROK, Japan) Cooperation in the Resolution of the North Korean Nuclear Crisis', *Pacific Focus*, vol. 19, no. 2 (Fall 2004), p. 68.
30 Scott Snyder, 'Alliance and Alienation: Managing Diminished Expectations for US-ROK Relations', *Comparative Connections* (Pacific Forum, CSIS, August 2004), p. 3, available at <www.csis.org/pacfor/ccejournal.html>.

US troops near the Demilitarized Zone (DMZ) was outdated and the Second Infantry Division located near the DMZ would be moved to south of the Han River. He continued that if South Korea did not want American forces, they would leave 'at any time, even tomorrow.'[31] Rumsfeld has been restructuring US troops worldwide in view of new technology and new threats. The Pentagon was reassessing the location and size of US bases and the number of troops stationed abroad.

In June 2004, the Pentagon presented a detailed plan to South Korea for withdrawing one-third (12,500) of its 37,000 troops by the end of 2005. This would be the first troop reduction since 1992.[32] The US announced that by 2006 all American troops would be moved from positions near the DMZ to new locations south of the Han River, out of artillery range of the North. The repositioning would mean the abandonment of the trip-wire strategy designed to ensure the automatic involvement of the US in a future Korean war. US officials stated that, despite the planned US troop reduction and redeployment, US commitment to the US–ROK alliance remained firm, pointing out that the US plan to spend $11 billion during the next five years to upgrade its military firepower in Korea.[33] The ROK government wanted the planned US troop repositioning to south of the Han river postponed until after the North Korean nuclear issue was resolved. Many South Koreans feared that such move was the first step for the US to launch a preemptive attack on North Korea. The Roh government also wanted the proposed troop reduction to be carried out gradually over 10 years. Washington and Seoul discussed these matters intensively in the following months. At the sixth round of Future of the Alliance Policy Initiative talks, held in Hawaii in January 2005, Seoul and Washington agreed that the Yongsan Garrison will be moved completely from downtown Seoul to the Osan-Pyongtaek area. According to the agreement, the ROK-US Combined Forces Command (CFC) and the UN Command (UNC) would be moved to the new site south of the Han River by the end of 2007.[34]

GPR clearly shows how functional issues overrode alliance considerations.[35] These moves alarmed the South Korean government, whose interests were defined primarily in terms of peace and stability on the Korean peninsula. The US perceives Kim Jong-Il's regime as a major threat to its security because of North Korea's

---

31 Cited from Jinwung Kim, 'Ambivalent Allies: Recent South Korean Perceptions of the United States Forces Korea (USFK)', *Asian Affairs*, vol. 30, no. 4 (Winter 2004), p. 147.

32 In 1992, 7,000 US troops in Korea were withdrawn in accordance with the 1989 Nunn-Warner amendment. The amendment called for a three-stage US troop reduction, but the plan was suspended due to the North Korean nuclear crisis of 1993.

33 James Brooke and Thom Shanker, 'US May Cut Third of Troops In South Korea', *The New York Times*, June 8, 2004; 'Fewer but deadlier', *Economist*, June 12, 2004.

34 The two sides agreed that the Dragon Hill Lodge, a liaison office of about 50 men, and communications offices for the Commander in Chief of Combined Forces Command (a four-star US general) and the Deputy Commander in Chief (a four-star Korean general) would remain in Yongsan. Yu Yong-weon, 'All US Military Facilities to Go South of the Han River', *Chosun Ilbo*, January 18, 2005.

35 Snyder, 'Alliance and Alienation', p. 4.

weapons of mass destruction (WMD) capabilities. The Bush administration is prone to apply forceful means (economic sanctions and military force) to remove the threat. The Proliferation Security Initiative (PSI) announced by Bush on May 31, 2003 was an attempt to 'prevent the flow of WMD, their delivery systems, and related materials on the ground, in the air and at sea to and from countries of proliferation concern,' and reflected the US tendency to apply coercion rather than negotiations to cope with proliferation.[36]

In contrast, South Korea's paramount goal is to prevent war on the Korean peninsula. Another Korean war would bring about unspeakable sufferings to the Korean people and devastate Korea's economy. As far as South Koreans are concerned, nuclear nonproliferation is secondary to war prevention, and nothing can justify an internecine conflict on the Korean peninsula. ROK's engagement policy with the DPRK was thus based on a realistic assessment of external environment.

Both Kim Dae-Jung's sunshine policy and Roh Moo-Hyun's 'peace and prosperity' policy were products of aroused Korean nationalism, the need for survival, and realistic assessments of shifted external environment. The basic objective of Kim Dae-Jung's sunshine policy was to improve inter-Korean relations by promoting reconciliation, cooperation, and peace. It was designed to engage the North through exchanges and cooperation and encourage it toward further opening and changes. This policy was predicated upon three principles – no tolerance of North Korea's armed provocation, no intention to absorb North Korea, and inter-Korean reconciliation and cooperation to resolve inter-Korean hostility.[37] As long as North Korea's nuclear ambitions were under check after the 1994 Agreed Framework and the Clinton administration was willing to try a negotiated solution to the North Korean nuclear issue, the sunshine policy did not cause frictions to US–ROK relations. G.W. Bush's hardline policy vis-à-vis North Korea, however, was not compatible with the sunshine policy.

Roh Moo-Hyun's 'policy for peace and prosperity,'[38] which was the continuation of his predecessor's sunshine policy with only cosmetic modifications, caused further friction and irritation in US–ROK relations. The Roh government stated that its North Korea policy would build upon the sunshine policy. Roh's peace and prosperity policy 'aims at balanced emphasis on between security and the economy, or between peace and prosperity' and postulates that peace and prosperity on the Korean peninsula will resolve a major security concern in Northeast Asia and eventually contribute to the promotion of peace and prosperity in the region. Its goals include the promotion of peace on the Korean peninsula, pursuit of mutual prosperity

---

36 Through the PSI, the US sought in cooperation with other states 'to develop a broad range of legal, diplomatic, economic, military and other tools to interdict shipments of such items.' For further details on the PSI, go to <http://www.state.gov/t/np/rls/fs/32725.htm>.

37 For an official policy, see *Policy Toward North Korea for Peace, Reconciliation and Cooperation* (Seoul, Korea: Ministry of Unification, ROK, 1999).

38 For further details on Roh's policy, see *The Policy of Peace and Prosperity*, Ministry of Unification, 2003, available at <http://www.globalsecurity.org/wmd/library/news/rok/2003/eng0403_91A.pdf>.

for South and North Korea, and contribution to prosperity in Northeast Asia.[39] The Roh government opposes North Korea's nuclear armament and vows to play the leading role in resolving the North Korean nuclear issue. Roh is opposed to applying sanctions or military force against North Korea. Roh's peace and prosperity policy, however, is neither original nor imaginative; it did not introduce new initiatives vis-à-vis the North. ROK's conciliatory stance vis-à-vis North Korea caused uneasiness and confusion in Washington.

Once G.W. Bush and Kim Dae-Jung (and Roh Moo-Hyun) defined their national interests and foreign policy goals the way they did, deterioration of US–ROK relations was inevitable.

Perception and attitudes

South Koreans' perception and attitudes toward North Korea and the US have changed substantially and irrevocably since 2000. To most South Koreans, North Korea is no longer viewed as a military threat and North Koreans are now viewed mostly as poor compatriots who need help. At the same time, an increasing number of South Koreans have come to perceive the US as a bully, a threat to peace, and an obstacle to inter-Korean reconciliation and unification. The Bush administration and American public, on the other hand, construed as signs of ingratitude, disloyalty, and betrayal, Kim Dae-Jung and Roh Moo-Hyun governments' assertiveness and refusal to follow the US lead, especially on the North Korean nuclear issue and their passive role in dissipating anti-American sentiments in South Korean society. The changing perception and attitudes on both sides contribute to US–ROK tensions and distrust.

Kim Dae-Jung's sunshine policy led to South Koreans' psychological metamorphosis by 'demystifying North Korea and undermining its image as the sworn enemy of the South.'[40] The inter-Korean summit in June 2000 left a lasting, indelible impact on South Koreans. For the first time, a South Korean leader (President Kim Dae-Jung) went to Pyongyang and met with the North Korean leader (Kim Jong-Il), and at the end of their talks the two leaders issued the June 15 declaration. Following the summit meeting, inter-Korean dialogue and personal exchanges increased and joint economic projects were pushed through. Nearly 10,000 visited North Korea in the first half of 2004. Around 800,000 South Koreans have visited Mt.Geumgang in North Korea. Roads connecting North and South Korea opened, and people traveled to and fro on land. In September 2002, North Korea sent 159 athletes to the Busan Asian Games along with 347 cheerleaders and dance troupes. In 2004, the athletes

---

39 Roh's North Korea policy professes to bring about peace and prosperity (or economic benefits) in Korea and Northeast Asia, but does not provide any strategy plan or blueprint to achieve the goals. For an analysis of Roh's policy for peace and prosperity, see Byung Chul Koh, 'Inter-Korean Relations under Roh Moo-Hyun', *Korea and World Affairs* (Spring 2003), pp. 5–17.

40 'Korea Backgrounder: How the South Views Its Brother From Another Planet', *Crisis Group Asia Report*, No 89 (Seoul & Brussels: December 14, 2004), p. 3.

of the two Koreas entered together the opening ceremony of the Athens summer Olympics under one 'Unification' flag. In May–June 2004, inter-Korean talks on security issues led to a mutual agreement to remove propaganda signs, institute a hotline, and jointly develop a communications system to help avoid accidental conflicts in the Yellow Sea (West Sea). The Gaesung industrial park in North Korea opened in 2005, with a pilot project of 19 South Korean companies.

Unlike his predecessors, President Kim Dae-Jung allowed non-governmental organizations (NGOs) to develop direct contacts with North Koreans. People-to-people contacts provided the impetus for the South Korean public's perception change. Through separated-family reunions, tourist visits, and NGO activities, South Koreans realized that North Koreans belonged to the same nation with a common language, culture, and history. Sports exchanges and cooperation and South Korean media's coverage of the sport events and interviews with North Korean athletes brought South Koreans much closer to North Koreans. Despite periodic armed clashes and crises on the Yellow Sea off the west coast and threats from Pyongyang, most South Koreans now consider North Korea not as a threatening regime but as a group of compatriots to be embraced.

Progressive South Koreans and the Roh government do not see the nasty, brutal aspects of Kim Jong-Il's regime and instead highlight the commonalities with the North Korean people. Many South Koreans tend to focus on the changed aspects (reforms) of North Korea while overlooking unchanged aspects (communist dictatorship) of the regime. It is a combination of 'projection of its own images' and 'wishful thinking' that led the South Korean government and progressive South Koreans to project an overly optimistic view of North Korea. In this context, Scott Snyder aptly said: 'Many South Korean leaders came to project their hopes onto Kim Jong-il in the initial months following the summit, presuming without hard evidence that Kim had decided or would decide to emulate Park Chung Hee's economic policies as a vehicle for achieving North Korea's economic recovery.'[41] The decision to drop the term 'main enemy' in reference to North Korea in a defense white paper for 2004, which is published by the Ministry of Defense, was in reaction to North Korea's persistent demand. The white paper will instead call North Korea a 'direct military threat.'[42] This controversial move was intended not to anger North Korea. It also reflects the Roh government's perception that North Korea no long is an imminent threat.

Although South Koreans increasingly came to view North Koreans in a favorable light, still substantial segments of South Korean society retain hostile attitudes toward Kim Jong-Il's regime. The division is mostly along the generational and ideological lines. Older people (50 or older) and those who classify themselves as conservative are more likely to view North Korea with suspicion and be critical of Seoul's engagement policy. The younger generation (20s–30s) and those who

---

41 Snyder, 'Alliance and Alienation', p. 6.
42 'N. Korea no Longer "Main Enemy" in Defense White Paper', *Chosun Ilbo*, January 28, 2005; 'South Korea to Stop Tagging North Its "Main Enemy"', *Reuters*, January 31, 2005.

classify themselves as progressive are more likely to view North Koreans as brothers and support the engagement policy with the North. South Korean society is also still divided over US troops in Korea. While older South Koreans and conservative politicians are generally concerned about the prospect of US troop withdrawal, younger people (30s–40s) and progressive politicians typically welcome it.

South Koreans' favorable perception and attitudes vis-à-vis North Korea were closely linked to the rising tide of anti-Americanism in South Korea. Anti-Americanism has grown steadily since the 1980s when the US supported dictatorial governments in Seoul. But there was rapid and intense growth in anti-American sentiment after G.W. Bush came to power. Anti-American sentiment spread in South Korea with an atmosphere of inter-Korean reconciliation and cooperation. Bush's hardline policy toward North Korea is perceived by many South Koreans as an effort to perpetuate Korean division and obstruct inter-Korean reconciliation and unification. Survey results indicate that South Koreans are more concerned with the threat posed by the US than by North Korea. Only a minority of South Koreans believes that North Korea would actually attack South Korea. A majority of South Koreans think that the North's nuclear program is for defensive purposes. And most South Koreans don't believe North Korea will actually use nuclear weapons against the South. The Bush administration's hardline policy vis-à-vis North Korea had a chilling effect on inter-Korean relations and, along with North Korea's intransigency, contributed to the second North Korean nuclear crisis. Bush's hardline policy toward North Korea, the 'axis of evil' speech, and his loathing of Kim Jong-Il heightened fears among South Koreans that the US might be bent on invading North Korea.

Anti-Americanism in South Korea is also linked to South Koreans' demand for equal and fair treatment from the US With rapid economic growth and political democratization, South Koreans became self-confident and assertive and readily pointed out injustices and unfair practices vis-à-vis the US. While North Korea's military threats were overwhelming and US forces in Korea served as an effective deterrent against North Korea's aggression, South Koreans cultivated US friendship and welcomed US military presence. But after North Korea's military threats dwindled and South Korea's socio-economic conditions improved, South Koreans became increasingly impatient with US heavy-handed, self-centered attitudes and behavior.

Under Roh's presidency, South Korea's political scene and societal mood have moved to the left on the ideological spectrum. The Roh government is the most leftist and least experienced in South Korea's political history. President Roh is leftist, stubborn, self-righteous, and incapable of accepting constructive criticisms. He is surrounded by like-minded staff. Roh's staunch supporters belong to the so-called '386 generation' (people in their 30s who were born in the 1960s and attended colleges in the 1980s) who now occupy key power positions. This group of people, often likened to the Taliban or President Roh's 'red-guards' by their critics, are headstrong outsiders with no experience or expert knowledge, no respect for the traditional bureaucracy and the establishment, and full of half-baked radical ideas. They are bent on the destruction of the existing order in the name of reforms, but do not have the slightest idea where their 'reforms' are headed. Two of South Korea's national TV networks are either government controlled (KBS) or dominated by its trade union, and their coverage often is critical of the US, reflecting their leftist bias. *Chungyojo* (South Korea's national teachers' union) teachers have become well-entrenched in the South Korean school system and often expose students to views critical of the US.

South Koreans' discontents with the existing SOFA, which stipulates the legal status of US forces in Korea, were the immediate cause for the recent wave of anti-Americanism in South Korea and frictions in US–ROK relations. The SOFA issue has been a major source of anti-American protests since the 1980s because many Koreans believe the agreement is unfair and unequal for Korea. A survey conducted in August 2000 revealed that 75.7 per cent of respondents considered the agreement 'unequal' and 18.9 per cent considered it 'equal.'[43] Despite persistent anti-American demonstrations, a majority of South Koreans want the US troops to remain. According to a *Joongang Ilbo* survey in January 2003, 13.8 per cent of those responded demanded a complete withdrawal of US troops and 41.5 per cent answered that US troops in Korea should stay at the current level.[44]

South Koreans complain the US–ROK SOFA agreement does not provide the same kind of rights to the host country as the US–Japan or US–German SOFA agreements. This lack of proper respect and treatment by the US hurts South Koreans' pride and leads to their resentment. The US–ROK SOFA agreement, first signed in July 1966, was revised in 1991 and 2000. Even after the revisions, South Koreans still felt the SOFA was unfair. In June 2002, two South Korean middle school girls were killed by an armored personnel carrier driven by American soldiers. The South Korean government's request to try the case was denied by the US authorities (the current SOFA stipulates that the US military has primary jurisdiction over personnel who commit crimes on duty). The two soldiers were tried in an American military court and subsequently acquitted of the changes of homicide. The acquittal was followed by fierce protests against the US and anti-American sentiment mounted. In November, President Bush expressed 'sadness and regret' over the incident through Ambassador Thomas Hubbard, and in December, Secretary of Defense Rumsfeld also expressed regret in person at the Thirty-fourth ROK–US security consultative meeting held in Washington D.C.[45] Nevertheless, anti-American protests over the incident continued into 2003. Many South Koreans turned out on Seoul streets to mourn the death of the two girls and express their desire for revising the SOFA. Many in the crowd also called for the withdrawal of the 37,000 US troops stationed in South Korea. Three in four South Koreans believe that the United States does not take South Korean interests into account when making international decisions.[46]

---

43 Cited from Jinwung Kim, 'Ambivalent Allies', p. 145.
44 Cited from Jinwung Kim, 'Ambivalent Allies', p. 156.
45 Jinwung Kim, 'Ambivalent Allies', p. 164.
46 Bruce Stokes, 'Nuclear Crisis Tests US-South Korean Ties, *National Journal*, vol. 35, no. 36 (September 6, 2003); Tim Shorrock, 'A Dangerous Game in Korea', *Nation*, January 27, 2003.

Since 1945, the US has been by far the most important partner for the ROK in political, economic, cultural, and military spheres. Seoul's ties with Beijing have strengthened rapidly ever since the two countries established diplomatic relations in 1992. In 2004, China for the first time surpassed the US as South Korea's number one trading partner. South Korea is China's largest source of new foreign investment. Furthermore, South Korea's geographical proximity, cultural affinity, and increased personal contacts and exchanges with China are drawing the two countries closer. As Seoul–Beijing relations have expanded and deepened, Seoul has come to feel less dependent on Washington or on the US–ROK alliance.

South Koreans' idealistic image and expectations of China were shaken in summer 2004 over the status of Korea's ancient kingdom Goguryeo. At the time, China's state-controlled New China News Agency depicted Goguryeo as a 'subordinate state that fell under the jurisdiction of the Chinese dynasties and was under the great influence of China's politics, culture and other areas.'[47] China thus tried to characterize the Korean kingdom as one of China's vassal states. Goguryeo was an independent Korean kingdom (37 BC to AD 668) of hunting tribes in control of much of today's North Korea and Manchuria. Koreans take great pride in the achievements and heritage of the kingdom and, in fact, the state title of Korea originated from Goguryeo. Chinese authorities were trying to 'rewrite' the history of the kingdom in an effort to stem what they feared was a 'greater Korea' movement to unite with the two million ethnic Koreans in Northeastern China.

This episode stirred Korean nationalism, and China's 'big-power' arrogance and insensitivity displayed in handling the issue aroused fears of China's aggressive intensions, inciting anti-Chinese sentiments in South Korean society. This dispute had an immediate and deep impact on South Koreans' perception and attitudes vis-à-vis China. In early 2004, 80 per cent of South Korean law-makers responded to a survey that China was South Korea's most important economic partner. In August 2004, only 6 per cent of those surveyed responded the same way.[48] And newspaper editorialists issued warnings of 'Sinocentrism' and China's dominance in East Asia. Beijing and Seoul sought to prevent this history issue from escalating into a major diplomatic dispute. Chinese Deputy Foreign Minister, Wu Dawei, and ROK Foreign Minister, Ban Ki-Moon, after hours of talks in Seoul, issued a loosely worded five-point verbal 'understanding.' This episode along with the recent resurgence of China's nationalistic outbursts made South Koreans reassess China as a harmless, friendly neighbor and provided an opportunity to appreciate the US as a valuable friend.

---

47 James Brooke, 'Seeking Peace in a Once and Future Kingdom', *The New York Times*, August 25, 2004.
48 Ibid.

The North Korean nuclear issue

The North Korean nuclear issue is at the heart of ROK–US discord. Bush's hardline policy vis-à-vis North Korea failed to make the US safer from North Korea's nuclear threats. On Bush's watch, North Korea has been openly developing nuclear weapons and may already possess as many as a dozen. Kim Dae-Jung's sunshine policy and Roh Moo-Hyun's policy for peace and prosperity have not constrained Kim Jong-Il's nuclear ambitions, either. Seoul's unconditional and unprincipled engagement policy toward Pyongyang neither tamed North Korea's bellicosity nor increased Seoul's leverage over Pyongyang in regard to the nuclear issue.

The second crisis over the North Korean nuclear issue flared up in the winter of 2002–2003 in the wake of Bush's special envoy James Kelly's visit to Pyongyang in early October 2002. James Kelly stated that the DPRK admitted a HEU program, and the US asserts that its claims regarding DPRK's HEU program are based on solid intelligence as well as the confessions of a Pakistani scientist who admitted providing uranium enrichment-related technology to North Korea. According to former US envoy to North Korea, Jack Pritchard, James Kelly did not confront North Korean officials at the time with evidence of their secret HEU program.[49] Kang Sok-Ju, whom Kerry quoted as having admitted to the secret nuclear program, flatly rejected the allegation. According to Kang, he told Kerry, 'We are entitled to have a nuclear program.'

The US halted fuel oil shipments to North Korea beginning in December. North Korea, in response, declared the 1994 Agreed Framework null and void and removed monitoring devices and expelled International Atomic Energy Agency (IAEA) international inspectors. North Korea then resumed its nuclear program in Yeongbyun, which had been mothballed since October 1994. North Korea reopened a sealed plutonium-reprocessing plant at Yongbyon. On January 10, North Korea announced its decision to withdraw from the Nuclear Non-proliferation Treaty (NPT). The US considered imposing sanctions and a blockade against North Korea, and the latter in turn declared that it would consider these measures an act of war.

Available evidence suggests that Kelly's confrontation with North Korea in October 2002 was motivated to derail inter-Korean reconciliation and Pyongyang–Tokyo normalization talks that were gaining momentum at the time. In April 2002, the two Koreas agreed to implement the plans for inter-Korean railroad links and for the joint development of an industrial complex at Gaesung in North *Korea (*about 1,000 South Korean firms were expected to move into the Gaesung complex). These conciliatory projects met with strong resistance from the US. The US 'refused to approve the de-mining, and threatened to block the Gaesung project by restricting the use of US-licensed and other sensitive technology by companies investing

---

49 'Former US Envoy: US Did Not Confront DPRK with Uranium Enrichment Proof', *Yonhap*, November 20, 2003.

in the zone.'⁵⁰ In September 2002, Japanese Prime Minister Junichiro Koizumi visited Pyongyang to discuss the normalization of relations. The US learned of the planned visit three weeks before it occurred. When Deputy Secretary of State Richard Armitage presented suspicions of North Korea's secret HEU program in an effort to dissuade him from making the trip, Koizumi still refused to cancel it. The Bush administration feared that it might lose control over the North Korean issue if DPRK's relationship with the ROK and Japan rapidly warmed up and decided to regain control by making an issue of North Korea's suspected HEU program.

Three rounds of six-party talks were held (August 2003, February 2004, and June 2004) involving the US, North Korea, South Korea, China, Russia, and Japan without producing breakthroughs in the North Korean nuclear stalemate. The US for the first time made a concrete proposal to resolve the North Korean nuclear issue in June 2004 at the third round of the six-party talks. This proposal, based on the Libya model, called for North Korea's complete and quick dismantling of its nuclear programs before the provision of security guarantee and economic aid to North Korea.⁵¹ The parties to the six-party talks were divided about the North Korean nuclear issue.⁵² South Korea as well as China and Russia became frustrated and critical of the inflexible attitudes of the US. South Korea was urging the US to show flexibility with regard to the North Korean nuclear issue and was pleased to see a detailed proposal from the US. The Bush administration's fundamental position did not change, insisting that North Korea should take steps to dismantle its nuclear programs first before the US provided security and economic rewards. The DPRK rejected the June 2004 US proposal, arguing that North Korea's freeze of its nuclear program and US rewards should proceed simultaneously. The Roh government maintained that the US should be more flexible and take into account North Korea's security and economic needs. It insisted that the North Korean nuclear issue should be resolved peacefully and resisted any US attempt to further isolate, pressure, or overthrow North Korea.

The fourth round of six-party talks was held in July–September 2005.⁵³ The sticking point this time around was North Korea's demand for a light-water reactor

---

50 Selig Harrison, 'Did North Korea Cheat?' *Foreign Affairs*, vol. 84, no. 1 (January/February 2005), p. 128.

51 For a detailed analysis of the US proposal, see Robert J. Einhorn, 'The North Korea Nuclear Issue: The Road Ahead', *Northeast Asia Peace and Security Network Forum Online* (September 14, 2004), available at <http://www.nautilus.org/fora/security/0433A_Einhron.html>.

52 At the six-party talks, a '1–3–2' formulation emerged: 'North Korea on its own; South Korea, Russia, and China favoring a more conciliatory approach of offering incentives to North Korea and more emphasis on a nuclear freeze instead of dismantlement; and Japan and the United States preferring a mix of dialogue and pressure on Pyongyang.' See Mark E. Manyin, Emma Chanlett-Avery, and Helene Marchart, 'North Korea: A Chronology of Events, October 2002-December 2004', CRS Report for Congress, Order Code RL32743 (January 24, 2005), p. 5.

53 For a detailed and in-depth analysis of the fourth round of six-party talks, see Chapter 2.

(LWR) as a condition for its dismantling its nuclear programs. The ROK government supported the DPRK's position on the condition that it should rejoin the NPT, accept IAEA inspections and dismantle all its nuclear programs first. The Bush administration opposed DPRK's acquiring a LWR and retaining the right to peaceful use of nuclear energy. On September 19, the six nations at the talks issued a joint statement. This statement marked the first agreement since the six-party talks began in August 2003. It was a result of compromise between the US and the DPRK, and contained provisions for North Korea to dismantle its nuclear weapons programs and for other parties to provide economic aid, diplomatic relations and other incentives to North Korea.[54] Some parts of the agreement were vague and ambiguous. Still, the 9.19 joint statement was an important breakthrough and may pave the road to a peaceful resolution of North Korea's nuclear crisis.

Concluding Remarks

Diverging approaches to the North Korean nuclear issue, Roh's assertive and independent postures, anti-American sentiment in South Korea, and Bush's abrasive and self-centered behavior all led to the friction, distrust, and awkwardness in US–ROK relations in the 2000s. After Bush entered his second term of presidency, differences, tensions, and discomfort between the US and the ROK on diplomatic and security fronts persisted. The US and the ROK relations are now in transition, and it will take a lot of imagination, patience, and effort on both sides to sustain friendship and the alliance.

The June 2000 inter-Korean summit meeting and drastic improvement in inter-Korean relations in subsequent years had a deep, lasting impact on US–ROK relations. Through personal contacts, exchanges, and joint economic projects with North Koreans, South Koreans came to realize that all Koreans are the same, and nationalistic aspirations gradually overshadowed ideological schism. North Korea was now viewed not as an 'evil' communist threat to be crushed but as a poor, helpless state of compatriots to be embraced. Coexistence and peaceful unification with the North became ROK's paramount foreign policy goal. The Bush administration never understood how Korean nationalism changed South Koreans' perception and attitudes toward the North. The 9/11 terrorist attacks had a profound impact on the US government and American public mood. The Bush administration's foreign policy turned radical and Americans became much more tolerant of extreme measures for national security. In Bush's global war on terrorism, North Korea's nuclear ambitions were an imminent threat. The Roh government did not clearly understand the repercussions of 9/11.

Friction in US–ROK relations is also ascribable to emotionalism and simplistic approaches on both sides. President Roh was naïve enough to believe he could talk President Bush into changing his hardline policy toward North Korea and reshape

---

54 'Text of Joint Statement from Nuclear Talks', *New York Times*, September 19, 2005.

US–Korea relations as equals. He did not understand that an equal relationship would take more than bombastic slogans and empty talks. President Bush also did not understand the profound changes that have been taking place in South Korean society in recent years and the potency of Korean nationalism. He expected that the US could prevail over any country by using superior military and economic capabilities, but had to face stubborn resistance from South Korea and other friends.

The US still remains ROK's most important friend as a political interlocutor, military ally, and economic partner. President Roh continues to vow to reestablish US–ROK relations on an equal footing and to achieve North Korea's denuclearization through peaceful means. Are the US and the ROK equal politically? Is it realistic or practical for the ROK to demand equality in its relationship with the US? The fact of the matter is the US is the sole remaining global superpower and the ROK is not. The ROK needs to assert itself, defending its own national interests vis-à-vis the US, but should not confuse aspirations (equality) with political reality. Bush's global war on terrorism and unilateralism suffered multiple setbacks, incurring diplomatic isolation and alienating many of former allies and friends. The Bush government should realize that 'soft power' is often more persuasive and effective than hard power and that even the global superpower cannot manage international affairs alone without cooperation and support from interested states.

Despite a certain degree of tension and distrust, US–ROK relations are now stable and manageable. But the North Korean nuclear issue will test the US–ROK alliance. To date, both the US and the DPRK have been patient and constrained – the US has not resorted to economic sanctions or military force against North Korea and North Korea has fallen short of carrying out nuclear weapons' testing. Still, the North Korean nuclear issue will not disappear through inaction or negligence. It would be prudent for the US and the ROK to get their acts together on North Korea and coordinate their policies at the six-party negotiation table. From a pragmatic and long-term perspective, Seoul and Washington should also begin discussing the future of the US–ROK alliance.

Chapter 4

Korea, the US, China and Japan: The Rise of Asian Regionalism

Claude E. Barfield and Jason Bolton

This goal of this chapter is to analyze evolving trade and investment patterns and relations among the US, South Korea, and China, with a special focus on the implications of rising Asian regionalism for the three countries. The research will also suggest optimal responses for the US and Korea to these new trends and trade policy shifts. The chapter is organized as follows. The first section will describe the growth of Korea as a trading nation as well as its trading relationship with major partners in the last decade. The second section will analyze the bilateral relationship of Korea and its four largest trading partners, including the US, China, Japan, and ASEAN. Included in the second section, the research examines Korea's recent strong economic performance and its emergence as a powerful regional and world trading power. The third, and final, section of the chapter will trace the growth of Asian regional trading patterns and describe recently concluded and proposed bilateral, sub-regional and regional Asian free trade agreements (FTAs). The chapter will conclude with discussion and recommendations regarding optimal responses for the US and Korea to the new realities of Asian trade and regionalism.

In the trade arena, throughout the entire post-war period, East Asian nations largely eschewed bilateral or sub-regional FTAs (ASEAN was the exception, but until quite recently, little or no trade liberalization had been fostered among its member states). As their political leaders pointed out, even though worldwide almost all nations belonged to one or more FTAs or customs unions, East Asia had flourished – with higher economic growth and per capita income rates – as individual nations outside of any trade bloc. During the 1990s, however, important new factors and pressures produced major changes in trade policies and priorities for the region. First, because many East Asian economies were heavily dependent on the US market as an export source, the signing of the North American Free Trade Agreement (NAFTA), with the potential of substantial trade diversion to Mexico, caused a wave of uneasiness. This uneasiness was heightened by the announced plans to negotiate a FTA encompassing all of Central and South America by the year 2005. Then came the financial crisis of 1997, which resulted in further reexamination of the traditional go-it-alone stance. Many Asian leaders felt that the US and the International Monetary Fund (IMF) had

Table 4.1 Progress of regionalism in East Asia

FTAs	Discussion	Joint Study	Progress Negotiation	Conclusion	Implementation
AFTA					V
AFTA–China			V		
AFTA–Japan		V			
AFTA–Korea		V			
AFTA–India	V				
AFTA–US	V				
China–Japan–Korea	V				
East Asian FTA	V				
Japan–Chile		V			
Japan–Canada	V				
Japan–Mexico			V		
Japan–Taiwan	V				
Japan–Singapore					V
Korea–Chile					V
Korea–Japan			V		
Korea–Mexico	V				
Korea–New Zealand			V		
Korea–Singapore			V		
Korea–Thailand		V			

Note: AFTA: ASEAN free trade agreement.
Source: Inkyo Cheong, 'Korea's FTA Policy: Focusing on Bilateral FTAs with Chile and Japan', Discussion paper 02-02 (Seoul: KIEP, September 2002).

reacted unsympathetically, advancing draconian policy prescriptions to the plight of beleaguered governments.

Only in 1999, however, did the real break with the past occur, when both Japan and Korea embarked on an historic course of action by advancing the possibility of negotiating a series of bilateral, sub-regional, and regional – and even cross-regional – trade agreement with other nations. Previously, both nations had limited their trade objectives to membership in the multilateral system of the General Agreement on Tariffs and Trade (GATT) and World Trade Organization (WTO),[1] though trade experts in each nation had at times called for special bilateral relations with the US.

Led by Japan and Korea, the East Asian region has witnessed a wave of proposals over the past several years for various bilateral and sub-regional combinations, including proposed FTAs between Japan and Singapore, Korea and Japan, Singapore and Australia, Singapore and New Zealand, China ASEAN, and Japan, Korea and China (Table 4.1).

---

1 WTO, 'Mapping of Regional Trade Agreements' (WT/REG/W/41, 2000). This document can be downloaded from the WTO website at <http://www.wto.org/>.

Table 4.2 Korea balance of trade, selected years: 1960–2004 (000s USD)

Year	Exports	Growth (%)	Imports	Growth (%)	Trade Balance
1960	32,827	48	343,527	-22	-310,700
1965	175,082	433	463,442	35	-288,360
1970	835,185	377	1,983,973	328	-1,148,788
1975	5,081,016	508	7,274,434	267	-2,193,418
1980	17,504,862	245	22,291,663	206	-4,786,801
1985	30,283,122	73	31,135,655	40	-852,533
1990	65,015,731	115	69,843,678	124	-4,827,947
1991	71,870,122	11	81,524,858	17	-9,654,736
1992	76,631,515	7	81,775,257	0	-5,143,742
1993	82,235,866	7	83,800,142	2	-1,564,276
1994	96,013,237	17	102,348,175	22	-6,334,938
1995	125,057,988	30	135,118,933	32	-10,060,944
1996	129,715,137	4	150,339,100	11	-20,623,963
1997	136,164,204	5	144,616,374	-4	-8,452,171
1998	132,313,143	-3	93,281,754	-35	39,031,388
1999	143,685,459	9	119,752,282	28	23,933,177
2000	172,267,510	20	160,481,018	34	11,786,492
2001	150,439,144	-13	141,097,821	-12	9,341,323
2002	162,470,528	8	152,126,153	8	10,344,375
2003	193,817,443	19	178,826,657	18	14,990,786
2004	253,844,672	31	224,462,687	26	29,381,985

Source: Korea International Trade Association (KITA), *Database: Korea Trade Statistics*, various, 2005, available at <http://www.kita.net>.

Korean Trade since 1960

Korea's trade statistics show dramatic export growth between 1960 and 1980 (Table 4.2). Spurred by the government's industrial policy, Korea's industrialization focused on increasing exports, and export growth rates during the period outpaced import growth rates. In the 1980s, both export and import growth rates slowed, and trade became more balanced. The trade balance began to deteriorate in 1990, however, and reached a deficit record of negative $20.6 billion in 1996. As a result of the 1997 financial crisis, growth stagnated even though the Korean *won* dropped precipitously in value. Exports dropped slightly, but imports decreased dramatically. As Korea's economy was restored, both imports and exports rebounded, showing healthy year-on-year growth. Although Korea's economy experienced a setback in 2001 – with negative growth rates for both imports and exports – Korea has run successive annual trade surplus since. By 2004 both exports and imports reached record nominal trade levels.

Table 4.3   Korea per annum total trade: 1996–2004 (000s USD)

Year	Imports	Exports	Total Trade
1996	150,339,100	129,715,137	280,054,237
1997	144,616,374	136,164,204	280,780,578
1998	93,281,754	132,313,143	225,594,897
1999	119,752,282	143,685,459	263,437,741
2000	160,481,018	172,267,510	332,748,528
2001	141,097,821	150,439,144	291,536,965
2002	152,126,153	162,470,528	314,596,681
2003	178,826,657	193,817,443	372,644,100
2004	224,462,687	253,844,672	478,307,359

Korea's major trading partners

Korea's most significant trading partners include China, the US, and Japan. The list also includes Hong Kong, Germany, Taiwan, and the UK. For the purpose of this research, the top three trading partners – China, the US, and Japan – are considered, due to their continued dominance in international/regional trade and their large volume in Korean imports and exports. Moreover, in light of the regional focus herein, and the implications for import and export patterns in the near horizon, ASEAN partners are also investigated.

In advance of the bilateral and intraregional trade analyses, the subsequent tables help identify Korea's 1996–2004 total trade growth and the import/export trends of

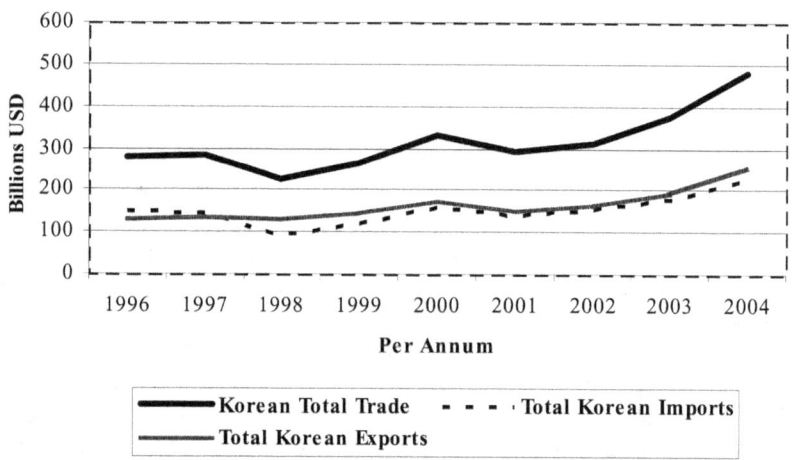

Figure 4.1   Korea's total trade
Source: KITA, *Database: Korea Trade Statistics*, various, 2005, available at <http://www.kita.net>.

Table 4.4 Korea per annum imports: 1996–2004, selected blocs and nations (000s USD)

Year	ASEAN	China	Japan	US	Europe	Total
1996	12,073,822	8,538,568	31,448,636	33,305,379	26,244,234	150,339,100
1997	12,548,804	10,116,861	27,907,108	30,122,178	23,687,605	144,616,374
1998	9,135,142	6,483,958	16,840,409	20,403,276	14,280,732	93,281,754
1999	12,249,476	8,866,667	24,141,990	24,922,344	16,579,165	119,752,282
2000	18,173,436	12,798,728	31,827,943	29,241,628	20,069,931	160,481,018
2001	15,915,658	13,302,675	26,633,372	22,376,226	18,861,330	141,097,821
2002	16,756,588	17,399,779	29,856,228	23,008,635	21,802,567	152,126,153
2003	18,458,465	21,909,127	36,313,091	24,814,134	24,758,673	178,826,657
2004	22,383,147	29,584,874	46,144,463	28,782,652	30,535,455	224,462,687

Source: KITA, *Database: Korea Trade Statistics*, various, 2005, available at <http://www.kita.net>.

Korea's largest trading partners. Korea's export surplus continues into 2004; however, the destination and bilateral contribution of Korea's total trade have fluctuated. Most of Korea's imports originate from East Asia, and, increasingly, a larger proportion of Korea's exports are landing in the same East Asian nations.

Total Korea trade rose near $200 billion from 1996 to 2004 (Table 4.3 and Figure 4.1). The marked increases in Korean export percentage originate from much higher demand levels in ASEAN, China, and Japan. This is not the case in Korea's exports, however, as the EU, US, and most recently, China, have maintained strong demand for Korean goods.

Tables 4.4 to 4.7 provide an historical picture of Korea's total trade involving imports and exports, and the contribution percentages of Korea's major trading partners.

Table 4.5 Percentage of total per annum import

Year	ASEAN	China	Japan	US	Europe	Total
1996	8	6	21	22	17	150,339,100
1997	9	7	19	21	16	144,616,374
1998	10	7	18	22	15	93,281,754
1999	10	7	20	21	14	119,752,282
2000	11	8	20	18	13	160,481,018
2001	11	9	19	16	13	141,097,821
2002	11	11	20	15	14	152,126,153
2003	10	12	20	14	14	178,826,657
2004	10	13	21	13	14	224,462,687

Source: KITA, *Database: Korea Trade Statistics*, various, 2005, available at <http://www.kita.net>.

Table 4.6 Korea per annum exports: 1996–2004, selected blocs and nations (000s USD)

Year	ASEAN	China	Japan	US	Europe	Total
1996	20,310,764	11,377,068	15,766,827	21,670,465	21,395,385	129,715,137
1997	20,365,332	13,572,463	14,771,155	21,625,432	24,817,284	136,164,204
1998	15,327,871	11,943,990	12,237,587	22,805,106	28,749,403	132,313,143
1999	17,707,934	13,684,599	15,862,448	29,474,653	26,091,213	143,685,459
2000	20,133,786	18,454,540	20,466,016	37,610,630	28,141,378	172,267,510
2001	16,458,982	18,190,190	16,505,766	31,210,795	23,958,093	150,439,144
2002	18,400,241	23,753,586	15,143,183	32,780,188	27,010,302	162,470,528
2003	20,253,388	35,109,715	17,276,137	34,219,402	31,898,993	193,817,443
2004	24,024,265	49,763,175	21,701,337	42,849,193	44,592,658	253,844,672

Source: KITA, *Database: Korea Trade Statistics*, various, 2005, available at <http://www.kita.net>.

Korea's major import partners (1980–2004)

Throughout the past two decades, Japan has been Korea's biggest import partner, followed by the US. (Table 4.8 provides an effective snap-shot in charting this historical relationship.) However, the trade contribution percentages of Japan and the US have reduced significantly, owing much to the growing importance of China as one of Korea's major sources of imports. China represented only 3 per cent ($2.27 billion) of Korea's total imports in 1990; however, China's share grew to 8 and 13 per cent, respectively, of total imports by 2000 and 2004.

Like Japan and the US, Saudi Arabia has been one of Korea's five main sources of imports since 1980 (ranked 6 in 1990), reflecting the importance of oil imports for the Korean economy, in particular during the 1980s. Saudi Arabia provided 15 per cent ($3.29 billion) of Korea's total imports in 1980, a share that decreased significantly by 1990 ($1.72 billion); however, Saudi Arabia's contribution increased markedly

Table 4.7 Percentage of total per annum export

Year	ASEAN	China	Japan	US	Europe	Total
1996	16	9	12	17	16	129,715,137
1997	15	10	11	16	18	136,164,204
1998	12	9	9	17	22	132,313,143
1999	12	10	11	21	18	143,685,459
2000	12	11	12	22	16	172,267,510
2001	11	12	11	21	16	150,439,144
2002	11	15	9	20	17	162,470,528
2003	10	18	9	18	16	193,817,443
2004	9	20	9	17	18	253,844,672

Source: KITA, *Database: Korea Trade Statistics*, various, 2005, available at <http://www.kita.net>.

Table 4.8 Nation/bloc source of Korea imports: 1980, 1990, 2000, 2004 (000s USD)

1980				2000			
Total Imports 21,949,891				Total Imports 160,481,018			
Rank	Nation/Bloc	Per cent	Import Total	Rank	Nation/Bloc	Per cent	Import Total
1	Japan	27	5,857,810	1	Japan	20	31,827,943
2	US	22	4,890,248	2	US	18	29,241,628
3	Saudi Arabia	15	3,288,406	3	China	8	12,798,728
4	Kuwait	8	1,753,192	4	Saudi Arabia	6	9,641,492
5	Australia	3	680,019	5	Australia	4	5,958,700
1990				2004			
Total Imports 69,843,678				Total Imports 224,462,687			
Rank	Nation/Bloc	Per cent	Import Total	Rank	Nation/Bloc	Per cent	Import Total
1	Japan	27	18,573,851	1	Japan	21	46,144,463
2	US	24	16,942,472	2	PRC	13	29,584,874
3	Germany	5	3,283,546	3	US	13	28,782,652
4	Australia	4	2,589,117	4	Saudi Arabia	5	11,799,580
5	PRC	3	2,268,137	5	Germany	4	8,485,567

Source: KITA, *Database: Korea Trade Statistics*, various, 2005, available at <http://www.kita.net>.

through 2004, reaching $11.8 billion. Korea's imports from other countries continued to increase between 1980 and 2004, a trend indicating Korea's diversification of imports. Excluding Korea's five major trading partners in imports, the number of countries that provided more than 1.4 per cent of Korea's total imports increased from 6 in 1980 to 10 in 1990. The number reached 12 in 2002, reflecting Korea's continuing import diversification. These countries included countries of Southeast Asia and East Asia (Indonesia, Malaysia, and Taiwan), Europe (Germany, the UK, Italy, and France), and the Middle East (United Arab Emirates and Kuwait).

Korea 1996–2004 imports

Korean import demand of European and US goods fell near 4 and 10 per cent, respectively, from 1996–2004 levels. The demand for ASEAN and Chinese goods, however, has supplanted European and US import loss, accounting for 10 and 13 per cent, respectively, of Korea's 2004 imports.

Import levels from Japan, in contrast to declines in European and the US, maintained per annum Korean import levels near 20 per cent. Japan remains the only Korea trading partner that exceeds 15 per cent of Korea's total per annum imports. The four other partners converge in the 10 to 15 per cent import contribution range. The US holds the largest net import loss, from 22 to 13 per cent in 10 years, and China the largest net gain, from 6 to 13 per cent (Table 4.8 and Figure 4.2).

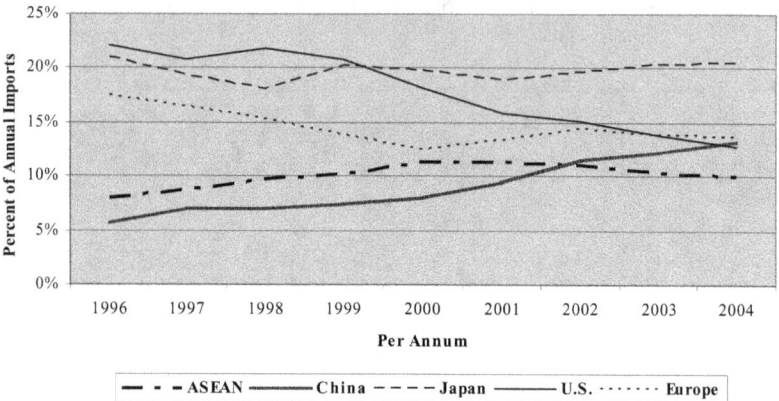

Figure 4.2   Korea 1996–2004 imports: Nation or bloc source contribution
Source: KITA, *Database: Korea Trade Statistics*, various, 2005, available at <http://www.kita.net>.

Korea's major export partners (1980–2004)

From 1980 to 2002, the US was Korea's largest export market. This is no longer the case. The contribution share of Korea's exports to the US has decreased significantly since 1990, from 30 per cent in 1990 to 22 per cent in 2000 to 17 per cent in 2004. The most influential trend affecting this decline proved fast-growing demand from China for Korean exports. In 1980 and 1990, the amount of Korea's exports to China was insignificant; however, in 2000 China took in 11 per cent ($18.5 billion) of Korea's total exports and 20 per cent ($49.8 billion) in 2004, supplanting the US and Japan as Korea's largest export destination (Table 4.9).

The growing share of the Chinese market for Korea's exports is also a sign of Korea's export-market diversification. Before the surge of exports to China, more than 40 per cent of Korea's exports headed to the US and Japan. China's emergence as a major importer of Korean products, however, has reduced Korea's heavy export concentration in the US and Japanese markets. Figure 4.1 shows that the shares of Korea's three major export markets became more evenly distributed by 2000 and 2004. Moreover, Hong Kong sustained its share – near 5 per cent and rising – of Korea's total exports in the 1990–2004 period. In 2004, non-top-five import countries took 43 per cent of Korea's total exports, which proved slightly smaller than their 44 per cent share in 2000. The number of countries whose share of Korea's exports was greater than 1.4 per cent grew from 8 in 1980 and 1990 to more than 14 in 2004. These countries included Southeast Asian and East Asian countries (Indonesia, Thailand, and Singapore), European nations (UK, Netherlands, France, and Germany), Canada, and Australia.

Table 4.9   Nation/bloc source of Korea exports: 1980, 1990, 2000, 2004 (000s USD)

1980				2000			
Total Exports 17,369,618				Total Exports 172,267,510			
Rank	Nation/Bloc	Per cent	Export Total	Rank	Nation/Bloc	Per cent	Export Total
1	US	27	4,606,625	1	US	22	37,610,630
2	Japan	17	3,039,408	2	Japan	12	20,466,016
3	Saudi Arabia	5	946,111	3	China	11	18,454,540
4	Germany	5	876,389	4	Hong Kong	6	10,708,094
5	Hong Kong	5	823,318	5	Taiwan	5	8,026,625
1990				2004			
Total Exports 65,015,731				Total Exports 253,844,672			
Rank	Nation/Bloc	Per cent	Export Total	Rank	Nation/Bloc	Per cent	Export Total
1	US	30	19,359,997	1	China	20	49,763,175
2	Japan	19	12,637,879	2	US	17	42,849,193
3	Hong Kong	6	3,779,949	3	Japan	9	21,701,337
4	Germany	4	2,849,165	4	Hong Kong	7	18,127,112
5	Singapore	3	1,804,587	5	Taiwan	4	9,844,215

Source: KITA, *Database: Korea Trade Statistics*, various, 2005, available at <http://www.kita.net>.

Korea 1996–2004 exports

Regional contributions to the Republic of Korea's exports have risen, in large part, due to increased demand in China. From 1996 to 2004, Korean exports to ASEAN countries fell near 5 per cent. European demand for Korean goods, from 1996 to 2004, permitted levels exceeding 15 per cent each year. The US, Europe, and China hold a similar contribution margin, nearing 17, 18, and 20 per cent, respectively, of total Korean exports in 2004.

The Asian crisis clearly initiated a sharp decline in export demand in ASEAN nations. However, the 5 per cent margin in ASEAN import reduction in 1997–98 did not mimic Europe or the US in this period. The per cent contribution demand levels, not nominal levels, from ASEAN nations have not recovered in 10 years, and China's rapidly rising demand levels prove a counterbalance, having more than doubled since 1996 (see Figure 4.3).

Korea's Major Trading Partners Examined

As mentioned above, again, Korea's most significant trading partners in 2004 included China, the US, and Japan. In addition, the ASEAN trading partners also drove much of Korea's regional trade numbers. The subsequent paragraphs examine each of the partners mentioned, and describe to the reader the macroeconomic relationships from an import and export perspective. The last eight years – from 1996 to 2004 – presented numerous changes in trade patterns in the North East Corridor, most significantly, the

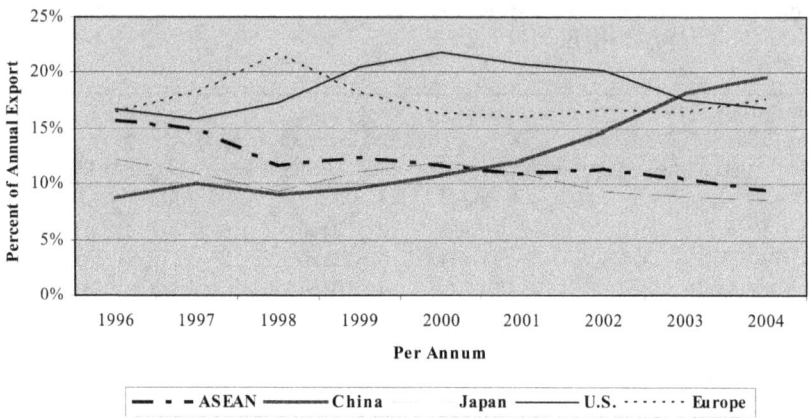

Figure 4.3 Korea 1996–2004 exports: Nation or bloc source contribution
Source: KITA, *Database: Korea Trade Statistics*, various, 2005, available at <http://www.kita.net>.

rise in intra-regional trade. Korea's bilateral relationships involving China, the US, Japan, and the ASEAN bloc serve as effective illustrations of this enhanced intra-regionalization in trade policy and the need for responsive US trade policies.

Korea–US trade: Asymmetrical but crucial

The trade relationship between the US and Korea, historically, has always proven asymmetrical. The US is no longer Korea's most important trading partner, this fact consistent with the trends in shifting market share observed in 2000. In 2000, Korea's exports to the US accounted for 22 per cent of its total exports, the highest among Korea's trading partners at the time. This asymmetrical relationship is also reflected in import contributions in the 1980s, when (Table 4.10) almost one-third of Korea's exports went to the US. Times have changed, clearly! In the last 15 years, Korea's imports from the US have shrunk from 24 per cent of total in 1990 to 13 per cent in 2004. Korea, historically, is not as important a trading partner for the US as the US is for Korea; the tides in bilateral contribution percentage have shifted some. Nevertheless, Korea still ranks as the seventh largest trading partner of the US (behind Canada, Mexico, Japan, China, Germany, and the UK) and as the seventh-largest recipient of US exports in 2004. Moreover, Korea took in 4 per cent total US exports in 2004 and supplied 3 per cent of total US imports. The asymmetrical dependence of Korea and the US also proves evident in measuring the ratio of bilateral trade volume to GDP in each country. The ratio in 2004 is estimated at 39 per cent for Korea and only 6 per cent for the US.

Although bilateral trade between Korea and the US grew tremendously in size, until 1981 the bilateral trade balance was persistently – with the exception of 1978 – in favor of the US. The balance of payments shifted into Korea's favor beginning

Table 4.10   Korea's bilateral US trade relationship: 1980-2004 (000s USD)

		1980	1985	1990	1995	2000	2004
Korea	Total Exports	17,369,618	30,283,122	65,015,731	125,057,988	172,267,510	253,844,672
	Exports to US	4,606,625	10,754,100	19,359,997	24,131,474	37,610,630	42,849,193
	Percentage of Total Exports to US	27	36	30	19	22	17
	Total Imports	21,949,891	31,133,006	69,843,678	135,118,933	160,481,018	224,462,687
	Imports from US	4,890,248	6,489,322	16,942,472	30,403,515	29,241,628	28,782,652
	Percentage of Total Imports from US	22	21	24	23	18	13
	Total BoP	-4,775,574	-860,586	-4,827,947	-10,060,944	11,786,492	29,381,985
	Bilateral BoP	-283,622	4,264,778	2,417,525	-6,272,042	8,369,002	14,066,541
US	Total Exports	224,250,000	215,915,000	392,975,794	583,030,524	780,418,628	817,935,849
	Exports to Korea	4,890,248	6,489,322	16,942,472	30,403,515	29,241,628	28,782,652
	Percentage of Total Exports to Korea	2	3	4	5	4	4
	Total Imports	249,750,000	338,088,000	496,037,579	743,505,251	1,216,887,535	1,469,670,757
	Imports from Korea	4,606,625	10,754,100	19,359,997	24,131,474	37,610,630	42,849,193
	Percentage of Total Imports from Korea	2	3	4	3	3	3

Source: KITA, *Database: Korea Trade Statistics*, various, 2005, available at <http://www.kita.net>.

in 1982 and has since grown significantly, reaching a peak at $14 billion in 2004. Korea showed a trade deficit with the US in 1991 and 1992 and also from 1994 through 1997; however, Korea has maintained a balance of payments surplus since the economic crisis of 1997.

Korea's 1998 recession, during which its gross domestic product shrank by 6.7 per cent, led to a sharp decline in its demand for imports from all countries, including the US.[2] Conversely, Korea's exports to the US rose significantly between 1998 and 2001, propelled by the strong US economy, which increased US demand for foreign goods and services, and by the depreciation of the *won*, which made Korean products cheaper for Americans to buy. In 2002, the slowing US economy led US imports from Korea to stagnate. From 2002 to 2004, the emboldened US economy led to further increases in imports from Korea.

Korea began its outward-oriented economic development in the mid-1960s, and Korea's access to the US market has proven critical for export-led growth. Recent trends in regional demand have clearly altered the US contribution percentages; however, the total value of the US imports remains inherent to Korea's dependence on the demand levels of the US. In addition to the total trade value, the intrinsic reliance of Korea on US trade is made more acute in examining the leading export sectors.

---

2   Raymond J. Ahearn, *South Korea's Economic Prospects* (Washington, DC: Congressional Research Service, RS 20041, February 1, 1999).

Korea's exports to the US (reference Table 4.11)

From 1996 to 2004, Korea's total and top ten exports to the US rose near 80 per cent and 90 per cent, respectively. Total exports from Korea neared $39 billion in 2004, from near $22 billion in 1996. Top ten exports, in total, reached $34 billion in 2004, from $18 billion in 1996; as a percentage of total exports, the top ten categories of Korea–US export trade rose from 83 to 87 per cent of total US exports. From 2000 to 2004, total Korea export trade to the US rose near $1.5 billion, in real terms. The total rise in 2004 exports from total 2000 levels is minimal (4 per cent), in comparison to the $17 billion increase from 1996 to 2004. The periodic variations in contribution ratios remain, however, especially involving automotive and machines and equipment exports.

Total electrical machinery and equipment exports – Korea's largest export commodity in US trade for the last 10 years – made up over 34 per cent of Korea's export trade in 2004, marking a 3 per cent rise from 2000 and a 9 per cent decline from 1996. Korea's current account information also exhibits the rise in Korea's automotive exports to the US, in 2004 replacing parts and mechanical appliances as the 2nd largest export category, next to electronics. In 2004, automotive parts and vehicles made up 25 per cent of total exports to the US. Reactors, machinery and appliances fell to 14 per cent of total export in 2004, from near 25 per cent of total in 2000. Textile and apparel export items have fallen in 2004 from levels seen in 1996 and 2000.

Emerging export categories in 2004, in addition to automotive and machinery, include rubber and rubber derivative products (1.7 per cent of US export total) – not in 1996 or 2000 respective top exports – and mineral fuels, mineral oils, and mineral waxes (2 per cent of export total). The largest periodic increases for top ten commodities in 2004 included electronics, automotives, and plastics. However, despite these independent trade fluctuations, the top three categories of commodity export in 2004 – including electrical machinery, parts and mechanical appliances, and automotive products – are also the top three in 1996 and 2000. For each four-year measured period, from 1996 through 2004, these three categories, collectively, advanced over 3 per cent, in real terms.

Korea's imports from the United States (reference Table 4.12)

Total imports from the US to Korea declined 22 per cent from 1996 to 2004, near $7 billion in reduced trade. Top ten commodity types – making up, on average, 75 per cent of US import totals – lost near $5 billion from 1996 to 2004, in real terms. The largest categorical product decline from 2000 import levels was electrical machinery and equipment, losing 8 per cent in reduced value (near $3 billion). In 2004, top ten imports from the US to Korea made near 74 per cent of total US–Korea imports, with electrical machinery and equipment representing near 29 per cent of total US imports. Top three imports – electrical machinery, parts and mechanical appliances,

Table 4.11 Republic of Korea exports to the US: 1996, 2000, 2004

Rank	1996 Commodity (Total Exports: $21,670,465,000)	US$ in Thousands	% of Total Exports	2000 Commodity (Total Exports: $37,610,630,000)	US$ in Thousands	% of Total Exports	2004 (M1-11) Commodity (Total Exports: $38,996,071,000)	US$ in Thousands	% of Total Exports
1	Electrical Machinery and Equipment and Parts thereof (85)	9,375,218	43.3	Electrical Machinery and Equipment and Parts thereof (85)	11,660,807	31.0	Electrical Machinery and Equipment and Parts thereof (85)	13,392,208	34.3
2	Nuclear Reactors, Boilers, Machinery, and Mechanical Appliances Parts thereof (84)	3,219,886	14.9	Nuclear Reactors, Boilers, Machinery, and Mechanical Appliances Parts thereof (84)	9,202,785	24.5	Vehicles other than Railway or Tramway Rolling-Stock, and Parts thereof (87)	9,839,076	25.2
3	Vehicles other than Railway or Tramway Rolling-Stock, and Parts thereof (87)	1,903,810	8.8	Vehicles other than Railway or Tramway Rolling-Stock, and Parts thereof (87)	5,552,990	14.8	Nuclear Reactors, Boilers, Machinery, and Mechanical Appliances Parts thereof (84)	5,550,971	14.2
4	Articles of Apparel and Clothing Accessories, not Knitted or Crocheted (62)	888,216	4.1	Articles of Apparel and Clothing Accessories, not Knitted or Crocheted (62)	1,260,693	3.4	Articles of Iron or Steel (73)	804,061	2.1
5	Articles of Apparel and Clothing Accessories, Knitted or Crocheted (61)	553,052	2.6	Articles of Apparel and Clothing Accessories, Knitted or Crocheted (61)	1,008,750	2.7	Articles of Apparel and Clothing Accessories, Knitted or Crocheted (61)	802,105	2.1
6	Articles of Iron or Steel (73)	512,646	2.4	Articles of Iron or Steel (73)	803,805	2.1	Mineral Fuels, Mineral Oils, Bituminous Substances, Mineral Waxes (27)	785,993	2.0
7	Iron and Steel (72)	432,197	2.0	Mineral Fuels, Mineral Oils, Bituminous Substances, Mineral Waxes (27)	779,075	2.1	Iron and Steel (72)	757,170	1.9
8	Plastics and Articles thereof (39)	341,634	1.6	Iron and Steel (72)	769,575	2.0	Plastics and Articles thereof (39)	689,416	1.8
9	Footwear, Headgear, Umbrellas, Walking-Sticks, Whips, Riding Crops (64)	328,249	1.5	Plastics and Articles thereof (39)	496,265	1.3	Rubber and Articles thereof (40)	682,117	1.7
10	Railway or Tramway Locomotives, Rolling-Stock and Parts thereof (86)	327,990	1.5	Optical, Photographic, Cinematographic, Measuring, Checking, Precision, Medical or Surgical Instruments and Apparatus, Parts and Accessories thereof (90)	477,124	1.3	Articles of Apparel and Clothing Accessories, not Knitted or Crocheted (62)	665,998	1.7
-	Sum of Top 10 Exports	17,882,898	82.5%	Sum of Top 10 Exports	32,011,869	85.1%	Sum of Top 10 Exports	33,969,715	87.1%

Source: KITA, *Database: Korea Trade Statistics*, various, 2005, available at <http://www.kita.net>.
Note: Numbers in parentheses refer to the HSK classification (commodity) code.

and optical measuring and instrument parts – represented nearly 50 per cent of total imports from the US.

Machinery parts and mechanical appliances fell from 21 per cent in 1996 to 15 per cent in 2004. Electrical machinery and equipment entered the top ten imports in 2000 as the number 1 import, nearing 37 per cent of total US imports. Electrical machinery and equipment parts, and optical measuring and instrument parts, supplanted automotive and aircraft part positions in 2000. However, electrical machinery and equipment did decline 8 per cent in 2004, as imports like organic chemicals and cereals increased. In 2004 import data, automotive is no longer in the top ten imports from the US (less than 2 per cent of total) and aircraft parts fell from 7 per cent of total US imports in 1996 to 3 per cent in 2004.

From 1996 to 2004 there is a periodic (per 4 years) decline in Korea–US importation, nearing $4 billion in reduced US product. Iron and steel imports rose notably in 2004, making 3 per cent of total US imports in 2004 from only 2 per cent in 1996 and less than 2 per cent in 2000. Meat and raw hides fell from the top ten imports in 2004, shedding roughly $1 billion from total US imports. Mineral derivatives, plastics and organic chemical, moreover, drove much of the increase in importation percentage in 2004. Pulp and timber products, in addition to the meat and hides, also fell, in percentage terms, from the top ten US imports. In addition to the removal of aircraft parts and automotive from the top import categories in 2004, there remain only two import categories that have risen since 1996, including organic chemicals and optical and precision measurement.

China's emergence as a trading nation

In particular, since the mid-1990s, China has become an increasingly important trading nation in both world[3] and East Asian regional markets. During the 1990s, China emerged as a major player in the world trade regime; no other country has ever expanded its role so rapidly. China has sustained an enviable growth performance for most of the last decade. Real GDP growth as measured by official figures[4] averaged

---

3   As in 2002, world trade accounted for US$ 6,347 billion, with China's annual total trade representing US$ 621 billion. As means of comparison, world trade hit the level of US$ 3,382 billion in 1990, and China's annual total trade reached US$ 117 billion (IMF, *Direction of Trade Statistics Yearbook* (Washington, DC: IMF, various years)).

4   Various studies suggest that official figures may overstate China's average real growth during the reform period by about 2 to 3 percentage points. Improvements in statistical methods during the 1990s and other factors probably have reduced the overstatement on average, but the bias probably varies with other circumstances. Alternative estimates developed by Thomas G. Rawski ('Measuring China's Recent GDP Growth: Where Do We Stand?', *China Economic Quarterly*, vol. 2, no. 1 (October, 2002), pp. 121–138) suggest that real growth in 1998 may have been less than half the official figure of 8 per cent. But even so, China's performance appears broadly comparable with that of other countries that have grown exceptionally rapidly during the post-war period, notably Japan and the Republic of Korea, and more recently several other 'Asian Tigers.'

Table 4.12 Republic of Korea imports from the US: 1996, 2000, 2004

Rank	1996 Total Imports: $33,395,379,000 Commodity	US$ in Thousands	% of Total Imports	2000 Total Imports: $29,241,628,000 Commodity	US$ in Thousands	% of Total Imports	2004 (M1-11) Total Imports: $26,156,483,000 Commodity	US$ in Thousands	% of Total Imports
1	Nuclear Reactors, Boilers, Machinery, and Mechanical Appliances Parts thereof (84)	6,977,284	20.9	Electrical Machinery and Equipment and Parts thereof (85)	10,783,550	36.9	Electrical Machinery and Equipment and Parts thereof (85)	7,485,527	28.6
2	Vehicles other than Railway or Tramway Rolling-Stock, and Parts thereof (87)	6,801,063	20.4	Nuclear Reactors, Boilers, Machinery, and Mechanical Appliances Parts thereof (84)	5,103,785	17.5	Nuclear Reactors, Boilers, Machinery, and Mechanical Appliances Parts thereof (84)	4,024,514	15.4
3	Aircraft, Spacecraft and Parts thereof (88)	2,360,385	7.1	Optical, Photographic, Cinematographic, Measuring, Checking, Precision, Medical or Surgical Instruments and Apparatus, Parts and Accessories thereof (90)	1,952,798	6.7	Optical, Photographic, Cinematographic, Measuring, Checking, Precision, Medical or Surgical Instruments and Apparatus, Parts and Accessories thereof (90)	2,004,209	7.7
4	Optical, Photographic, Cinematographic, Measuring, Checking, Precision, Medical or Surgical Instruments and Apparatus, Parts and Accessories thereof (90)	1,861,979	5.6	Organic Chemicals (29)	991,504	3.4	Organic Chemicals (29)	1,399,808	5.4
5	Cereals (10)	1,844,281	5.5	Plastics and Articles thereof (39)	650,929	2.2	Cereals (10)	995,972	3.8
6	Organic Chemicals (29)	1,143,433	3.4	Pulp of Wood or of other Fibrous Cellulose Material, Waste of Paper (47)	598,488	2.0	Iron and Steel (72)	807,810	3.1
7	Mineral Fuels, Mineral Oils, Bituminous Substances, Mineral Waxes (27)	915,722	2.7	Mineral Fuels, Mineral Oils, Bituminous Substances, Mineral Waxes (27)	597,760	2.0	Aircraft, Spacecraft and Parts thereof (88)	737,580	2.8
8	Raw Hides and Skins (other than Fur Skins), Leather (41)	793,671	2.4	Meat, Edible Meat Offal (02)	595,888	2.0	Mineral Fuels, Mineral Oils, Bituminous Substances, Mineral Waxes (27)	698,623	2.7
9	Plastics and Articles thereof (39)	727,556	2.2	Raw Hides and Skins (other than Fur Skins), Leather (41)	590,783	2.0	Plastics and Articles thereof (39)	679,872	2.6
10	Iron and Steel (72)	690,247	2.1	Aircraft, Spacecraft and Parts thereof (88)	556,160	1.9	Miscellaneous Chemical Products (38)	532,192	2.0
-	Sum of Top 10 Imports	24,115,621	72.2%	Sum of Top 10 Imports	22,421,645	76.7%	Sum of Top 10 Imports	19,366,107	74.0%

Source: KITA, *Database: Korea Trade Statistics*, various, 2005, available at <http://www.kita.net>.

Note: Numbers in parentheses refer to the HSK classification (commodity) code.

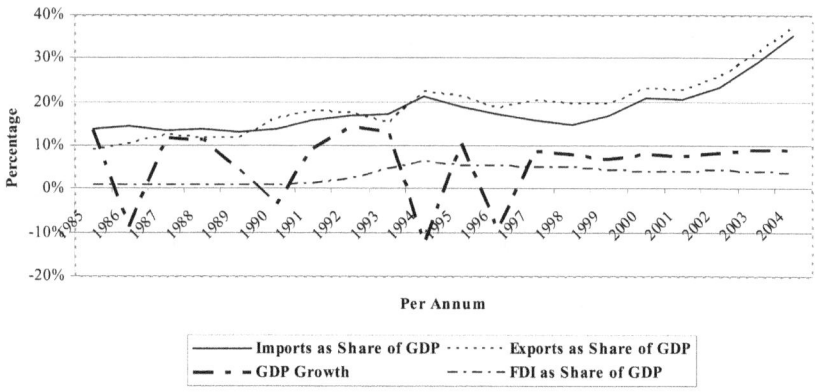

Figure 4.4   China's production response to trade and FDI inflows: 1985–2004

Sources: International Monetary Fund (IMF), International Trade Administration (ITA), and United Nations Statistics Division (UNSD), various, 2005.

more than 10 per cent during the 1990s (Figure 4.4). Exports and imports have grown even more rapidly than GDP during the 1990s. As a result, China's economy is now substantially more open to international trade than it was at the beginning of the 1990s. China's relative openness is also evident in examination of recipient foreign direct investment (Figure 4.4).

China's foreign trade exploded, with its exports and imports increasing from near $18 billion and $20 billion in 1980 to $62 billion and $53 billion in 1990, and then to $593 billion and $561 billion in 2004, respectively. By 2002, its share of world trade had almost tripled compared with its share in 1990, with exports and imports totaling 6 per cent and 4.3 per cent of world total imports and exports.[5] China successfully kept strong momentum for its exports and imports expansion with an average annual growth rate of 14.4 per cent throughout the period of 1980-2002. Moreover, China enjoyed a trade surplus with the rest of the world, and in particular, the trade surplus in 2004 ($32 billion) hit the record level, reflecting their recent economic boom after the WTO accession.

With its strong growth potential, deriving from its huge population and largely underdeveloped market, China has increasingly emerged as a major center for trade and investment. As China has pursued market-oriented economic reform, foreign direct investment (FDI) inflows to China have increased substantially. In 2004, China received $54.25 billion, the largest FDI inflow in the world. Large-scale investments in China will continue as a result of political stability and more liberal FDI regulations.

China's manufacturing sector receives 50 per cent of its FDI. As a manufacturing center, China's export shares in the world trade have been growing significantly.

---

5   IMF, *Direction of Trade Statistics Yearbook* (Washington, DC: IMF, 2003).

China's exports of manufacturing goods represented 4.7 per cent of world exports in 2000, a huge increase from 1.7 per cent in 1990. China's share of total US imports was 8.9 per cent in 2002, up from 3 per cent in 1991. In the same period, China's share of Korea's total imports increased to 10 per cent from 4 per cent.

Along with its strong increase in exports, imports into China have grown rapidly. As China's industrialization has proceeded, China has demanded more material and machinery to expand its production capacity. Asian Development Bank (ADB)[6] statistics demonstrate a close relation between China's import growth and industrialization. Throughout the 1990s, more than 70 per cent of China's imports fell into three standard international trade classification (SITC) categories – chemicals, basic manufactures, and machine and transport equipment. China has increasingly – and particularly during the 1990s – imported what it needs from Asian Newly Industrialized Economies (ANIE) countries; their share of China's total imports grew to 26 per cent in 2000 from 9 per cent in 1991.

Although most imports have gone into China's manufacturing sector, local markets for consumer goods have also strengthened. China's rapid economic development has created local demand for imported consumer goods and has provided more opportunities for foreign companies to profit from Chinese consumers. Samsung Electronics, for example, considers China as one of its priority markets. It sold $1.81 billion worth of consumer electronics in China in 2002 and expects to triple these sales figures by 2005.[7] In particular, Samsung is promoting its high-end products, and its success shows that growing numbers of Chinese consumers can afford and demand expensive and sophisticated goods.

Positive growth will continue as long as China's labor-intensive exports expand. In addition, a more integrated China will benefit neighboring Asian countries. China's accession to the WTO is forecast to increase its economic output by 2.2 to 5.5 per cent annually.[8]

Korea's growing dependence on the Chinese market

Korea is becoming increasingly dependent on the Chinese market for its exports; Korea's exports to China increased from 1.4 per cent in 1991 to 20 per cent in 2004. (Table 4.8 illustrates the trade balance between Korea and China.) By contrast, during the same time period, Korea's export dependence on the US and Japan fell from 26 per cent and 17 per cent, respectively, to 17 per cent and 9 per cent.

---

6   ADB, *Key Indicators of Developing Asian and Pacific Countries, 2002* (Manila: ADB, 2002).

7   Dexter Roberts and Ilhwan Moon, 'How Samsung Plugged into China', *Business Week*, available at <www.businessweek.com/magazine/content/02_09/b3772138.htm> (March 2002).

8   Nicholas R. Lardy, *Integrating China into the Global Economy* (Washington, DC: Brookings Institution Press, 2002).

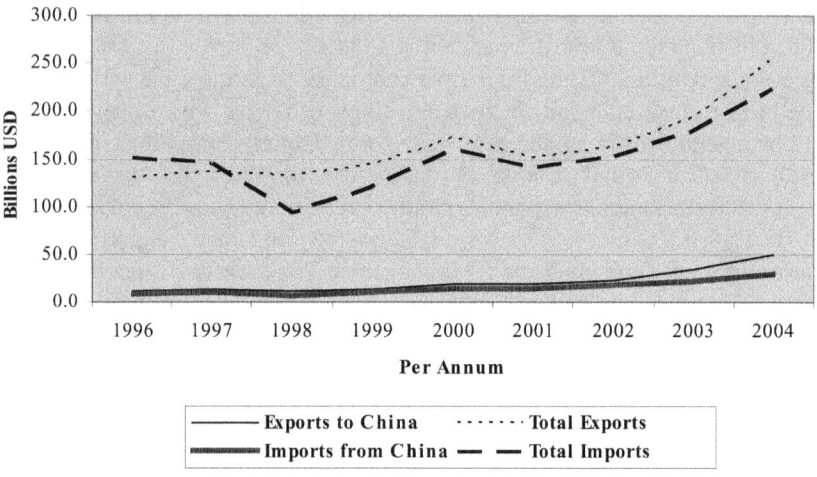

Figure 4.5   Korea's trade with China: 1996–2004
Source: KITA, *Database: Korea Trade Statistics*, various, 2005, available at <http://www.kita.net>.

Over the years, China's major exports to Korea have been textile materials and products, crude oil and petroleum, corn, coal, and other raw materials. Other bulk export commodities include chemical raw materials, rolled steel, leather goods, shoes, fodder, and mechanical and electrical products. In recent years, China's sales to Korea of electronic components and other products with high added value (i.e. telecommunications equipment) have been mounting steadily. Chemicals, electronics, and iron and steel are China's major imports from Korea. The specifics to the 2004 bilateral trade relationship merits further attention.

Korea's exports to China (reference Table 4.13)

Korea's 2004 exports to China exceeded $45 billion, a 298 per cent and 146 per cent increase, respectively, from 1996 and 2000 export numbers (see Figure 4.5). Top ten 2004 export categories represented 86 per cent of the total per annum exports to China. This is in contrast to 1996 and 2000, at 76 per cent and 82 per cent, respectively. Top three Korean exports in 2004 – electrical machinery and equipment, parts and mechanical appliances, and organic chemicals – represent 53 per cent of total 2004 exports to China. This contrasts slightly from 1996 and 2000 numbers, when top three exports reached 36 per cent and 40 per cent, respectively. Further periodic dissimilarities in top three Korean exports to China in 1996 and 2000 include trade in plastics in 1996 and 2004, and rising trade in electronic machinery and equipment.

In addition to plastics – that fell from 12.9 per cent of total export to China in 1996 to 6.7 per cent in 2004 – iron and steel and man-made filaments also fall in contribution percentage and/or in total export dollar value. Emerging from outside the top ten, in the preceding 1996 and 2000 periods, copper and products thereof, optical measuring and precision equipment, and motor vehicle and parts thereof, made it to the top ten in 2004; collectively, these three represented $5 billion in export value and 11 per cent of total 2004 export. The 2004 numbers emphasize the export concentration in electrical machinery and equipment, and in parts and mechanical appliances.

The gradual departure of man-made filaments from the top ten exports to China, from 6 per cent in 1996, 3.6 per cent in 2000, and 1.2 per cent in 2004, much like other traditional large export items, is deceiving. The reduction in percentage terms does not always reflect a reduction in product export value, and thus should be measured carefully. Emerging products and their rising importance in Korea's export portfolio to the China market might simply replace the percentage value of another export, but not deplete the former exports value in real terms.

Korea's imports from China (reference Table 4.14)

Total imports from China neared $27 billion in 2004, rising 212 per cent from 1996 import levels. The top 10 imports from China prove more concentrated in total imports, and marked a 121 per cent and 248 per cent increase from 2000 and 1996 levels, respectively. Total imports more than doubled from 2000. Korea's top three imports from China in 2004, including electrical machinery and equipment, parts and mechanical appliances, and iron and steel, represent 45 per cent of total imports. The difference in top three import percentage numbers from 2004 to 1996 and 2000, respectively, is 7 per cent and 7 per cent. Most relevant, however, is the make-up and individual percentage changes in each import classification.

Korea's rising demand levels in iron and steel led to a near 400 per cent increase, from 2000 to 2004, in iron and steel imports from China. Electrical machinery and equipment remain the top import from 2000, and nearly doubled in import value each four-year period, from 1996 forward. Mineral fuels and mineral oils declined in percentage terms in 2000 to 2004, near 4 per cent, following the long import decline from 13.7 per cent in 1996 to 5 per cent in 2004. Non-knitted or crocheted apparel and clothing remains at over 4%, a consistent percentage from 1996 to 2004. Missing from the 2004 top ten list from 2000 are cereals, man-made staple fibers, and cotton, representing, collectively, near 12 per cent of total imports from China in 2000.

Reductions, in percentage terms, of footwear and silk in 2000 and 2004 numbers, leave these imports outside the top ten. Fish and other aquatic invertebrates remain in the 3–4 per cent range, from 1996 to 2004, and represent over $600 million in 2004. Rising into the top ten ranks in 2004 are also knitted or crocheted articles of clothing, at 3.5 per cent of imports, and aluminum products, at 4.1 per cent of total imports from China. Optical and medical and measuring instruments remain a large factor in 2004, rising from 2.4 per cent in 2000 to 2.9 per cent, in contribution percentage terms, and doubling in total trade value at near $620 million.

Table 4.13 Republic of Korea exports to China: 1996, 2000, 2004

Rank	1996 Total Exports: $11,377,068,000 Commodity	USD in Thousands	% of Total Exports	2000 Total Exports: $18,454,540,000 Commodity	USD in Thousands	% of Total Exports	2004 (M1-11) Total Exports: $45,308,228,000 Commodity	USD in Thousands	% of Total Exports
1	Nuclear Reactors, Boilers, Machinery, and Mechanical Appliances Parts thereof (84)	1,526,154	13.4	Electrical Machinery and Equipment and Parts thereof (85)	3,430,123	18.6	Electrical Machinery and Equipment and Parts thereof (85)	10,925,623	24.1
2	Plastics and Articles thereof (39)	1,463,454	12.9	Nuclear Reactors, Boilers, Machinery, and Mechanical Appliances Parts thereof (84)	2,033,029	11.0	Nuclear Reactors, Boilers, Machinery, and Mechanical Appliances Parts thereof (84)	8,945,369	19.7
3	Electrical Machinery and Equipment and Parts thereof (85)	1,133,525	10.0	Plastics and Articles thereof (39)	1,908,884	10.3	Organic Chemicals (29)	4,360,333	9.6
4	Mineral Fuels, Mineral Oils, Bituminous Substances, Mineral Waxes (27)	822,240	7.2	Organic Chemicals (29)	1,880,992	10.2	Plastics and Articles thereof (39)	3,449,939	7.6
5	Iron and Steel (72)	741,157	6.5	Mineral Fuels, Mineral Oils, Bituminous Substances, Mineral Waxes (27)	1,854,722	10.1	Iron and Steel (72)	3,046,994	6.7
6	Raw Hides and Skins (Other Than Fur skins), Leather (41)	739,536	6.5	Iron and Steel (72)	1,203,282	6.5	Mineral Fuels, Mineral Oils, Bituminous Substances, Mineral Waxes (27)	2,510,218	5.5
7	Man-Made Filaments (54)	678,896	6.0	Raw Hides and Skins (Other Than Fur skins), Leather (41)	755,739	4.1	Optical, Photographic, Cinematographic, Measuring, Checking, Precision, Medical or Surgical Instruments and Apparatus, Parts and Accessories thereof (90)	2,404,003	5.3
8	Organic Chemicals (29)	640,590	5.6	Man-Made Filaments (54)	665,933	3.6	Vehicles other than Railway or Tramway Rolling-Stock, and Parts thereof (87)	1,898,823	4.2
9	Man-Made Staple Fibers (55)	583,412	5.1	Man-Made Staple Fibers (55)	508,733	2.8	Copper and Articles thereof (74)	683,571	1.5
10	Paper and Paperboard, Articles of Paper Pulp, of Paper or of Paperboard (48)	371,658	3.3	Impregnated, Coated, Covered or Laminated Textile Fabrics (59)	896,128	4.9	Man-Made Filaments (54)	544,139	1.2
-	Sum of Top 10 Exports	8,700,622	76.5%	Sum of Top 10 Exports	15,137,565	82.0%	Sum of Top 10 Exports	38,769,012	85.6%

Source: KITA, *Database: Korea Trade Statistics*, various, 2005, available at <http://www.kita.net>.

Note: Numbers in parentheses refer to the Harmonized System of Korea (HSK) classification (commodity) codes.

Table 4.14 Republic of Korea imports from China: 1996, 2000, 2004

Rank	1996 Total Imports: $8,538,568,000 Commodity	USD in Thousands	% of Total Imports	2000 Total Imports: $12,798,728,000 Commodity	USD in Thousands	% of Total Imports	2004 (M1-11) Total Imports: $26,647,249,000 Commodity	USD in Thousands	% of Total Imports
1	Mineral Fuels, Mineral Oils, Bituminous Substances, Mineral Waxes (27)	1,172,840	13.0	Electrical Machinery and Equipment and Parts thereof (85)	2,704,137	21.1	Electrical Machinery and Equipment and Parts thereof (85)	6,970,568	24.5
2	Machinery Specialized for Particular Industries (72)	1,085,041	12.7	Mineral Fuels, Mineral Oils, Bituminous Substances, Mineral Waxes (27)	1,158,208	9.0	Nuclear Reactors, Boilers, Machinery, and Mechanical Appliances Parts thereof (84)	2,846,582	5.6
3	Electrical Machinery and Equipment and Parts thereof (85)	956,087	11.2	Nuclear Reactors, Boilers, Machinery, and Mechanical Appliances Parts thereof (84)	1,051,921	8.2	Iron and Steel (72)	2,232,393	5.3
4	Man-Made Staple Fibers (55)	506,141	5.9	Iron and Steel (72)	759,324	5.9	Mineral Fuels, Mineral Oils, Bituminous Substances, Mineral Waxes (27)	1,922,491	4.9
5	Articles of Apparel and Clothing Accessories, Not Knitted or Crocheted (62)	368,803	4.3	Cereals (10)	700,724	5.5	Articles of Apparel and Clothing Accessories, Not Knitted or Crocheted (62)	1,229,136	4.3
6	Nuclear Reactors, Boilers, Machinery, and Mechanical Appliances Parts thereof (84)	325,067	3.8	Articles of Apparel and Clothing Accessories, Not Knitted or Crocheted (62)	560,707	4.4	Aluminum and Articles thereof (76)	830,479	4.1
7	Organic Chemicals (29)	296,125	3.5	Fish, Crustaceans, Mollusks, other Aquatic Invertebrates (03)	468,447	3.7	Fish, Crustaceans, Mollusks, other Aquatic Invertebrates (07)	736,893	3.9
8	Silk (50)	242,262	2.8	Man-Made Staple Fibers (55)	413,466	3.2	Articles of Apparel and Clothing Accessories, Knitted or Crocheted (61)	706,731	3.5
9	Footwear, Headgear, Umbrellas, Walking-Sticks, Whips, Riding Crops (64)	205,973	2.4	Optical, Photographic, Cinematographic, Measuring, Checking, Precision, Medical or Surgical Instruments and Apparatus, Parts and Accessories thereof (90)	309,448	2.0	Optical, Photographic, Cinematographic, Measuring, Checking, Precision, Medical or Surgical Instruments and Apparatus, Parts and Accessories thereof (90)	622,159	3.0
10	Fish, Crustaceans, Mollusks, other Aquatic Invertebrates (03)	195,255	2.3	Cotton (52)	309,320	2.4	Organic Chemicals (29)	543,315	2.9
-	Sum of Top 10 Imports	5,353,594	62.7%	Sum of Top 10 Imports	8,435,702	65.9%	Sum of Top 10 Imports	18,640,747	70.0%

Source: KITA, *Database: Korea Trade Statistics*, various, 2005, available at <http://www.kita.net>.

Note: Numbers in parentheses refer to the HSK classification (commodity) code.

Trade in the Japan–Korea relationship

The historical impact and inherent role of Japan in shaping Korea's economic production cycles and trade flows is undeniable. Bilateral trade remained strong in 2004, making Japan the largest source of Korean imports and fifth among large partners in total demand for Korean exports. These contributions, in addition to solidifying formal trading relationships, also have influenced intraregional trade patterns and FTAs. The subsequent descriptions of Korea-Japan exports and imports provide insight into the inherent regional and supply-chain relationships maintained by these two Northeast Asian countries (NEC) nations.

Korea's exports to Japan (reference Table 4.15)

From 1996 to 2004, total export to Japan increased near 25 per cent, leaving the two leading trade product categories intact – electrical machinery and equipment and mineral fuels, mineral oils, and mineral waxes. However, from 2000 to 2004, Korean trade in exports fell near 4 per cent, in real terms. In accord with the total periodic (1996–2004) gains in export, the top three categories of export commodity also rose in 2004, nearing 56 per cent of export totals. These included electrical machinery and equipment, mineral fuels, mineral oils, and mineral waxes, and parts and mechanical appliances. Top ten exports neared $16 billion in 2004 – 81 per cent of total 2004 exports – marking a 10 per cent rise from 1996 numbers and a slight 1 per cent increase from 2000.

Large periodic fluctuations, for top ten exports to Japan, include declines in mineral products (fuels, oils, and waxes), and in exported parts and mechanical appliances, falling near 10 and 6 per cent, respectively. Numerous top ten categories increased from export levels in 2000 to 2004, including articles of iron and steel (from 3 to 4 per cent), optical measurement and precision tools (from 2 to 3 per cent), iron and steel (from 6 to 7 per cent), plastics (from 5 to 7 per cent), and organic chemicals (from 4 to 6 per cent). The 2000 to 2004 percentage declines, in addition to the large declines in mineral derivatives and parts and mechanical appliances, also includes fish and aquatic exports (from 5 to 4 per cent).

Emerging in 2004, top ten exports to Japan, at 3 per cent of total exports, is the automotive product line, a commodity category that missed the 1996 and 2000 top ten. Furthermore, removed from the 2000 and 2004 tables is the precious stone and metals category that formerly, in 1996, had 2 per cent of bilateral export to Japan. From 1996 export levels forward, the strongest periodic and categorical rises to 2004 export data include parts and mechanical appliances (from 5 to 8 per cent) and plastics (from 2 to 7 per cent). Iron and steel remains Korea's fourth largest export to Japan, holding its position from 2000 in the 2004 trade table, and increasing near $300 million from 2000 numbers.

Table 4.15 Republic of Korea exports to Japan: 1996, 2000, 2004

Rank	1996 Commodity Total Exports: $15,766,827,000	US$ in Thousands	% of Total Exports	2000 Commodity Total Exports: $20,466,016,000	US$ in Thousands	% of Total Exports	2004 (M1-11) Commodity Total Exports: $19,702,900,000	US$ in Thousands	% of Total Exports
1	Electrical Machinery and Equipment and Parts thereof (85)	3,906,414	24.8	Electrical Machinery and Equipment and Parts thereof (85)	4,593,835	17.8	Electrical Machinery and Equipment and Parts thereof (85)	5,579,037	20.0
2	Mineral Fuels, Mineral Oils, Bituminous Substances, Mineral Waxes (27)	1,728,120	11.0	Mineral Fuels, Mineral Oils, Bituminous Substances, Mineral Waxes (27)	3,678,671	17.3	Mineral Fuels, Mineral Oils, Bituminous Substances, Mineral Waxes (27)	3,005,967	7.7
3	Iron and Steel (72)	1,311,534	8.3	Nuclear Reactors, Boilers, Machinery, and Mechanical Appliances Parts thereof (84)	3,478,349	13.5	Nuclear Reactors, Boilers, Machinery, and Mechanical Appliances Parts thereof (84)	2,517,000	7.6
4	Articles of Apparel and Clothing Accessories, Knitted or Crocheted (61)	902,443	5.7	Iron and Steel (72)	1,163,132	6.1	Iron and Steel (72)	1,450,592	7.4
5	Fish, Crustaceans, Mollusks, Aquatic Invertebrates (03)	871,121	5.5	Fish, Crustaceans, Mollusks, Aquatic Invertebrates (03)	834,503	5.3	Plastics and Articles thereof (39)	788,597	6.8
6	Nuclear Reactors, Boilers, Machinery, and Mechanical Appliances Parts thereof (84)	785,609	5.0	Articles of Apparel and Clothing Accessories, Knitted or Crocheted (61)	699,947	5.1	Organic Chemicals (29)	699,765	6.4
7	Articles of Iron or Steel (73)	441,295	2.8	Plastics and Articles thereof (39)	696,256	4.6	Articles of Iron or Steel (73)	552,075	4.3
8	Articles of Apparel and Clothing Accessories, not Knitted or Crocheted (62)	396,866	2.5	Organic Chemicals (29)	404,072	3.7	Fish, Crustaceans, Mollusks, Aquatic Invertebrates (03)	536,038	3.9
9	Pearls, Precious or Semi-Precious Stones, Precious Metals, Coin (71)	379,735	2.4	Articles of Iron or Steel (73)	404,035	2.7	Optical, Photographic, Cinematographic, Measuring, Checking, Precision, Medical or Surgical Instruments and Apparatus, Parts and Accessories thereof (90)	476,590	3.4
10	Plastics and Articles thereof (39)	374,101	2.4	Optical, Photographic, Cinematographic, Measuring, Checking, Precision, Medical or Surgical Instruments and Apparatus, Parts and Accessories thereof (90)	255,931	1.9	Vehicles other than Railway or Tramway Rolling-Stock, and Parts thereof (87)	308,681	3.4
-	Sum of Top 10 Exports	11,097,238	70.4%	Sum of Top 10 Exports	16,208,731	79.2%	Sum of Top 10 Exports	15,914,342	80.8%

Source: KITA, *Database: Korea Trade Statistics*, various, 2005, available at <http://www.kita.net>.
Note: Numbers in parentheses refer to the HSK classification (commodity) code.

Korea's imports from Japan (reference Table 4.16)

Imports from Japan exceeded $42 billion in 2004, marking a 34 and 32 per cent rise from respective levels in 1996 and 2000. From 1996 to 2000, little changed in total Korea imports from Japan. Top ten imports from Japan in 2004 represent near 88 per cent of total imports. Top three imports in 2004, including electrical machinery and equipment, parts and mechanical appliances and iron and steel, represent near 58 per cent of total Japan importation. In 1996 and 2000, top ten imports measured 86 per cent and 85 per cent, respectively, of total imports from Japan. Top three import concentration for 1996 and 2000 was 61 per cent per annum. For each period, the three top import categories included parts and mechanical appliances and electrical machinery and equipment. However, in 2004, iron and steel imports replaced optical measuring and precision equipment, the third highest imports for Korea in 1996 and 2000.

Total imports in 1996 and 2000 neared $31 and $32 billion, respectively. The 1996 and 2000 contribution import percentages, however, reflect periodic dissimilarities. In 2000, Korea, from 1996 numbers, increased imports of parts and mechanical appliances 2 per cent, parts and mechanical appliances 2 per cent, and imports of electrical machinery and equipment 20 per cent. From 1996 to 2000, Korean import reductions included optical measurement and precision instrumentation (minimal), organic chemicals (minimal), mineral derivatives, and articles of iron and steel (not the same as the 'iron and steel' demarcation). Korea import reductions in 2000–2004 data included copper (and articles thereof), and photographic and film products.

Most top ten import commodities remain from 2000 tables in 2004 import numbers. Korea's higher 2004 import in iron and steel imports, electrical machinery and equipment, and parts and mechanical appliances further concentrate bilateral imports from Japan. Mineral derivatives (fuels, oils, and waxes) and glass products emerge in the top ten in 2004, at 2 and 2 per cent, respectively. In automotive, having suffered a near 2 per cent decline (in import contribution, not product value) in 2000, there proved more demand in 2004, rising more than 2 per cent in 2004 (and 300 per cent in product value).

Korea and ASEAN: Korea's trading bloc neighbors

The Korean–ASEAN trade relationship remains integral in examining patterns in Korea's regional import and export numbers and also in discussing prospects for a sub-regional trade agreement. The subsequent paragraphs articulate the demand levels of the member nations in ASEAN for Korean exports, and also the imported and exported commodity descriptions from 1996–2004.

Korea's exports to ASEAN (reference Table 4.17)

Korea export totals to ASEAN nations in 2004 neared $22 billion and marked a slight increase of 8 and 8 per cent, respectively, from 1996 and 2000. Top ten

Table 4.16 Republic of Korea imports from Japan: 1996, 2000, 2004

Rank	1996 Commodity (Total Imports: $31,448,636,000)	US$ in Thousands	% of Total Imports	2000 Commodity (Total Imports: $31,827,943,000)	US$ in Thousands	% of Total Imports	2004 (M1-11) Commodity (Total Imports: $42,038,239,000)	US$ in Thousands	% of Total Imports
1	Nuclear Reactors, Boilers, Machinery, and Mechanical Appliances Parts thereof (84)	8,932,497	19.1	Electrical Machinery and Equipment and Parts thereof (85)	9,923,475	31.2	Electrical Machinery and Equipment and Parts thereof (85)	11,327,346	27.0
2	Electrical Machinery and Equipment and Parts thereof (85)	7,486,043	11.0	Nuclear Reactors, Boilers, Machinery, and Mechanical Appliances Parts thereof (84)	6,555,548	20.6	Nuclear Reactors, Boilers, Machinery, and Mechanical Appliances Parts thereof (84)	7,794,173	18.5
3	Optical, Photographic, Cinematographic, Measuring, Checking, Precision, Medical or Surgical Instruments and Apparatus, Parts and Accessories thereof (90)	2,644,927	9.2	Iron and Steel (72)	2,858,805	9.0	Iron and Steel (72)	5,284,040	12.6
4	Iron and Steel (72)	2,218,720	8.9	Optical, Photographic, Cinematographic, Measuring, Checking, Precision, Medical or Surgical Instruments and Apparatus, Parts and Accessories thereof (90)	2,651,322	8.3	Optical, Photographic, Cinematographic, Measuring, Checking, Precision, Medical or Surgical Instruments and Apparatus, Parts and Accessories thereof (90)	4,444,606	10.6
5	Organic Chemicals (29)	1,575,810	7.0	Plastics and Articles thereof (39)	1,547,058	4.9	Plastics and Articles thereof (39)	1,980,220	4.7
6	Plastics and Articles thereof (39)	1,029,774	5.0	Organic Chemicals (29)	1,148,989	3.6	Organic Chemicals (29)	1,932,101	4.6
7	Vehicles other than Railway or Tramway Rolling-Stock, and Parts thereof (87)	646,713	4.4	Miscellaneous Chemical Products (38)	798,081	2.5	Miscellaneous Chemical Products (38)	1,161,989	2.8
8	Miscellaneous Chemical Products (38)	1,269,654	3.6	Vehicles other than Railway or Tramway Rolling-Stock, and Parts thereof (87)	658,971	2.1	Vehicles other than Railway or Tramway Rolling-Stock, and Parts thereof (87)	1,875,198	4.5
9	Mineral Fuels, Mineral Oils, Bituminous substances, Mineral Waxes (27)	536,619	3.0	Copper and Articles thereof (74)	439,498	1.4	Glass and Glassware (70)	670,851	1.6
10	Articles of Iron or Steel (73)	535,851	2.1	Photographic and Cinematographic Goods (37)	417,831	1.3	Mineral Fuels, Mineral Oils, Bituminous substances, Mineral Waxes (27)	637,995	1.5
-	Sum of Top 10 Exports	26,876,608	85.5%	Sum of Top 10 Exports	26,999,578	84.8%	Sum of Top 10 Exports	37,108,519	88.3%

Source: KITA, *Database: Korea Trade Statistics*, various, 2005, available at <http://www.kita.net>.
Note: Numbers in parentheses refer to the HSK classification (commodity) code.

Table 4.17 Republic of Korea exports to ASEAN: 1996, 2000, 2004

Rank	1996 Commodity (Total Exports: $20,310,764,000)	US$ in Thousands	% of Total Exports	2000 Commodity (Total Exports: $20,133,786,000)	US$ in Thousands	% of Total Exports	2004 (1-11) Commodity (Total Exports: $21,845,138,000)	US$ in Thousands	% of Total Exports
1	Electrical Machinery and Equipment and Parts thereof (85)	6,514,037	32.1	Electrical Machinery and Equipment and Parts thereof (85)	8,460,906	42.0	Electrical Machinery and Equipment and Parts thereof (85)	7,665,771	35.1
2	Pearls, Precious or Semi-Precious Stones, Precious Metals, Coin (71)	2,630,165	12.9	Nuclear Reactors, Boilers, Machinery, and Mechanical Appliances Parts thereof (84)	2,243,199	11.1	Nuclear Reactors, Boilers, Machinery, and Mechanical Appliances Parts thereof (84)	3,284,196	15.0
3	Nuclear Reactors, Boilers, Machinery, and Mechanical Appliances Parts thereof (84)	2,121,834	10.4	Mineral Fuels, Mineral Oils, Bituminous Substances, Mineral Waxes (27)	1,037,167	5.2	Iron and Steel (72)	1,336,525	6.1
4	Iron and Steel (72)	1,048,435	5.2	Plastics and Articles thereof (39)	928,215	4.6	Vehicles other than Railway or Tramway Rolling-Stock, and Parts thereof (87)	1,206,399	5.5
5	Vehicles other than Railway or Tramway Rolling-Stock, and Parts thereof (87)	826,018	4.1	Iron and Steel (72)	773,615	3.8	Plastics and Articles thereof (39)	1,196,852	5.5
6	Plastics and Articles thereof (39)	763,743	3.8	Vehicles other than Railway or Tramway Rolling-Stock, and Parts thereof (87)	740,240	3.7	Mineral Fuels, Mineral Oils, Bituminous Substances, Mineral Waxes (27)	1,156,181	5.3
7	Mineral Fuels, Mineral Oils, Bituminous Substances, Mineral Waxes (27)	620,385	3.1	Organic Chemicals (29)	659,878	3.3	Organic Chemicals (29)	570,081	2.6
8	Man-Made Filaments (54)	581,608	2.9	Man-Made Filaments (54)	585,528	2.9	Man-Made Filaments (54)	455,127	2.1
9	Ships, Boats and Floating Structures (89)	529,383	2.6	Impregnated, Coated, Covered or Laminated Textile Fabrics (59)	379,866	1.9	Knitted or Crocheted Fabrics (60)	380,376	1.7
10	Articles of Iron or Steel (73)	465,530	2.3	Pearls, Precious or Semi-Precious Stones, Precious Metals, Coin (71)	363,174	1.8	Ships, Boats and Floating Structures (89)	336,861	1.5
-	Sum of Top 10 Exports	16,101,138	79.3%	Sum of Top 10 Exports	16,171,788	80.3%	Sum of Top 10 Exports	17,588,369	80.5%

Source: KITA, *Database: Korea Trade Statistics*, various, 2005, available at <http://www.kita.net>.
Note: Numbers in parentheses refer to the HSK classification (commodity) codes.

exports in 2004 represented 81 per cent of total exports to ASEAN, more or less consistent with top ten percentage numbers in 1996 and 2000; incremental increases of 9 per cent occur in the top ten in 2000 and 2004. The contribution of the top three to Korea's total exports to ASEAN, however, did modify over the measured periods. For instance, in 2004, electrical machinery and equipment, the top export classifications, changed from 32 and 42 per cent to near 35 per cent, respectively, in 1996, 2000, and 2004. Korea's exports of machinery and mechanical appliances, moreover, also shifted in this periodic measure, from 10 and 11 per cent in 1996 and 2000, respectively, to 15 per cent in 2004.

Top ten exports, again, measured 81 per cent of total exports to ASEAN in 2004. This percentage, nearing $18 billion, contrasts significantly from previous periods. For instance, iron and steel numbers nearly doubled in 2004, and knitted and crocheted fabrics, and ships and floating structures, each climbed in the top ten export list. There remain in the data, however, incremental contribution and/or value increases in exported iron and steel, plastics, electrical machinery and equipment, and machinery and mechanical appliances.

The decreasing exports, from 1996 to 2004, in the top ten lists include precious and semi-precious stones, and laminated textile fabrics. Export figures from 2004 signal the rapid reduction in ASEAN demand for Korea's precious semi-precious stones, falling, in percentage terms, near 11 per cent of total bilateral export. The reemergence of ships and floating structures in export in 2004, moreover, signals a revival in ASEAN demand and Korea's production lines. However, important to note, the 2004 bilateral export levels in ships and floating structures represent half those of 1996.

Korea's imports from ASEAN (reference Table 4.18)

Korea's import totals to ASEAN for 2004 neared $20 billion, marking a 68 and 12 per cent increase from 1996 and 2000, respectively. Top ten imports from ASEAN represented near 84 per cent of total bilateral imports in 2004, more or less (inside 2 per cent) the contribution percentages in 1996 and 2000. Top three imports from ASEAN in 2004 totaled 72 per cent of imports from ASEAN. Korea's mineral fuels and oil imports and imports of electrical machinery and equipment measured near 66 per cent of total bilateral imports, leaving machinery and mechanical appliance parts in third at 6 per cent of total imports. The top three import classifications have remained the largest three in 1996, 2000, and 2004.

In addition to the top three Korean imports from ASEAN, the 4th and 5th ranked, in per annum contribution percentage, imports have remained consistent in all the reported periods. These last two include wood and articles of wood and rubber and rubber articles.[9] Measures of 2004 Korean imports from ASEAN also illustrate

---

9 Note, however, that Korea's wood imports from ASEAN nations are increasingly moribund.

Table 4.18 Republic of Korea imports from ASEAN: 1996, 2000, 2004

Rank	1996 Total Imports: $12,073,822,000 Commodity	US$ in Thousands	% of Total Imports	2000 Total Imports: $18,173,436,000 Commodity	US$ in Thousands	% of Total Imports	2004 (M1-11) Total Imports: $20,284,102,000 Commodity	US$ in Thousands	% of Total Imports
1	Mineral Fuels, Mineral Oils, Bituminous Substances, Mineral Waxes (27)	4,386,033	36.3	Mineral Fuels, Mineral Oils, Bituminous Substances, Mineral Waxes (27)	5,893,208	32.4	Mineral Fuels, Mineral Oils, Bituminous Substances, Mineral Waxes (27)	6,755,891	33.3
2	Electrical Machinery and Equipment and Parts thereof (85)	1,931,733	16.0	Electrical Machinery and Equipment and Parts thereof (85)	4,765,586	26.2	Electrical Machinery and Equipment and Parts thereof (85)	6,606,047	32.6
3	Nuclear Reactors, Boilers, Machinery, and Mechanical Appliances Parts thereof (84)	1,045,022	8.7	Nuclear Reactors, Boilers, Machinery, and Mechanical Appliances Parts thereof (84)	3,014,284	16.6	Nuclear Reactors, Boilers, Machinery, and Mechanical Appliances Parts thereof (84)	1,234,471	6.1
4	Wood and Articles of Wood, Wood Charcoal (44)	1,029,535	8.5	Wood and Articles of Wood, Wood Charcoal (44)	573,185	3.2	Wood and Articles of Wood, Wood Charcoal (44)	509,711	2.5
5	Rubber and Articles thereof (40)	493,424	4.1	Rubber and Articles thereof (40)	290,737	1.6	Rubber and Articles thereof (40)	498,243	2.5
6	Miscellaneous Chemical Products (38)	334,785	2.8	Ores, Slag, Ash (26)	256,326	1.4	Organic Chemicals (29)	365,995	1.8
7	Sugars and Sugar Confectionery (17)	244,979	2.0	Organic Chemicals (29)	233,719	1.3	Miscellaneous Chemical Products (38)	259,861	1.3
8	Iron and Steel (72)	172,919	1.4	Pulp of Wood or of other Fibrous Cellulose Material, Waste of Paper (47)	212,293	1.2	Pulp of Wood or of other Fibrous Cellulose Material, Waste of Paper (47)	256,315	1.3
9	Copper and Articles thereof (74)	162,652	1.3	Miscellaneous Chemical Products (38)	206,724	1.1	Iron and Steel (72)	245,052	1.2
10	Animal or Vegetable Fats, Oils and Waxes, Prepared Edible Fats (15)	161,709	1.3	Pearls, Precious or Semi-Precious Stones, Precious Metals, Coin (71)	205,415	1.1	Fish, Crustaceans, Mollusks, other Aquatic Invertebrates (03)	235,475	1.2
-	Sum of Top 10 Imports	9,962,791	82.5%	Sum of Top 10 Imports	15,651,477	86.1%	Sum of Top 10 Imports	16,967,061	83.6%

Source: KITA, *Database: Korea Trade Statistics*, various, 2005, available at <http://www.kita.net>.
Note: Numbers in parentheses refer to the HSK classification (commodity) code.

Table 4.19 Total Asia trade and intraregional trade

Trade	Date	China (US$)	Japan (US$)	Korea (US$)
Total Trade (USD)	1996	290,114,000,000	713,700,000,000	280,054,237,000
	2000	473,855,000,000	808,100,000,000	332,748,528,000
	(2003 for China) 2004	851,086,000,000	1,076,700,000,000	478,307,359,000
Trade with	1996	105,324,000,000	288,900,000,000	123,346,075,000
Asia (USD)	2000	172,050,000,000	334,400,000,000	151,354,452,000
	(2003 for China) 2004	301,627,000,000	505,900,000,000	240,771,717,000
Intraregional:	1996	36	40	44
Total Trade (%)	2000	36	41	45
	2004	35	47	50

Source: China Trade Numbers (IMF Direction of Trade Statistics, 1993–2003); Korea Trade Numbers (KITA, March, 2005); Japan Trade Numbers (Jetro, March 2005).

that imports of iron and steel and fish and aquatic invertebrates are rising and that chemical products are also in high demand.

Top ten departures in 2000 included sugar and sugar confectionery and copper. There is no sign of reemergence, in contribution import percentage, in 2004. In 2004, pearls, precious and semi-precious stone and ores, slag, and ash also fall from the top ten import listings, in contribution terms. In real terms, there is a top ten increase of 70 and 8 per cent in 2004, respectively, from 1996 and 2000 value numbers.

The Rise of Asian Regionalism

Intraregional trade is an important element in the total composition of trade for East Asia. Petri[10] concludes that intraregional trade has always been a substantial part of the region's trade composition. Some scholars even attribute intraregional trade as a source of steady East Asian growth throughout the 1990s, despite a worldwide recession during the period between 1990 and 1992.[11] The relevance of regional trade patterns affecting NEC trade flows and, more specifically, Korean bilateral interests, is not in doubt. More relevant here is the per annum regional percentage fluctuations and the trends in affecting trade policies in Asia and also US interests. Table 4.19 presents the scale and intraregional contribution percentages that are driving this discussion.

---

10 Peter Petri, 'The East Asian Trading Bloc: An Analytical History', in Jeffrey Frankel and Miles Kahler, eds, *Regionalism and Rivalry: Japan and the US in Pacific Asia* (Washington, DC: National Bureau of Economic Research, 1993).

11 Claude E. Barfield, 'Trade, Investment, and Emerging US Policies for Asia', *Expanding the US-Asian Trade and Investment* (Washington, DC: American Enterprise Institute, 1997).

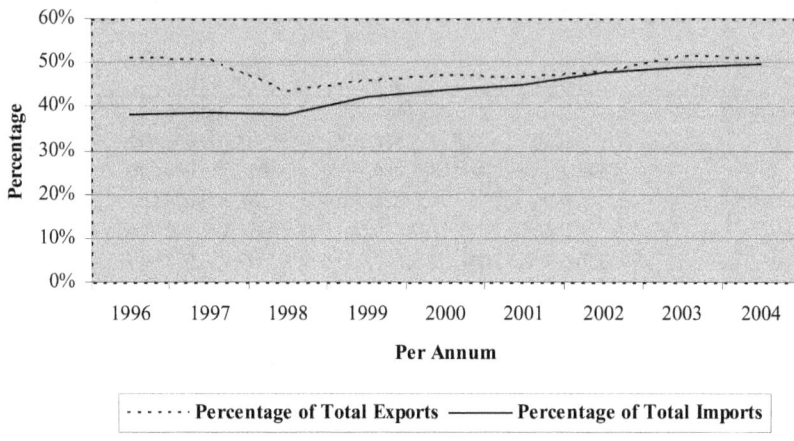

Figure 4.6 Total regional (Asia) trade as percentage of total trade
Source: KITA, *Database: Korea Trade Statistics*, various, 2005, available at <http://www.kita.net>.

Total Korea regional trade as a percentage of total trade

Korea's regional imports in 2004, near 50 per cent of total per annum Korean trade, represent an increase of 20 per cent from 1996 trade figures. Exports in the region remained near 1996 levels in 2004, at 51 per cent of total trade, and recovered from a 5 per cent decline in the period 1997–1998. Figure 4.6 illustrates the rise in regional imports in 1998–1999 and the proceeding per annum rise of 1 per cent through 2004.

The convergence of Korea's regional imports and regional exports, as a percentage of Korea's total trade, occurs in 2002; regional imports and exports arriving near 48 per cent of total Korea trade. In 2003, however, regional exports exceed 50% of total trade, and imports reach close to 50 per cent, at 49 per cent. The increasing regional contribution, imports and exports, of Korea's total trade has no precedence (Tables 4.11 and 4.14).

Nation and trade bloc specified intraregional trade numbers further reflect the regional preferences, and also exhibit the pace of per annum regional trade growth. Figures 4.7 and 4.8 illustrate the regional import and export trends throughout East Asia. From the data and trade flows portrayed, there is clearly more disparity in the respective regional export percentages over time than in the regional import flows. Near 50 per cent, the regional import figures are the most striking, altering the non-regional demand patterns in trade dependence and flows that previous decades reflected. Regional export patterns remain more cyclical, responding more acutely to global economic demand/market patterns than regional imports; thus, regional import levels prove measured and in the last 10 years, constantly rising.

Total regional trade levels (Figure 4.8) are evaluated using ASEAN+4 consolidated numbers, including Japan, Korea, China (mainland), and Hong Kong. The benefit in

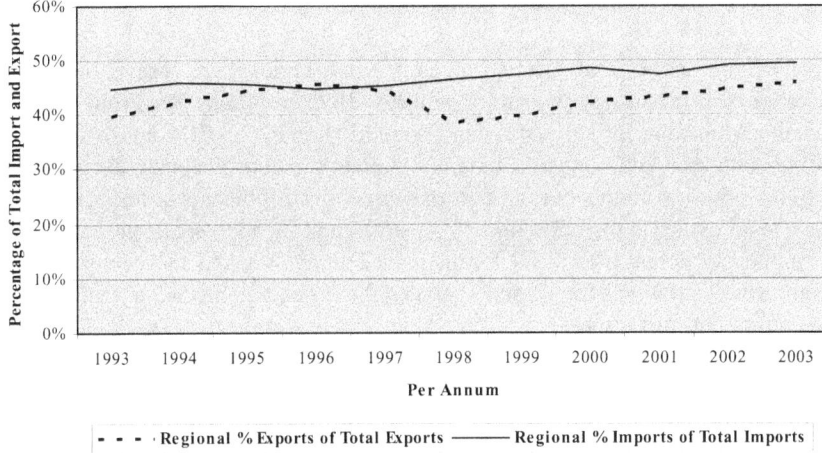

Figure 4.7 ASEAN+4: Regional import and export percentage of total world import and export
Source: IMF Direction of Trade, 1993–2003.

this particular East Asia grouping is the removal of large south Asian nations, such as India, that tend to skew the trade East Asian measurements. Having previously included all Asia and NEC data sets, the ASEAN+4 measures thus provide the most logical and concise intraregional trade depiction, in light of this report's purpose.

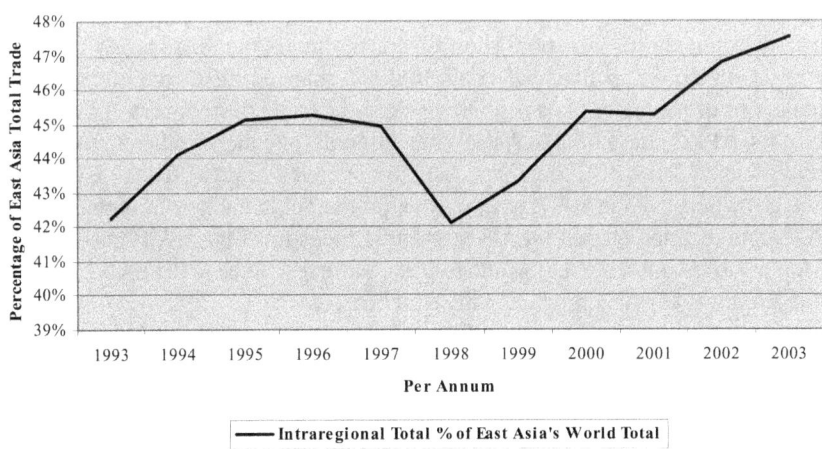

Figure 4.8 Intraregional total trade (ASEAN+4) as percentage of East Asia's total world trade
Source: IMF Direction of Trade, 1993–2003.

East Asia regionalism and formal institutional arrangements

The first premonitions of the rise of East Asian regionalism rose initially from the ashes of a proposal put forward in 1991–1992 by Malaysian Prime Minister Mahathir Mohamad for an East Asian Economic Group (EAEG), consisting of the ASEAN countries plus, Japan, China and Korea, but conspicuously excluding the US. This proposal foundered through the force of US objections, but at the same time a less hostile (to the US) effort by Australia and Japan to create an Asia Pacific Economic Cooperation (APEC) forum gained impetus when the newly installed Clinton administration adopted and upgraded the concept as the major vehicle for its trade policy for East Asia.

Thus began what might be called an APEC phase of East Asian integration, when the US led a region-wide trade liberalization movement, anchored by the first high-level meetings of chiefs of state in Seattle in 1993, and followed by the Bogor declaration in 1994, whereby APEC countries pledged to achieve free trade in the region by 2010 for developed countries and 2020 for developing countries. Ultimately, APEC proved far too ambitious, not least because the various leading parties had very different goals for the negotiating forum. For the East Asian members, APEC represented a means possibly of curbing US unilateral trade sanctions, while keeping Asian trade a top priority for the United States Trade Representative (USTR). Instead, the US made it clear that its trade remedy actions were not on the negotiating table, and with the conclusions of NAFTA in 1994 and the Miami declaration the same year, pledging free trade in the Americas by 2005, the US seemed to veer back toward a hemisphere-first trade policy. The drift of US policy away from APEC was hastened by the failure of its strong drive for APEC-based trade liberalization in the Early Voluntary Sectoral Liberalization (EVSL) initiative.[12]

Meanwhile, APEC also did not satisfy the desire of Asian countries for a regional forum of economic cooperation, short of drastic trade liberalization. At this point, the onset of the Asian financial crisis in 1997 changed all of the equations and calculations of the major players, both inside and outside the region.[13] It marked the end of the APEC phase of East Asian integration despite the fact that, to the dismay and anger of Asian APEC members, the US continued to press for the EVSL even as the crisis deepened in 1997. In turn, disappointment in the lack of momentum for APEC liberalization caused the US to shift its focus to China's WTO accession as the top priority within the region and to place more resources in the Free Trade Area of the Americas (FTAA) process in the Americas.

Against the background, the ASEAN+3, a gathering of ASEAN countries plus China, Japan and Korea, held its first leaders' meeting in December 1997. Though it would become an important forum for intra-East Asian policy discussions, ASEAN+3 was too diverse to form the basis for economic integration through a formal free

---

12 Naoka Munakata, *Whither East Asian Economic Integration* (Washington, DC: Brookings Institution Press (Mimeograph), June, 2002).
13 Ibid.

trade arrangement. Thus, from the outset, even as the Asian financial crisis caused a wholesale revamping of individual economies, a search began for more practical alternatives, such as bilateral or smaller sub-regional trade agreements. The key change, as noted above, were the decisions by Japan and Korea in 1999 to break with their long-standing policy of exclusive multilateralism and launch multi-track trade policies that included bilateral, sub-regional, and even cross-regional trade arrangements. Within Asia, Singapore led the way; acting independently of its ASEAN partners, Singapore announced that it intended to become the hub of a number of FTAs (Table 4.1). Thus, Singapore started negotiations with New Zealand and Australia, followed by talks with the US and then Japan. Similarly, Korea started negotiations with Chile and also with Singapore. Singapore's independent moves sparked a response among its ASEAN partners, and ASEAN began exploring FTAs with Australia and New Zealand and then with China, Korea and Japan.

In 2001, as it was completing the accession process for membership in the WTO, China entered the regionalism equation with some force. Earlier, China had proposed discussions with ASEAN of an FTA, and then in November 2001 China and ASEAN agreed to negotiate an FTA within 10 years. The sweetener that sealed the deal was the offer by China of an 'early harvest' by which China would reduce tariffs of interest and concern to new ASEAN members (Vietnam, Cambodia, et al.) early on. China, as always the 'elephant in the room', both fascinated and alarmed its regional trading partners. On the one hand, they greatly feared that China would swamp them in third markets such as the US and Europe; and the governments feared the 'hollowing out' effect as Japanese, Taiwanese and Korean businessmen poured billions of dollars into green field plants on the mainland. On the other hand, there was the huge allure of the internal Chinese market itself and the division from within each nation caused by businessmen seeking to counter 'hollowing out' fears with the prospect of repatriated profits and re-exports to other continents.

Meanwhile, in January 2002, Japanese Premier Koizumi proposed a Japanese/ASEAN 'economic partnership', and his announcement was followed by an announcement from Seoul that Korea likewise was considering a future FTA with ASEAN. In March 2002, during a trip by Japanese PM Koizumi to Korea, the two nations announced that, despite continuing political problems, they would officially begin discussions leading to a Japan–Korea FTA. The bottom line is that by mid-2004 all East Asian countries (plus Hong Kong and Taiwan, separately) were engaged in talks or negotiations leading to bilateral or sub-regional preferential trade arrangements. Japan had successfully completed negotiations with Singapore and Mexico; Korea had signed an agreement with Chile and was moving toward serious negotiations with Japan, Mexico, New Zealand, and Singapore; China completed its negotiations with ASEAN in 2004; and on the periphery, the US had concluded FTAs with Singapore and Australia and was in serious talks with Thailand (Table 4.1).[14]

---

14 Inkyo Cheong, 'Korea's FTA Policy: Focusing on Bilateral FTAs with Chile and Japan', Discussion paper 02-02 (Seoul: KIEP, September 2002).

The rise of Asian regional agreements: US and Korean perspectives

The sudden increase in the number of negotiated and proposed regional and sub-regional trade agreements over the past few years has taken both trade officials and scholars by surprise. Although trade economists have long studied the potential effects of various FTAs around the world, recent events and proposals have spawned a veritable cottage industry of studies by academics and national departments of trade. Economic effects constitute one important basis for judging the pros and cons of individual new trade agreements; however, a number of geopolitical factors – security, diplomatic, and political goals and realities – are also relevant and must be factored in.

Costs and benefits of new trade agreements by Asian countries, whether with one another or with other trading partners, will likely depend as much on geopolitical factors as economic consequences. This is particularly true with regard to the US and Korea because the exigencies created by the Cold War and a divided Korean peninsula (never more intrusive than at present) created a relationship in which political and security issues are inextricably entwined with economic issues.

Selected larger sub-regional trade arrangements would have other economic effects and impacts on the US and Korean economies as well as non-economic consequences. To simplify this analysis, the results of one set of simulations[15] will form the basis for judgment. Scollay and Gilbert[16] constructed their simulations using a computable general equilibrium model (CGE) (see Table 4.20). This model takes cross-sectional data from a single base period, not only for trade but also for production and consumption, and imposes a detailed theoretical structure on the interactions among different data elements. Using certain constraining assumptions, the models are put to use by changing the underlying data and observing how the remaining variables adjust.

Scollay and Gilbert used a static CGE model that captures only short-term effects, but not dynamic, longer-term effects, such as the exploitation of economies of scale and the impact over time of positive changes in investment and productivity. Their model is therefore likely to be at the lower bound of positive effects. These results are not, of course, exact and should be taken as giving the range and direction of change. In many circumstances, CGE models such as these have produced conflicting results, but simulations of liberalization by various APEC countries have shown a broad consistency among earlier and current studies. For Korea, from a purely welfare gain–loss perspective, the larger Asian FTAs yield the most positive results:

- an APEC preferential liberalization under which APEC members remove tariffs against each other, but not against nonmembers, would boost Korea's economy by an additional 1.63 per cent of GDP;

---

15 Rober Scollay and John P. Gilbert, *New Regional Trading Arrangements in the Asia Pacific?* (Washington, DC: Institute for International Economics, 2001).
16 Ibid.

Table 4.20 Effects of various Asian trade agreement formations on Korea and US welfare and trade

	Korea Welfare	Korea Δ in... Exports	Korea Imports	US Welfare	US Δ in... Exports	US Imports
[APEC Formation]						
APEC MFN basis	1.08	23.4	23.15	0.01	7.16	6.56
APEC preferential basis	1.63	26.28	26.08	-0.01	7.26	6.69
APEC MFN (excluding US)	0.94	22.17	21.92	0.06	1.58	1.43
APEC MFN (excluding US and Japan)	0.93	22.06	21.81	0.05	1.34	1.2
AFTA–CER–Japan–Korea–China (Western Pacific)	1.2	23.66	23.54	-0.06	-1.33	-1.26
[East Asia and Western Pacific Formation]						
Japan–Korea	-0.28	8.21	8.12	-0.01	-0.25	-0.23
Japan–Korea (excluding agriculture)	-0.15	6.24	6.16	-0.01	-0.23	-0.22
Japan–Korea–China	0.8	19.49	19.42	-0.02	-0.35	-0.34
AFTA–Japan–Korea	0.18	12.07	11.96	-0.02	-0.67	-0.64
AFTA–Japan–Korea–China (East Asia)	1.18	22.96	22.85	-0.03	-0.8	-0.78
AFTA–CER–Japan–Korea–China (Western Pacific)	1.2	23.66	23.54	-0.06	-1.33	-1.26
AFTA–CER–Japan–Korea	0.19	12.94	12.83	-0.05	-1.16	-1.08
AFTA–CER	-0.05	-0.3	-0.3	-0.01	-0.21	-0.2
[FTAA, APEC, East Asian Bloc Formation]						
FTAA	-0.1	-0.62	-0.62	0.06	3.69	3.43
APEC MFN and FTAA	1.01	22.9	22.65	0.07	9.59	8.82
APEC preferential and FTAA	1.56	25.71	25.5	0.06	10.02	9.26
Western Pacific bloc and FTAA	1.12	23.13	23.01	0.01	2.29	2.1
[Global]						
Global liberalization	**1.83**	**39.96**	**39.38**	**-0.05**	**19.98**	**18.48**

Source: Scollay and Gilbert, 2001.

Notes:
- Welfare # = % of initial GDP.
- Exports # = Export value FOB, % Δ from base.
- Imports # = Import value CIF, % Δ from base.
- ***APEC MFN basis***: Basic scenario in which it is assumed that APEC members continue to practice 'open regionalism', understood in the sense of collective implementation of unconditional MFN liberalization, or 'concerted unilateralism.'
- ***APEC preferential basis***: It is assumed that members remove tariffs against each other, but not against nonmembers.
- ***CER***: Australia–New Zealand Closer Economic Relations Trade Agreement.
- ***FTAA***: Free Trade Area of the Americas.
- ***AFTA***: ASEAN Free Trade Area.

- a Western Pacific (AFTA12–CER–Japan–Korea–China) FTA would boost Korea's GDP by 1.20 per cent;
- an AFTA–Japan–Korea–China (East Asia) FTA would add 1.18 per cent;
- an APEC most-favored-nation (MFN) liberalization under which APEC members remove tariffs against each other *and* against nonmembers would add 0.94 per cent of GDP to Korea's economy;
- an APEC FTA, excluding the US, would boost Korea's economy by 0.94 per cent; and
- an APEC FTA, excluding Japan, would boost it by 0.93 per cent.

The Scollay–Gilbert model indicates that potential bilateral FTAs with Japan have a negative effect on Korea's GDP, -15.0 per cent, with agriculture excluded; 0.28 per cent, with agriculture included.

For the US, the picture is more complicated; several explanatory points need to be made before tracking the impact of individual FTAs on US GDP. First, in most cases, the impact is miniscule and, given the imprecision of CGE model results, the best interpretation would be that these FTAs would have practically no positive or negative impact on US GDP. Second, given the size of the US economy, it may well be (though this is not inevitable) that the future dynamic effects (economies of scale and productivity enhancement) of trade liberalization that are not captured would produce much more positive results. Third, given the relative openness of the US market in manufacturing and agriculture, the real welfare gains from future liberalization may come in the services sectors, where current models are inadequate and may well understate future positive benefits.

In general, however, progressively more comprehensive East Asian–Western Pacific trade blocs that exclude the US result in progressively greater welfare losses for the US. Thus, the US would be negatively impacted most by a Western Pacific FTA at -0.06 per cent of GDP followed by a Japan–Korea–CER–AFTA (South Asia, plus Japan and Korea) FTA at -0.015 per cent and an East Asia FTA (Japan–Korea–China–AFTA) at -0.013 per cent. On the other hand, various APEC-based liberalizations generally yield small but positive welfare gains for the US.

For many of the proposed or consummated Asian FTAs, trade diversion from countries excluded from each particular pact is pervasive though often small. For Korea, particularly, the impact of trade diversion from US companies will present an important calculation and problem. For the US, although the amount of diversion may be small in terms of GDP, for the affected industries and sectors the impact might provoke substantial constituent opposition and pressure from the US Congress.

In the end, geopolitical factors in both the US and Korea will play significant roles, especially given recent events and trends in Asia. For example, China in the past several years has begun to move decisively toward a leadership role in trade with Southeast Asia, as evidenced by its persistent wooing of the nations of ASEAN for an FTA. Japan has signaled a redirection of its trade policy toward more intra-Asian trade agreements; however, unlike China and possibly because of a general stasis in Japanese internal politics, Japan has largely failed to carry through its new goals. Korea must decide whether it really wants to pursue bilateral or trilateral trade arrangements (Korea–Japan, Korea–China, or Korea–China–Japan) that will quite possibly lead to greater political involvement with these two powers and less with the US. Would a move toward integrating with US and Latin America make more sense for Korea from both an economic and a political standpoint?

While the US is much the larger economic and political power – indeed, the only superpower – it, too, faces real challenges in responding to the rapidly evolving patterns of Asian regionalism. Both economics and geopolitics dictate that the US cannot afford to be left out of these Asian trends; yet, little thought seems to have gone into the specifics of a US–Asia regional policy. USTR has trumpeted 'competitive liberalization' and has announced its intent to negotiate FTAs with many and sundry nations – Chile, Singapore, Jordan, Morocco, Australia, and Central America – but neither incumbent US Trade Representative Robert Zoellick/nominee Rob Portman, nor any other US official has provided a sense of priority or order to this process.

Optimal choices for the US and Korea

The best option for both the US and Korea is to take a leadership role and summon the political courage to make the necessary compromises to achieve a successful outcome to the WTO Doha Round.[17] A proliferation of numerous bilateral or trilateral FTAs would be the most negative outcome among the choices of various Asian regional pacts. For small-scale FTAs, in almost all cases the economic welfare of the participants is little enhanced; more important, each such arrangement would increase the level and complexity of trade diversion and create a bewildering set of new trade rules and rules of origin. A plethora of small FTAs would also most likely lead to greater trade tension and conflicts. Finally, the attention and resources that would need to be devoted to these small FTAs would divert human resources and political capital from the attainment of larger trade and investment goals.

Thus, as the economic studies cited above amply demonstrate, the first and best regional options revolve around APEC. For both the region as a whole and for individual nations, APEC-wide liberalization yields the most significant economic welfare gains. Politically, negotiations within the APEC framework get around the problem of integrating Taiwan, Hong Kong, and China into a trade framework. And both Australia and New Zealand, which are often left out of sub-regional FTA proposals, could be included.

The largest challenge to APEC today is the modality that hitherto has governed the negotiating process. So-called concerted unilateralism, by which each APEC nation liberalizes unilaterally and no reciprocal rules are applied, has not to date produced meaningful results; and APEC liberalization seems to have stalled. The US and Korea – and, most significantly, Japan and China, as the other major forces behind APEC liberalization – face crucial choices in the immediate future. One path,

---

17 Bernard K. Gordon, 'A High-Risk Trade Policy', *Foreign Affairs*, vol. 82 (July/August 2003), pp. 105–118.

which seems increasingly unlikely, is to reinvigorate concerted unilateralism. The other is to explore the possibility of adopting a more traditional modality: that is, converting APEC into a reciprocity-based and binding FTA.

Economic simulations show that, whatever the means to get there, an APEC preferential agreement does result in the greatest welfare gains for APEC members, both large and small; however, the problems inherent in this approach are enormous. Would Japan and Korea, for instance, agree to binding rules for agriculture? Would the US make unacceptable demands regarding labor and the environment? In addition, an APEC-wide FTA would have the strongest negative impacts on other regions such as Europe and Latin America in the multilateral trading system. This could increase trade friction and conflict or, conversely, it could spur these regions to take the lead in greater MFN liberalization through the WTO.

Two other obvious potential configurations in Asia are a Western Pacific FTA or an East Asian FTA. A Western Pacific trade bloc, joining Northeast Asia, Southeast Asia, and Australia–New Zealand would also generate substantial welfare gains for participants; but, as with an APEC FTA, it would have a negative impact on the economic welfare and terms of trade of nations outside the agreement – most notably the US. For Korea, and for other nations, the political consequences of joining such a bloc could be damaging if their membership produced a backlash from US industry that would translate into protectionist intervention by the US Congress. It is, therefore, in the interest of both the US and Korea to work to avoid either a Western Pacific or East Asian FTA that does not include the US. Both Korea and the US face the immediate problem of the disjuncture between the economic logic underlying Asian regional proposals and political realities. Asian nations today are busily proposing and negotiating small, bilateral FTAs, largely because they present fewer political problems. This trend, however, will result in a bad economic outcome and in greater political tensions and conflicts. Thus, it is in the interest of both the US and Korea to think beyond the short-term economic and political attractions of small FTAs and use their influence to channel the pressures for greater Asian regional arrangements toward large-scale economic agglomerations such as APEC or an inclusive Western Pacific-based FTA.

Chapter 5

The Realignment of USFK and the US–ROK Alliance in Transition

Seong-Ryoul Cho

The alliance between the US and the Republic of Korea (ROK or South Korea) conceived as a defense-oriented one against a North Korean military attack has been maintained thus far on the two pillars. One is the 'ROK–US Mutual Defense Treaty' (ROK–US MDT) and the other the US Forces in Korea (USFK). The alliance, however, has not changed its basic form in any fundamental way. But the current discussion on USFK's reduction differs from previous ones in one important way. Previously the issue focused merely on the number of troops, and the current discussion touches upon both the goals of this alliance and mission change of USFK.

The core of the US–ROK alliance lies in military issues. Thus, the role transformation or realignment of USFK will definitely make a profound impact on the overall nature of the US–ROK alliance. At a conceptual level, one can analyze USFK's realignment in two important ways – changes in the troop level and force structure, and changes in the role and status. Particularly changes in the role and status of USFK could bring about fundamental changes in the alliance.

In the past, USFK has changed in its troop level. US troop reduction may have led to changes in military capabilities, and air force elements played a secondary and supporting role. This force structure remains basically unchanged, even when troop level has been reduced. The US has reduced the number of troops stationed in South Korea five times since October 1953 when the US and the ROK signed the mutual defense treaty, and each reduction has led to a readjustment of USFK structure and its troop level.

The discussion on the role change of USFK began in 1990 when the Cold War came to an end. The 'static form' of USFK's role for Korea's defense was under review. As the range of military operations has widened, the missions of ROK and US forces have been changed. Therefore, 'Koreanization of South Korean Defense' has been promoted, which means that ROK armed forces will lead the Korean defense, and US forces will be supplementary.

The last step of USFK realignment will involve changes in the status of the forces or character of the alliance. The change in USFK character will lead to a fundamental transformation of the US–ROK alliance. The plan for the dissolution of the UN Forces Command or transforming USFK into peacekeeping forces (PKF) as asserted by some Korean non-government organizations (NGOs) will bring about changes in the status of USFK. The complete withdrawal of USFK could imply the annulment of the 'ROK–US MDT,' which would lead to the dissolution of the alliance beyond the change in its character.

The current reduction plan is occasioned by the 'US Military Transformation' and 'Global Defense Posture Review' (GPR). It shows role changes to the extent that part of frontline US army personnel on the Demilitarized Zone (DMZ) will be reduced, and the rest of USFK will be reorganized into the Stryker Brigade Combat Team (SBCT) and then will be relocated to Pyeongtaek in the rear, and the USFK operational ranges will expand beyond the Korean peninsula to Northeast Asia.

How then will such a role change affect the US–ROK alliance in the future? What is the desirable direction of the alliance in the 21st century? What can we do to bring this about? This chapter will address these questions.

Background

At the first meeting of the Future of the US–ROK Alliance (FOTA) in April 2003, the representatives of the ROK and the US agreed on the need to adapt the alliance to the new global security environment and to take into account Korea's status as a prosperous democratic country, and on the necessity of the transforming the alliance.[1] However, the direct cause for the transformation lies in threat perception and changes in the US view on the alliance. Additionally, the Korean people's perception has changed because of the ROK's growing national power spurred on by its rapid economic growth and democratization, and changes in economic relations between the two allies.

South Korea's request for alliance transformation

First of all, many South Koreans' attitudes to the alliance and to North Korea have been changed by the growth in national power. Since the democratic movement of 1986, South Korean society has been democratized. Then the democracy continued to mature towards a real civilian government in 1992. Despite its relatively short history of democracy, South Korea has entered a stable stage of democracy in which it can absorb quite strong external impacts. This is clearly shown in the response of the South Korean people to the North Korean threat. Its threat used politically by past South Korean authoritarian regimes has become less persuasive.[2] Such attitude changes resulted from South Korea's stable political system, which has the capacity to absorb shocks and demand alliance changes in the region.

---

1 Joint Statement on 'The Future of the ROK–US Alliance Policy Initiative', April 9, 2003.

2 'East Asia: Assassination Attempt, Impeachment Hint at Stability?', *Yonhap*, March 19, 2004.

South Korea has attempted to decrease its dependence on the US, while it has normalized its relations with North Korea, a tendency that became pronounced particularly after the South–North summit in June 2000. The ROK's perception change vis-à-vis the DPRK led to changes to its perception of threat from the North. In the *ROK Defense White Paper 2004* published in early February 2005, North Korea is no longer referred to as the 'main enemy' but a 'direct military threat.'[3] In South Korea, many people share the opinion that the ROK should maintain a more independent foreign and military policy by reducing its dependence on the US and achieve gradual reconciliation, cooperation and eventual unification with North Korea. This opinion is spreading from the general public to political circles. Therefore, the need for an equal alliance relationship with the US became an important factor behind the ROK's request for US–ROK alliance transformation.

Another factor was the emergence of China as a rising power in Northeast Asia and the reduced importance of US–ROK economic activities for South Korea's economy. The US–ROK security ties were predicated upon the blood pledge and the economic and other aid from the US after the Korean War. US economic aid for ROK's rehabilitation after the war became a solid basis for the alliance. Since the 1960s, the US has supported ROK's rapid economic growth in an effort to prevent the spread of Communist threat. It provided a market for South Korean exports by granting Korea a most favored nation status and supplying capital for economic development.[4]

By the early 1980s, the ROK laid down a foundation for economic development through trade with, and technology transfers from, the US. In the 1980s, as the US practiced economic protectionism, Washington and Seoul began to experience trade disputes. As US pressures for open trade and fair trade practices increased, Koreans became resentful of the US.

South Korea and China normalized their diplomatic relations in 1992, and subsequently ROK–China trade increased steadily while US–ROK and ROK–Japan trade declined in relative terms. Particularly ROK's trade with China accelerated in 2000, and China became ROK's number one trading partner, outpacing the US for the first time in 2003.[5] As Table 5.1 shows, the US was by far the most important ROK trading partner until 1990, but after ROK–China diplomatic normalization, the ROK's trade with China increased dramatically. China has also increased its political influence in Northeast Asia based on its economic capabilities and US leadership in the region weakened, eventually leading to changing power dynamics between the US and China in the region. Currently, China is the largest import partner for Japan

---

3 The ROK Ministry of National Defense, *The Defense White Paper 2004*, Seoul, February 2005.

4 See Yeong-Jae Chun, 'Issues on the ROK–US Relations and Our Tasks', Samsung Economic Research Institute, CEO Information No. 453, June 2, 2004, pp. 7–11.

5 Yong-Sang Syn, 'The Changes of Export-Import Structure in Korea and Their Policy Implications: The Meanings of employment-stagnated Growth' (in Korean), Korea Institute of Finance, March 19, 2004, p. 5.

Table 5.1 **Proportions of South Korea's trade with the US, China and Japan (%)**

	1990	1995	2000	2001	2002	2003	2004 (Jan 1–Feb 20)
The US	29.8	19.3	21.8	20.7	20.2	17.7	14.4
China (including. Hong Kong)	0.9 (6.7)	7.3 (15.9)	10.7 (16.9)	12.1 (18.4)	14.6 (20.9)	18.1 (25.7)	18.4 (27.7)
Japan	19.4	13.6	11.9	11.0	9.3	8.9	8.8

Source: Korean Traders Association.

and largest trade partner for South Korea. The emergence of China as an important power to reckon with became an important factor for the ROK's demand for US–ROK alliance transformation.

The 9/11 Attacks and Changes in the US View on the Alliance

Since the 9/11 terrorist attacks in 2001, US perception of the alliance has changed. International terrorism and the proliferation of weapons of mass destruction (WMD) emerged as new threats in the 21st century. The US wants to restructure the current alliance system to cope with the new threats. Traditionally, alliance means a self-help action to improve one's security using others' forces. Alliance is not based on friendship, but on calculated self-interests.[6] However, the Bush administration chose a short-term coalition, the 'Coalition of the Willing' which was formed with the nations willing to cooperate rather than traditional alliances to cope with its security threats.[7]

The strength of this coalition system lies in the capability to deal with problems immediately and to maintain an unchallenged role for the US in the course of problem solving. The US adopted this new strategy to deal with new challenges in a new global security environment.[8] Germany and France, as traditional alliance partners of the US, followed the US lead in the war in Afghanistan, but expressed clear opposition to the US war on Iraq. In contrast, former enemy nations of the US cooperated with the US war efforts in Iraq in pursuit of their national interests. China, India and Pakistan were unfriendly with the US in the past, and now they have closer cooperation with the US than France and Germany concerning some principal issues.

---

6   Seong-Ryoul Cho, *US Forces in Korea: Retrospect and Prospect*, (in Korean) Seoul: Hanul Publishing, 2003, p. 311.

7   Kurt M. Campbell, "The End of Alliance? Not So Far," *The Washington Quarterly* (Spring 2004), pp. 160–163.

8   Charles Wolf, Jr., 'A Test Determine Who's an Ally', *International Herald Tribune*, July 8, 2004.

As shown above, as relations among allies change according to perceived national interests, the US applies various standards and classifies countries as allies, enemy nations or possible cooperative nations for its diplomatic and security policy. Charles Wolf, Jr. classified allies in three categories, 'a new nuclear family,' 'new friends' and 'flings,' based on their degree of cooperation in terms of anti-terrorism.[9]

Korea has been a longtime core alliance partner of the US, but the US–ROK alliance relationship has been damaged since the two allies failed to narrow the gap in their perceptions of the North Korean threat. Moreover, the unilateral notification by the US of its decision to reduce USFK by 12,500 troops also damaged their relations. For this reason some in the US are skeptical about whether South Korea should be included in a new group of core alliances. However, the dispatch of 3,600 ROK soldiers to Iraq and the agreement on the removal of the Yongsan US base improved their relations. Also the positive change in the US perception of South Korea's cooperative economic activities with North Korea, such as the Gaesung industrial park project, has mitigated the conflict. But it does not mean that the US and the ROK can return to its alliance relationship of the Cold War era because there is a need to establish a new alliance in the 21st century in light of changed global security environment.

The Current Issues: Military Transformation, GPR and USFK Realignment

The US has pursued military transformation since the late 1990s in responses to the Revolution in the Military Affairs (RMA). The major points of the transformation are: improvement of long-range force projection capability, elevation of long-range strike capability, and improved coordination among the Army, Navy, Air Force and Marines. In the meantime, President Bush stressed on November 25, 2003, the need to implement military reform to deal with rogue states, international terrorism, and WMDs, and announced the Global Military Posture Review (GPR) based on the Quadrennial Defense Review (QDR). The GPR showed that the 'threat-based approach,' which focused on the double threat in the Middle East and Northeast Asia, has changed to a 'capability-based approach,' which is focused on unspecified threats in Northeast Asia, Southeast Asia, the Middle East, Southwest Asia and Western Europe.

US revisions of its military strategy after World War II did not realistically change US military composition or allocation. However, the recent announcement of military transformation and the GPR signaled substantial, large-scale changes in military, strategic and political spheres. 'QDR2001,' announced in September 2001, defined a new expected conflict area as the 'arc of instability,' which includes the Middle East, the Bengal Bay, and Southeast and Northeast Asia. At present, the is US reallocating its military forces to focus on this region. Regarding the GPR, the US announced that it would move its Army, Navy, Air Force and Marines headquarters in

---

9 Kurt M. Campbell, 'The End of Alliance', pp. 162–163.

the region to Japan, and endow it with an operational power in the arc of instability.[10] According to the GPR, the 1st US Corps Command, which is the main force of the US Army in the Pacific, now located in Washington State, will move to Zama Camp, and the 5th US Air Force Command in Yokoda Base in Tokyo will absorb the 13th US Air Force Command and then will move to Guam. The 3rd brigade of the 2nd Division and the 1st brigade of the 25th Division, which were reclassified as the SBCT, are planned to move to the command of the 1st US Corps Command, which will move to Japan.

Military transformation and the GPR are propelled by different strategic considerations, and the reform of USFK is part of the global restructuring of the US forces. The schedule of USFK reduction was agreed at the FOTA meeting: 5,000 in 2004 (first stage), 3,000 in 2005 and 2,000 in 2006 (second stage), 2,500 in 2007–08 (third stage). The USFK will be reduced by a total of 12,500 soldiers and the US will keep its 25,000 troops on Korean soil after October 2009.

As a result of FOTA meetings, the USFK will play a deterrent role against the North Korean threat in the short term, and if the North Korean threat decreases it will be attached to the Quick Reaction Force (QRF) for regional operations in the mid and long term. Thus, the USFK will hand over its role for South Korean defense to ROK military forces, and gradually refocus on its regional roles. The US also wants the US–ROK alliance to be able to expand in scope to include regional missions beyond the Korean peninsula. The reduction of USFK has been necessitated by anti-American sentiment in South Korea, shortages of military personnel after the wars in Iraq and Afghanistan, and the GPR and military transformation.

The characteristics of USFK reform are as follows. First, according to the 'military transformation', the 8th US Army Command is to be reformed into UEy (Unit of Employment Y), and the 2nd Infantry Division Command into UEx. The 1st Brigade of the 2nd Infantry Division will be reformed from part of a division-centered structure to a brigade-centered Unit of Action (UA). The UA will continue to keep high-level information technologies and facilities owned by a division, making it stronger than traditional brigades. The reduction of the 2nd brigade of the 2nd Infantry Division is based on the idea that it can meet the demands of other conflict areas and the reformed 1st brigade alone will have enough deterrent power against North Korea.

Secondly, USFK reduction and its relocation to south of the Han River were intended to have a flexible setup in order to cope with new threats and uncertainties from China. This was based on the plan that no large-scale military forces will be stationed in Korea, there will be two central hub bases (Pyongtaek-Osan, Daegu-Busan); these will be used to store armaments and equipment in peace time and reinforcements will arrive at them in an emergency. This plan was to minimize the conflict with Korean residents and to maintain a stable USFK presence and to expand the USFK brief to encompass regional roles.

---

10 Douglas J. Feith, 'Transforming the US Global Defense Posture', Center for Strategic and International Studies, Washington DC, December 3, 2003.

As discussed above, the realignment of the USFK results from a combination of factors, including GPR, military transformation and 'strategic flexibility.'

Issues between the ROK and the US

There were decade-long long quarrels between the US and Japan. One was over the wide-area command's transfer to the Zama camp in Japan, such as the 1st US Corps Command, which would command a broad area beyond the Far East. Another concerned the relocation of the Futenma US Marine Corps Air Station in Okinawa and of the home-porting a nuclear aircraft carrier in Yokosuka. The interim report on the transformation and realignment for the future of the US–Japan alliance was announced in late October 2005. The document is implicitly deferential to Japan's political processes.

The ROK and the US have had disagreements over guarantees of the 'strategic flexibility' of the USFK, the formation of the US–ROK QRF, and the regional coalition of the US, Korea, Japan and Australia. First, the primary issue is 'strategic flexibility.' The US asserts that the USFK's role is not in a 'static form' against a North Korean attack, but as a QRF that can move in and out for counter-terrorism wars. The US defines 'strategic flexibility' as a military intervention in international conflicts, including a China–Taiwan military clash. However, South Korea must be aware of a negative response from China. The USFK's intervention in military conflicts between China and Taiwan might lead to China attacking US military bases in Korea.

Second, the US wants the US–ROK combined forces to be part of the QRF serving as PKFs in Northeast Asia. Lieutenant General Charles C. Campbell, Chief of Staff, USFK/UNF/Combined Forces asserted in May 2004 that the operational range of the US–ROK Combined forces could be expanded from the Korean peninsula to the Northeast Asia region in the 21st century.[11] However, South Korean Foreign Minister Ban Ki-Moon clearly opposed to the idea of transforming the alliance from a defensive to an offensive one.[12]

Third, regarding the future of the US–ROK alliance, the US plans to transform bilateral relations with Korea, Japan and Australia into the framework of a multilateral security coalition. Condoleezza Rice, at confirmation hearings for the Secretary of State in January 2005, drew attention to this when she mentioned the intention to keep peace and prosperity in alliance with Korea, Japan and Australia against common threats in the Western Pacific.[13] The US plans military exercises, dubbed 'Valiant Dragon,' in 2006 in which the US, Korea, Japan and Australia will participate in preparing for an emergency in the Korean peninsula. It remains to

---

11 *Yonhap*, May 25, 2004.

12 *Yonhap*, May 27, 2004.

13 US Department of State, 'Confirmation Hearing for Dr. Condoleezza Rice', January 18, 2005, available at <http://www.state.gov/r/pa/ei/pix/b/40978.htm>.

be seen whether or not the US will implement the idea of a multilateral regional security coalition.

Fourth, it is expected that the US will ask Korea to participate in the formation of a US Pacific Command (PACCOM) Regional Maritime Security Initiative (RMSI) and an International Standing Forces (ISF), which can join multinational forces led by the US without the approval of the ROK National Assembly. Japan has already planned to create a permanent rapid reaction force that reports directly to the Director-General of the Defense Agency in case of emergency, such as a terrorist attack. A permanent rapid reaction force of 1,300 troops can be dispatched at the request of the US without a resolution of the UN Security Council.[14]

Factors Affecting the Future of the US–ROK Alliance

The US strategy toward China: Deterrence or dissuasion?

A report, 'Mapping the Global Future' by the National Intelligence Council (NIC), forecasts that China and India are likely to emerge as new major global players by 2020.[15] In the report, the Korean peninsula and Taiwan Strait crises are likely to take place by 2020, risking conflict with global repercussions.[16] The role of the US in Northeast Asia and Northeast Asian regional stability will be determined largely by the conflict factors caused by the rise of China and how it deals with the expected conflicts in Northeast Asia. Since conflicts in Northeast Asia are closely linked to Chinese interests, the transformation of the US–Korea and US–Japan alliance systems will be influenced by US–China relations in the future.

The US strategy vis-à-vis China could take the forms of either a 'deterrence strategy' or a 'dissuasion strategy,'[17] Depending on the choice of strategy, the direction of the US–ROK alliance and the enlargement of USFK will be determined. The first scenario is the deterrence strategy in which the US considers China as a strategic competitor, and reinforces triangle security cooperation among the US, Korea and Japan along with cooperation for transnational threats such as international terrorism. In this case, the US will pursue the 'Koreanization of South Korean defense' as early as possible, and then when the situation in Iraq stabilizes, it will carry out the enlargement of the role of USFK and use parts of the military forces in Korea and Japan to cope with terrorism in Southeast Asia and China's threat. For mid- and long-term plans, the US will organize coalition forces with USFK, US Forces in Japan (USFJ), and South Korean forces and Japanese Self Defense Force (SDF) for the same purpose.

---

14 See <http://www.jda.jp/j/kisha/2004/12/10.pdf>.

15 National Intelligence Council, 'Mapping the Global Future', December 2004, pp. 47–51.

16 Ibid., p. 55.

17 Department of Defense, 'Quadrennial Defense Review Report', September 30, 2001, pp. 11–13.

The second scenario is the dissuasion strategy in which the US considers China as a potential enemy and dissuades it from confronting the US through hostile policies or military competition, but persuades it instead to cooperate, so that China can deal with transnational threats. The dissuasion strategy, which intends to dissuade the counterpart from challenging the hegemon through persuasion, appeared in QDR2001 for the first time, and the gist included a wide range of political measures, including diplomacy and military tools. But the details have not been provided. In this case, the US will urge China to cooperate with the international community for a constructive role in the economic, political and security areas, and lead it to becoming an interest-sharing partner rather than a threat in East Asia and the world. As the US needs multilateral cooperation to deal with transnational threats such as terrorism and WMDs, it will pursue the establishment of a multilateral security organization in addition to bilateral alliance systems. Nevertheless, the US will expand its joint military exercises with US forces in Korea and Japan for its role as a stabilizer in the region and for its efficient operations against an international threat.[18]

South Korea's strategy toward North Korea: Confrontation or coexistence?

The most important factor affecting security on the Korean peninsula is the North Korean military threat (see Table 5.2). Assessment of the North Korean threat has changed since the South–North summit in June 2000. The US and the ROK have different assessments of the North Korean threat. South Korea's perception of the North Korean threat has greatly changed since the inter-Korean summit. The ROK government recognizes that the North Korean threat is dwindling. Consequently, the ROK government has shifted its security strategy from hostile confrontation to inter-Korean cooperation and peaceful coexistence. The 'Northern Diplomacy' initiated by President Roh Tae-Woo in 1989 and pursued by the Kim Young-Sam government became a formal security strategy of the Kim Dae-Jung government.[19]

The US, however, maintains that the North Korean threat remains unchanged. In February 2001, General Thomas A. Schwartz, Commander of the US–ROK Combined Forces, expressed his view on the North Korean threat by saying that an inter-Korean dialogue continued but North Korea's military forces had been bigger, better, closer and armed in a deadlier way since 2000.[20] The US recently showed a view similar to that of South Korea. This change is attributable to the international security environment surrounding the Korean peninsula: an imbalance of conventional military capabilities between the two Koreas in favor of South

---

18 Japan and the US for the first time mentioned in a joint statement 'Common Strategic Goals' that China's military build-up was a cause of concern on February 19, 2005 in Washington at the 'two-plus-two' meeting of Foreign and Defense Ministers.

19 Seong-Ryoul Cho, *US Forces in Korea*, pp. 151–152.

20 Statement of General Thomas A. Schwartz Before the Senate Armed Committee, March 27, 2001, p. 4.

Korea and the promotion of confidence building measures (CBMs) in military affairs between the two Koreas.

Charles C. Campbell, Chief of Staff, USFK/UNF/Combined Forces, assumed that the ROK and US combined military capabilities were much more powerful than those of North Korea, and added that 'such difference has been developed for the last few years.'[21] Congressional Research Service researcher, Larry A. Niksch, also analyzed that the reduction of the USFK was based on the judgment that North Korea's military power had weakened. He asserted that South Korea had become superior to North Korea in conventional military power since the 1990s and North Korea had lost its large-scale offensive power, and thus the US need not keep large-scale US forces in Korea.[22]

However, the US does not think that all of the North Korean threat has disappeared. The WMDs of North Korea pose a serious threat. Paul Wolfowitz, Deputy Secretary of Defense, stated at a hearing of the Senate Foreign Relations Committee on May 18, 2004: 'the US force is useless in the DMZ and it cannot function but as a tripwire that might have an adverse reaction.' This statement indicates that the US has to change its mission due to North Korea's WMD capabilities. What Wolfowitz emphasized was the threat of WMDs, but the testimony indicated that that North Korea's conventional military power had decreased. The US is worried that the DPRK may export nuclear-related materials and technologies to third-world countries or terrorist groups. In the spring of 2005, it was reported that North Korea had exported UF6 (Uranium Hexafluoride), the low-enriched uranium, to Libya.[23] The US believes that the ROK forces can deal with the North Korean threat from conventional weapons, and intends to change the role of the US forces to concentrate on the WMDs threat. This is the 'Koreanization of South Korean Defense' and coincides with the 'role sharing of the US and Korea with conventional weapons and WMDs.'

The CBMs between South Korea and North Korea in military affairs seem to affect the security environment on the Korean peninsula. Since the South–North summit, confidence building in political issues has made great progress, with many active exchanges and cooperation, but in military affairs, there has only been one inter-Korean defense ministers' meeting in September 2000; the communication channel for working-level military talks opened.

The first and second rounds of the South–North Korean high-level military talks were held on May 26 and June 3–4, 2004, and both sides reached an agreement. Even an agreement such as this was remarkable progress in inter-Korean relations. From now on, any action that may lead to an accidental military clash near the Northern Limited Line (NLL) on the Yellow Sea can be prevented, and both sides can build up their CBMs in the Military Demarcation Line (MDL). The direction of

---

21 Interview with Charles C. Campbell, *Yonhap*, May 25, 2004.
22 SBS *Evening News Show*, June 12, 2004.
23 Glenn Kessler, 'North Korea May Have Sent Libya Nuclear Material, US Tells Allies', *The Washington Post*, February 2, 2005.

Table 5.2 Differences between the ROK and US in relation to the alliance

Issues	ROK position	US position
Role of Alliance Factors of Change	First priority in Korean security, then security in Northeast Asia Formation of alliance suitable to its development of democracy and international status	Formation of regional security alliance beyond Korean security Change of static alliance to dynamic alliance according to the changed security environment (traditional alliance→coalition of the willing)
Mobilization of USFK	Opposed if it imposes a heavy burden on neighboring nations	For worldwide conflicts as well as regional conflicts
US–ROK QRF	Opposed to the US–ROK QRF and restrained by USFK activities in the Northeast Asia which negatively affect security of Korean peninsula	Possible in Northeast Asia as well as Korean peninsula in the 21st century as PFKs
Role of ROK Military in Alliance	Contribution for international community by Cooperative Self-Reliant Defense and US–ROK alliance	The alliance deals with Korea's defense, but Korea should contribute to the international community based on universal values, democracy and stability
Image of Future Alliance	Forming regional cooperative security system based on the US–ROK alliance in Northeast Asia	Multilateral security coalition including Korea, US, Japan and Australia

the US–ROK alliance will be affected by the progress of CBMs and arms control between the ROK and the DPRK.

Three Alternative Visions for the US–ROK Alliance

The factors influencing the future of the US–ROK alliance are as follows: the global security environment, US security policy toward East Asia, especially China, and South Korea's national security strategy, especially toward North Korea. A new US security policy can be found in the GPR, and Korea's national security strategy can be found in the 'cooperative self-reliant defense policy initiative.' Although the discussion on the future of the US–ROK alliance covers not only the military field but also diplomacy, economy, and so on, I will take the military aspect into account. I would like to discuss all possible forms of the US–ROK alliance considering the above two factors. Let us look at the alternative visions of the US–ROK alliance.[24] It should be noted that the possible repeal of the alliance has never been considered by either the US or the ROK.

---

24 See Jonathan D. Pollack and Young Koo Cha, *A New Alliance for the Next Century*, Washington DC: RAND's National Defense Research Institute, 1995.

An alliance for the Korean peninsula defense: A Korean view

As reduction of USFK may lead to an early realization of the self-reliant defense policy and military modernization of South Korea, North Korea is likely to strongly oppose this plan and build up its own military capabilities in both conventional weapons and WMDs. This situation may produce tensions on the Korean peninsula. The main goal of the US–ROK alliance will be then to defend South Korea from the North Korean threat. This type of alliance can be put in place if tensions arise on the Korean peninsula because of an accelerated arms race. This is the same format that has been sustained for the past 50 years, but it differs in that the role of dealing with WMDs has been added. In order to cope with WMDs, unlike conventional weapons, the ROK and the US need to build up an integrated defense system. For this reason, the US will strongly demand that the US–ROK combined forces maintain a more integrated military cooperation and South Korea participate in the Missile Defense (MD) system and Proliferation Security Initiative (PSI). In particular, the US has proposed establishing a combined force improvement plan (FIP) in order to enhance the US–ROK combined defense capability in 10 sections, some of which include a missile defense plan and surgical strike.

After the collapse of the former Soviet Union, the ROK government decided to participate in a worldwide cooperative program called 'Global Partnership against Proliferation of WMDs and Related Materials' in order to prevent the proliferation of WMDs in Russia.[25] If North Korea's nuclear issue remains unresolved and tensions on the Korean peninsula increase, the ROK government may have to seriously consider participating in the PSI. However, the type of alliance is likely to lose out due to the changes in US military strategy and the changing role of USFK. USFK are handing over its primary mission to the ROK military, and it will play only a supplementary role in defending South Korea.

The ROK government opposes the idea of changing the USFK to a QRF fearing that this plan would have a negative effect on its relationship with surrounding countries. It has clearly opposed its participation in the US-led Northeast Asia MD system, which may have negative effects on North Korea and China, and it has also turned down a proposal for a combined FIP in 10 fields, intended to accelerate the integration of US–ROK combined defense capabilities.

The fact that this type of alliance by nature is based on the assumption that it will strengthen the military integration between the ROK and the US is a stumbling block. In the recent development of the US–Japan alliance, we may find the same trend. So far, the role of the USFJ has been limited to its operation only in case of a Northeast Asian emergency, including the Korean peninsula. However, as a part of GPR and through US–Japan military integration, Japan may play a main role in the Middle East and Asia-Pacific regions in an emergency situation. We can see the same trend in the recent moving of the Air Self-Defense Force Command to

---

25 Sang-Heon Yi, 'Korea, Took part in "Global Partnership" of Proliferation', *Yonhap*, June 9, 2004.

Yokoda Base, where the US Air Force base is situated, in order to set up a combined operation with the Northeast Asia MD system. Judging from this trend, the ROK government is unlikely to accept this scenario.

An alliance for regional security: An American view

A regional security alliance is based on the assumption that military tensions on the Korean peninsula will be lessened. It is a constructive military relationship that works with the US–ROK combined forces to jointly confront various problems occurring in the Northeast Asian region, such as regional conflicts, terrorism, and piracy. In order to convert the US–ROK alliance into the regional security alliance, there has to be a dramatic enhancement in terms of the security environment on the Korean peninsula. As long as the North Korean threat exists, a US–ROK military cooperation beyond the Korean peninsula can only be restricted. However, if inter-Korean CBMs in military affairs are established, and the North Korean threat is reduced through arms control agreements, the current US–ROK alliance may possibly change into a regional security alliance.

In the regional security alliance system, the USFK will defend the Korean peninsula and also will act as a QRF that will consist of US–ROK combined forces, which will be sent to the Asia-Pacific region and Southeast Asia when a conflict occurs, and the ROK should be responsible for providing the base and logistics. This form of regional security alliance is the same as the existing alliance in terms of the fact that it gives a top priority to the strategic defense of South Korea, but it has a conspicuous difference in the point that the US–ROK combined forces or the US and its allies undertake an expansive responsibility throughout Northeast Asia as well as the Asia-Pacific region.

Under the regional security alliance system, the ROK military will take part in specific regional missions with minimum control, and the US army will be given permission to use the military base and the right to approach. The ROK military will also participate in regional peacekeeping operations. They will also receive necessary 'combined and joint exercises' and deploy combined operations in order to carry out their missions beyond the Korean peninsula. Regional tasks will be limited to Northeast Asia at the beginning, and later expand to other regions. In this case, mainly the air and naval forces may be in charge of the joint operation of the US–ROK combined forces, and ground troops of the US–ROK combined forces may take part in the tasks of peacekeeping operations. As mentioned earlier, Charles Campbell once commented that US–ROK combined forces would be transformed to PFKs for Northeast Asia.

Michael Green, the US National Security Council's Senior Director for Asia, also expressed a similar opinion. He emphasized the regional function of the US–ROK alliance, saying that it is necessary to readjust the alliance according to the new security environment based on the 'ROK–US MDT' if terrorism still exists in

Northeast Asia, even if the North Korean threat does not exist and peace arrives.[26] He stressed that North Korea is still the number one threat to the ROK, but it needs to be discussed how to use the characteristics of the US–ROK alliance if conflicts arise in the Northeast Asia region.

As discussed above, the US military authorities want to convert the current alliance into a regional security alliance. The decision makers in the Bush administration think it is too early for a change. Michael Green also has reservations about whether is it right to convert, claiming that it should be decided after a discussion between the two allies. Many think it is premature to transform to a regional security alliance because of the presence of the North Korean threat. But many believe that the developmental direction of the US–ROK alliance should be towards a regional security alliance system.

Strategic security alliance: An amicable view

It is doubtful whether the US–ROK alliance can successfully change to a regional security alliance when tensions still exist on the Korean peninsula. Since the ROK clearly opposes the concept of a regional security alliance, this second scenario is also unlikely to be realized in the near future. As long as tension on the Korean peninsula still fundamentally exists, the ROK government wants to cooperate, and work together with the US at a comprehensive level beyond bilateral military cooperation. Even if the North Korean threat does not completely disappear, the ROK hopes that active inter-Korean exchanges and cooperation will lessen tensions between the two Koreas, which will lead the US–ROK alliance to comprehensive cooperative relations at the level of national strategies, which not only cover the security of the Korean peninsula but also deal with the overall 21st century threats, such as WMDs, terrorism, drugs, and environmental pollution. This is why the third scenario of the future US–ROK alliance is called a strategic security alliance.

The strategic security alliance will focus on the security of the Korean peninsula where inter-Korean military confrontation still exists. But it also implies that the ROK military will have the primary responsibility for self-defense. The ROK military will be able to defend itself against the North Korean military threat without outside support, and construct a self-reliant military posture, the operational command system for initial defense around the DMZ. Only when the ROK military encounters heavy military attacks from the North beyond its capacity will it call for US military assistance.

In this scenario, the primary function of USFK is to accommodate swift reinforcements from the US. Providing a nuclear umbrella to the ROK, the US army's mission will be to support the ROK military in accordance with the 'ROK–US MDT' and wartime augmentation plan in the event of an all-out war. The key point of the strategic security alliance is how to effectively organize wartime reinforcements when a war breaks out. The remaining USFK will take the role of supporting the

---

26 Interview with Michael Green, *Yonhap*, June 4, 2004.

accommodation of the QRF in wartime, and maintaining a new deterrent against North Korea, assuring defense commitments by regular joint military exercises in peacetime. Although the size of the USFK may be smaller than that of the peninsula defense alliance, circular deployment of the SBCT may complement the military power loss resulting from reduction of the USFK.

The ROK and the US will keep the close US–ROK combined operational plan under the strategic security alliance, but the US army will usually serve as wartime reinforcements. As the role of USFK reduces for South Korea's security, a drastic change in USFK and the US–ROK combined system becomes inevitable. In this case, substantial reconfigurations are made in the relative function and sharing responsibility of defense.

Reduction of the US forces within the combined defense strategy and combined defense posture makes the rearrangement in scale and structure of the USFK inevitable. In this type of alliance, the remaining USFK takes over the role of wartime reinforcements, the lower part of the structure. The US–ROK Combined Forces Command (CFC) will be disintegrated and reduced to a smaller US–ROK Planning Command or the US–ROK Planning Unit, and the ROK military assumes the wartime operational control. Both the ROK and the US will perform periodic combined military training and exercises so that deterrent power against North Korea and defense cooperation may not be weakened. For this, US QRF could be stationed on circular basis.

Conclusion

The RAND has assessed US–ROK security interests and objectives as 'common interests' and 'compatible interests.' First, the common interests involve deterring and defeating North Korea's attack, preventing North Korea's nuclearization, fostering peaceful unification, preventing the rise of a hostile hegemon, maintaining regional stability against surviving threats from socialist countries, territorial conflicts and pirates, and so on. Secondly, the compatible interests involve countering proliferation of WMDs, shifting self-defense responsibility to ROK, fostering US and ROK prosperity, protecting overseas resources, sea lines of communication and fostering democracy.[27]

In this regard, the primary mission of the USFK is to protect US geo-political and geo-economic interests through guarding the security of Korea. In contrast, the USFJ carries out its role as an outpost for air force and navy operations in the Indian Ocean and the Persian Gulf as well as the role of a stabilizer for the Korean peninsula and the Taiwan Straits. But USFK, differently from the US Forces in other areas, has focused on its role as the deterrent of North Korea rather than as a stabilizer or an outpost.

---

27 Pollack and Cha, *A New Alliance for the Next Century*, p. 15.

There had been virtually no disagreement between the ROK and the US until 1998 to the idea that North Korea was a 'main enemy,' and both maintained a hostile policy toward China because it was a military ally of North Korea. There was no contradiction between the ROK security/military strategy and the US East Asian military strategy, and thus, the two allies organized the US–ROK CFC in 1978, and then transferred the wartime operational control, which ought to be under ROK Chairman of Joint Chiefs of Staff (CJCS), to the Commander of US–ROK Combined Forces, which was an additional post for the Commander of USFK (COMUSFK). On this ground, the combined forces could share 'Operation Plan 5027.'

However, the national security strategy and strategy in East Asia of both allies have changed since the inter-Korean summit in June 2000 and the 9/11 attacks in 2001. The 'National Security Policy Initiative of the Korean Participatory Government' published by the ROK National Security Council (NSC) is clearly based on the national security policy for reconciliation, cooperation and peaceful coexistence with North Korea, which was tacitly carried out by the Kim Dae-Jung administration.[28] The ROK security strategy has turned to inter-Korean reconciliation, cooperation and peaceful coexistence since the 'sunshine policy' was launched, and its military strategy is on the way to transforming itself accordingly.

Meanwhile, although the importance of Northeast Asia has increased in the new US strategy, the US perception of the North Korean threat remains almost the same. Especially, since October 2002 when North Korea allegedly admitted a highly enriched uranium (HEU) program, the US began changing its deterrence power from conventional weapons to WMD. The US plans, through FOTA meetings, to improve the military power of the USFK during the four years from 2004 for 150 items with US$11 billion. This plan indicates that the US still considers North Korea its main enemy in its East Asian military strategy and develops its strategy and operational plans accordingly.

However, since the US strategy in East Asia has continued with its previous intention to contain China, it has begun to conflict with South Korean security and military strategy. South Korea's policy for reconciliation, cooperation and peaceful coexistence no longer considers North Korea its main enemy, and South Korea cannot participate in containing China given the fact that ROK cooperation with China is essential to its economic interests as well as to the security of the Korean peninsula. The Korean security strategy, therefore, cannot be the same as that of the US in East Asia. Moreover, there is another disagreement on the form of the alliance. Although the mid- and long-term national interests of the ROK and the US coincide, the two allies cannot but show their disagreements in the short term. The future of the US–ROK alliance will depend on whether both allies can share a strategic harmony based on common interests and common responsibilities.

---

28 The Korea National Security Council, National Security Policy Initiative of Korean 'Participatory Government: Seeking for Peace and Prosperity' (in Korean) (March 2004).

Chapter 6

Assessing the Present and Charting the Future of US–DPRK Relations: The Political–Diplomatic Dimension of the Nuclear Confrontation

Bruce E. Bechtol, Jr

The diplomatic relationship between the US and North Korea over the past five years has been what can only be described as rocky and teetering on the edge of crisis. While many have argued varying reasons and some have placed the blame on the current presidential administration in Washington, depending on whether this relationship is being analyzed from a left-of-center or right-of-center perspective, there can be no doubt, that the primary sticking point in the extremely rocky relationship between these two governments is Pyongyang's nuclear weapons program.

Because North Korea's nuclear weapons program is the primary reason for the impasse in easing tensions between Washington and Pyongyang, it will be one of the primary issues addressed in this chapter. I will also address how the North's actions have caused a breakdown in the relationship between Washington and Pyongyang and why. In addition, I will discuss the troubling attempts that Kim Jong-Il's government made during 2004 to become involved in the internal politics of South Korea and the US, as well as recent evidence that indicates there may be a level of turmoil within the government of North Korea. Because of the fact that in the six-party talks during September of 2005, North Korea agreed to dismantle its nuclear program, I will address challenges that continue to face the US and Pyongyang's neighbors in the region as all parties move through the steps to ensure this happens in a transparent manner. Finally, I will address the strategy of the Bush administration during the nuclear confrontation, and perhaps as importantly, the effects of the ROK–US alliance on US–DPRK relations, highlighting the differing strategies of the Roh and Bush governments.

The Problems Involving North Korea's Nuclear Program

The diplomatic confrontation with North Korea that continues as of the writing of this chapter is generally agreed to have begun on October 3, 2002, when Assistant

Secretary of State for East Asian Affairs James Kelly told North Korean negotiators Kim Kye-kwan and Kang Sak-ju (at the first of formal unilateral talks held after the Bush administration took office) that Washington knew about North Korea's clandestine highly enriched uranium (HEU) weaponization program, demanding that it be dismantled. During the talks, Kang Sak-ju, the North's chief Deputy Foreign Minister, admitted to the program, and demanded a non-aggression treaty from the US.[1] The information from this meeting was made public almost immediately, and soon thereafter, Pyongyang denied having an HEU program.[2]

The problem with North Korea since that time has been two-fold; first of all, the US has been calling for a 'complete, verifiable, irreversible, dismantlement' of a two-track nuclear program (which includes both the plutonium-based weaponization program originating from Yongbyon and the HEU program), while North Korea has been calling for a 'freezing' of it's nuclear program.[3] This has led to the ongoing dilemma of 'freeze versus dismantlement.' The second part of the problem has been that North Korea continues to deny (as of November 2005) that it even has an HEU program, and has not agreed to date to even discuss a program it admitted to during the last unilateral talks during 2002.[4] This will no doubt be the largest hurdle in the six-party talks, as North Korea moves down the road of dismantling all elements of its two-track nuclear program. In fact, even in the first official statement ever made by the North Korean government where it acknowledged it had nuclear weapons (on February, 10 2005), there was no discussion specifically of an HEU program – only 'nukes.'[5] This continues to create an impasse in the process, as the US continues to assert that any discussion of the nuclear weapons program that Pyongyang has, must include both the plutonium and HEU programs.

The diplomatic problems between Washington and Pyongyang really began long before the talks in October of 2002. The reasons for this are extremely important.

---

1 Oh Young-hwan and Jeong Yong-soo, 'North's Uranium Put US in Policy Quandry', *Joongang Ilbo*, October, 11 2004, available at <http://joongangdaily.joins.com/200410/20041 01122312568099000092309231.html>.

2 Peter Hayes, 'The Multilateral Mantra And North Korea', *The Nautilus Institute Online*, February 20, 2004, available at <http://www.nautilus.org/DPRKBriefingBook/multilateralTalks/PHMultilateralMantra.html>.

3 Mark E. Manyin, Emma Chanlett-Avery, and Helene Marchart, 'North Korea: A Chronology of Events, October 2002-December 2004', CRS Report for Congress, Order Code RL32743 (January 24, 2005), p. 24.

4 'Roh Meets Bush Advisor on Nukes, Alliance', *Korea Update*, The Embassy of the Republic of Korea, July 20, 2004, available at <http://www.koreaemb.org/archive/2004/7_2/foreign/foreign5.asp>.

5 See 'Text Statement of the Democratic Peoples Republic of Korea', *KCNA*, February 10, 2005, available at <http://news.bbc.co.uk/2/hi/asia-pacific/4252515.stm>. See also 'DPRK "Manufactured" Nuclear Weapons, To "Suspend" 6-Way Talks for "Indefinite Period"', *Korean Central Broadcasting Station Statement*, full text of February 10, 2005 statement broadcast over North Korean Radio and Television, available at <http://www.nautilus.org/napsnet/sr/2005/0513A_KCBS.html>.

First of all, because of the hotly contested US presidential election in the fall of 2000, the Clinton administration had suspended sensitive talks that had been ongoing during that time frame. A scheduled trip by envoy Wendy Sherman was canceled.[6] Secondly, the strategy for the Bush and Clinton administrations for dealing with North Korea were extremely different, and because there was a delay (again, because of the difficulties with the presidential election) in getting their people in and conducting a thorough examination of what the strategy should be regarding North Korea, there was a period of several months where no discussion at all occurred between Washington and Pyongyang. This likely caused an already paranoid government in North Korea to become extremely apprehensive about their dealings with the new administration. This was exacerbated by the fact that the Bush and Kim Dae-Jung administrations had stated differences in the strategies they wished to pursue in dealing diplomatically with Pyongyang.[7] Originally the talks held in October were scheduled to be held in July, but were delayed even further because of a violent sea-battle between DPRK and ROK naval forces initiated by the North, that resulted in casualties on both sides, and the sinking of a ROK naval vessel.[8]

It is now known that the government in North Korea was extremely paranoid about dealing with a Republican administration that had openly stated during the elections of 2000 that the policies of the Clinton administration had been far too soft in dealing with the North Korean weapons of mass destruction (WMD) issues. In fact, according to Lim Dong-won, the head of the National Intelligence Service during the Kim Dae-Jung administration, Kim Jong-Il had planned to visit Seoul in the spring of 2001, months after holding a landmark summit with the former South Korean President. Lim, who also served as chief Presidential Security Advisor during the Kim Dae-Jung administration, remarked that Kim Jong-Il told him he 'had no choice' in canceling his visit, because of the outcome of the US elections, since his advisors had informed him that George W. Bush would take a hard-line policy that would 'threaten the North Korean regime.' Lim made his remarks at the Young Korean Academy Forum for Unification, in Seoul during June of 2004.[9]

---

6 Michael R. Gordon, 'How Politics Sank Accord on Missiles With North Korea', *New York Times*, March 6, 2001, available at <http://www.nytimes.com/2001/03/06/world/06MISS.html>.

7 'A Visit by South Korea's Leader', *New York Times*, March 6, 2001, available at <http://www.nytimes.com/2001/03/06/opinion/06TUE3.html>.

8 George Gedda, 'US Withdraws Offer to Hold Security Talks with North Korea Next Week', *Associated Press*, July 2, 2002, available at <http://www.nautilus.org/napsnet/dr/0207/JUL03.html#item2>.

9 See 'Former NIS Head Says N.K. Leader Had Planned S.K. Visit in 2001', *Digital Chosun Ilbo*, June 9, 2004, available at <http://english.chosun.com/cgi-bin/printNews?id=200406090013>. See also Bruce E. Bechtol, Jr, 'The Impact of North Korea's WMD Programs on Regional Security and the ROK-US Alliance', *International Journal of Korean Studies*, vol. 8, no. 1 (Fall/Winter 2004), p. 141.

The 'Freeze versus Dismantle' Debate of 2002–2005

Getting back to the two-fold issue of the nuclear program – 'freeze versus dismantle', and 'do they or do they not have an HEU program', there has been much debate about both aspects of this issue. To begin the discussion, I would first like to address the 'freeze versus dismantle' aspect. Unlike the 'do they or do they not have an HEU program' aspect of the North Korean nuclear program debate (which is primarily an argument about evidence), the 'freeze versus dismantle' debate within American policy circles and Asian policy circles has truly seemed to be an extremely polarizing political issue, with some arguing for a freeze with those with a clearly different perspective on the region arguing for dismantlement of North Korea's nuclear programs (CVID (Complete, Verifiable, Irreversible Dismantlement), if you will).[10] Some have argued for a 'freeze, then dismantle' strategy to deal with North Korea. During February of 2005, Leon V. Segal, Director of the Northeast Cooperative Security Project wrote:

> ... agreeing to normalize relations and provide written security assurances makes sense if North Korea agrees to freeze and eliminate any nuclear programs it has. That means not only plutonium reprocessing but also uranium enrichment, something it has not yet agreed to do. The details of a verifiable elimination of enrichment could be worked out in the future.[11]

While many have argued for a posture which would once again allow the North Koreans to once again freeze their two-track nuclear program (if they were even to publicly admit to having an HEU program – and then to allow inspectors in to verify such a freeze), there is reasonable precedent for being hesitant in pursuing such a policy. The North Koreans have previously formally agreed to freeze their nuclear program in return for alternative energy sources under the Agreed Framework of 1994.[12] But since 2002, numerous sources have revealed that North Korea in fact began pursuing a clandestine HEU weaponization program in 1997 as an alternate source – because of the fact that International Atomic Energy Agency (IAEA) inspectors were monitoring the plutonium-based facility at Yongbyon.[13]

---

10 See Robert Marquand and Donald Kirk, 'Ranks Breaking Over North Korea', *Christian Science Monitor*, June 22, 2004, available at <http://www.csmonitor.com/2004/0622/p01s04-woap.html>. See also Ralph A. Cossa, 'US Mantra: N Korea Nukes Must Go, But How?' *Asia Times*, May 8, 2004, available at <http://www.atimes.com/atimes/Korea/FE08Dg01.html>.

11 Leon V. Segal, 'North Korea's Tactics', *Boston Globe*, February 12, 2005, available at <http://www.boston.com/news/globe/editorial_opinion/oped/articles/2005/02/12/north_koreas_tactics/>.

12 Benjamin Friedman, 'Fact Sheet: North Korea's Nuclear Weapons Program', *Nuclear Issues: Center for Defense Information*, January 23, 2003, available at <http://www.cdi.org/nuclear/nk-fact-sheet-pr.cfm>.

13 See Daniel A. Pinkston, 'When Did the WMD Deals Between Pyongyang and Islamabad Begin?', *North Korea Special Collection, Monterey Institute of International Studies, Center for Nonproliferation Studies* (Monterey, CA: Monterey Institute of International Studies,

To further strengthen the argument of 'fool me once, shame on you, fool me twice, shame on me', the North Koreans then 'unfroze' their plutonium facility at Yongbyon following the talks with James Kelly, expelling the IAEA inspectors who had been monitoring the freeze at the facilities, and essentially rendering the Agreed Framework null and void.[14] Thus, when an analysis of using a nuclear freeze as an option is undertaken, there are two clear reasons why the option is flawed, (1) precedent shows the North Koreans will simply pursue an alternative path to nuclear weaponization; or (2) simply decide to 'unfreeze' their program, and then the US, our allies, and the region, are back to square one. Agreeing to a freeze – even a temporary freeze – is also tenuous because of the past precedent of brinkmanship that Pyongyang has engaged in, often breaking agreements as the government there saw fit.[15] The only thing close to a guarantee for a nuclear-free Korean peninsula would be dismantlement of Pyongyang's nuclear program – and even this will be extremely difficult to confirm.

How Strong is the Evidence Regarding North Korea's HEU Program?

The debate, both within the US policy and academic communities, and to a lesser extent, among allies, on whether or not North Korea actually has an HEU program, has been ongoing since the initial bilateral talks between the US and Pyongyang during October of 2002. To be sure, some have actually turned this into a 'left versus right' issue. In fact, during February of 2005, noted Korean analyst Selig Harrison of the Woodrow Wilson International Center for Scholars, remarked that '… the Bush administration presented a worst-case scenario as an incontrovertible truth and distorted its intelligence on North Korea (much as it did in Iraq) …'[16] Some in the American academic community, as well as some scholars in South Korea and other parts of Asia, also have agreed with this assessment.[17]

On the other hand, the US government has stated that the evidence has existed for quite some time that North Korea had been pursuing a secret HEU program

---

January, 2003), available at <http://cns.miis.edu/pubs/week/021028.htm>. See also Victor D. Cha, and David C. Kang, 'The Korea Crisis', *Foreign Policy*, September 29, 2003, available at <http://www.foreignpolicy.com/story/story.php?storyID13620>.

14 'North Korea Expelling IAEA Inspectors', *CNN.COM*, December 27, 2002, available at <http://archives.cnn.com/2002/WORLD/asiapcf/east/12/27/nkorea.expulsions/>.

15 'IAEA Director General Cites DPRK Nuclear Brinkmanship', Texts of December 26 and 27 IAEA press releases on developments in North Korea, available at <http://japan.usembassy.gov/e/p/tp-20021230a7.html>.

16 Selig S. Harrison, 'Did North Korea Cheat?', *Foreign Affairs* (January/February 2005), available at <http://www.foreignaffairs.org/20050101faessay84109/selig-s-harrison/did-north-korea-cheat.html>.

17 'Dispute Imperils North Korea Nuke Talks', *Associated Press*, February 19, 2004, available at <http://www.military.com/NewsContent/0,13319,FL_korea_021904,00.html>.

– since the 1990s. As US Deputy State Department spokesman Adam Ereli stated in December of 2004:

> There are claims made in the article that we learned about the uranium enrichment program from the North Koreans [when US envoy James Kelly visited Pyongyang in October 2002]. That's not the case.... We were already aware of the program before they ever talked to us and we informed them of our knowledge about it in October 2002. And it was at that time that North Korea acknowledged to senior US officials that it was pursuing such a covert program.[18]

Others in the academic community have also stated that there is very strong evidence that North Korea is pursuing an HEU program, most notably Robert L. Galluci, a former official in the Clinton administration who had access to highly classified information during the critical time period of the late 1990s (Galluci is not a Bush supporter, and in fact has often been critical of Bush policies). In 2004, Galluci went so far as to say that there is 'no doubt' that North Korea has the technology. He also stated in an online forum during 2004, that '... I think the North would like to keep its enrichment program as insurance against US actions. This is something we cannot allow them to do.'[19]

It is very important to discuss this key issue (whether or not North Korea actually has a covert HEU weaponization program) from an evidence-based perspective, and not from a political perspective. While the 'freeze versus dismantle' controversy may or may not have deserved to be debated among political pundits, academics, and those in the policy and national security communities, the question of whether to accept (or not) North Korea's denial of possessing an HEU program in this chapter will be based on evidence. It is the belief of the author that there has been enough unclassified evidence since early 2003 to make a clear assessment regarding the existence of Pyongyang's HEU program.

The evidence pointing to the existence of North Korea's HEU program starts with activities that really began during the mid-1990s. According to high-ranking North Korean defector Hwang Jang-yop, the program was specifically conceived and started because of a desire to possess nuclear weapons separately from the plutonium-based program – which was being closely monitored by the IAEA. Hwang describes his meeting with a high-ranking North Korean official saying, '... before the fall of

---

18 Heo Yong-beom, 'N.K. Uranium Program Known for Years: US State Department', *Chosun Ilbo*, December 12, 2004, available at <http://english.chosun.com/w21data/html/news/200412/200412120019.html>.

19 See Stephanie Ho, 'North Korea Pursuing Two Paths Toward Nuclear Weapons', *Voice of America*, June 21, 2004, available at <http://www.iwar.org.uk/news-archive/2004/06-21-3.html>. See also Robert L. Gallucci, 'North Korean Nuclear Crisis: An Online Question and Answer Session', *Washington Post*, June 23, 2004, available at <http://discuss.washingtonpost.com/wp-srv/zforum/04/world_gallucci062304.htm>.

1996, he said we've solved a big problem. We don't need plutonium this time. Due to an agreement with Pakistan, we will use uranium.[20]

Following James Kelly's accusation to the North Koreans during October of 2002, and their subsequent admission to possession of an HEU program (later denied), a great deal more evidence became available, as noted Pakistani scientist A.Q. Khan admitted to selling HEU technology to Pyongyang. Khan reportedly confessed to supplying the North Koreans with centrifuge prototypes and blueprints, which enabled Pyongyang to begin its centrifuge enrichment program.[21] The program continued well into 2000–2001, and the evidence points to it being part of a 'nukes for missiles' deal between the two cash-strapped regimes in Islamabad and Pyongyang. During this time period, technology, equipment, and blueprints went from Pakistan to North Korea, as missiles went from North Korea to Pakistan. The barter deal between the two nations was of great benefit to both sides, with North Korea supplying Pakistan with missiles that could counter the Indian threat (the No Dong, later renamed the Ghauri once transferred to Pakistan).[22] Reportedly, North Korean missile technicians and Pakistani nuclear scientists were exchanged frequently between the two countries throughout the 1990s. The program continued well into 2001, even after an alliance had been formed between Washington and Islamabad to fight the Global War on Terrorism, and US troops were headed for Pakistan.

Of interest, the missiles and nuclear technology were reportedly being shuttled between North Korea and Pakistan on American-built C-130s.[23] In fact, according to several sources, to include defectors and press reports, the 'missiles-for-nukes' shuttles were carried out on American-made C-130s, previously sold to the Pakistanis through Chinese airspace – an interesting development given Beijing's many statements calling for a 'nuclear free Korean Peninsula.'[24] Reportedly, on one such trip, one of the C-130s being used to shuttle the weaponry and technology back and forth broke down at Sunan airfield near Pyongyang, causing quite a disruption in North Korea, since, of course, no spare parts existed there for the American-made aircraft.[25] More evidence regarding Pakistani involvement in the North Korean HEU

---

20 'Defector: North Korea Has Uranium Program', *Associated Press*, February 8, 2004, available at <http://www.nuclearpolicy.org/NewsArticlePrint.cfm?NewsID=1276>.

21 Mitchell B. Reiss and Robert L. Galluci, 'Red Handed', *Foreign Affairs* (March/April 2005), available at <http://www.foreignaffairs.org/20050301faresponse84214/mitchell-b-reiss-robert-gallucci/red-handed.html>.

22 David E. Sanger and James Dao, 'US Says Pakistan Gave (Nuclear) Technology to North Korea', *New York Times*, October 18, 2002, available at <http://membres.lycos.fr/tthreat/article24.htm>.

23 David E. Sanger, 'In North Korea and Pakistan, Deep Roots of Nuclear Barter', *New York Times*, November 24, 2002.

24 'High Stakes on the High Seas in Korean Blockade', *Sydney Morning Herald*, July 12, 2003, available at <http://www.smh.com.au/articles/2003/07/11/1057783354653.html>.

25 Greg Bearup, 'Pakistan's Nuclear Bazaar: Dr. Khan's Shady Nuclear Family', *South China Morning Post*, February 11, 2004, available at <http://www.worldpress.org/Asia/1825.cfm>.

program came to light in the summer of 2004 when Jeon Sung-hun of the Korean Institute for National Unification was quoted as saying, 'Nine Pakistani nuclear scientists have been missing since they left their country six years ago, and we cannot rule out the possibility that some of them are in North Korea', further stating, 'North Korea's enriched uranium program was at an early stage in its development.'[26]

Yet more evidence became available during 2004, when Colonel Ghadafi in Libya (in a completely transparent, Middle Eastern version of 'CVID') agreed to cease his effort to develop nuclear weapons. In doing so, he gave up all of the designs, equipment and materials, as well as the uranium that he had acquired from various sources, in exchange for an opening up of economic and diplomatic ties with the America and the West. American Vice-President Richard Cheney addressed this evidence in a speech given during April of 2004 at Fudan University in China where he stated:

> ... Libyans acquired their technical expertise, weapons design and so forth from Mr. A.Q. Khan, Pakistan.... Mr. Khan also provided similar capabilities to the North Koreans. So we're confident that the North Koreans do, in fact, have a program to enrich uranium to produce nuclear weapons.[27]

Finally, more evidence was revealed during Congressional testimony by the Director of the Defense Intelligence Agency, Lowell F. Jacoby, before the Senate Armed Services Committee during April of 2005. When asked by Senator Hillary Clinton whether it was his assessment that, 'North Korea has the ability to arm a missile with a nuclear device?' in response, he stated, 'my assessment is that they have the capability to do that, yes.' This is the first public statement by a US official that states an assessment of North Korea's ability to arm a missile with a nuclear device.[28] Because it is nearly impossible to arm a missile with a plutonium-based weapon (it is simply too big), if the assessment passed on to the US Senate Armed Services Committee is correct, then the most likely type of warhead would have to come from weaponized, HEU.

If one is to examine the question of whether or not North Korea has an HEU program from a purely evidence-based perspective, it certainly appears that there is not one 'smoking gun', there are many. The evidence shows a clear chart of why Pyongyang chose to pursue an HEU program, how they chose to pursue that program, and who they developed the program with. Indeed, if one is to contrast the evidence regarding North Korea's HEU program with the evidence regarding Iraq's WMD programs, it truly appears to be an 'apples and oranges' comparison.

---

26 'Missing Pakistani Nuclear Scientists in North Korea', *Agence France-Presse*, June 20, 2004, available at <http://www.pakistan-facts.com/article.php?story=20040620201344967>.

27 Richard Cheney, Vice President of the United States, 'Vice President Speaks at China's Fudan University April 15', speech given at Fudan University, China, April 15, 2004, available at <http://helsinki.usembassy.gov/servlet/PageServer?Page=today2.html>.

28 'Open Letter from Senators Clinton and Levin to Secretary Rice', *Web site of the United States Senate*, April 28, 2005, available at <http://clinton.senate.gov/4.28.05.html>.

There are two key questions that remain regarding the program; where is it being developed in North Korea, and how far along is the program? As of the writing of this chapter, these questions remain unanswered, but because of breakthroughs reached in the six-party talks during September of 2005 (where Pyongyang agreed to dismantle its nuclear programs, with specifics to be worked out at a later date) it is extremely unlikely that the nuclear issue will be resolved until North Korea makes it clear to the world the exact details of its HEU program. This will be discussed in great detail in a later section.

It is very clear from an examination of events that occurred during 2004 that, because of this program (the two-track nuclear program), Pyongyang took rather unprecedented steps regarding the internal political dynamics within both the US and South Korea – probably in the hopes of gaining a diplomatic advantage in the six-party talks that occurred that year, and perhaps because of the hope that these initiatives would move the US closer to bilateral talks.

Key Changes in Pyongyang's Strategy During 2004: Attempts at Involvement in US and ROK Internal Politics

As discussed earlier in this chapter, Lim Dong-won stated that during a visit to North Korea, he was informed of Kim Jong-Il's reasons for canceling his visit to South Korea during 2001 (the key reason being that he felt George Bush would take a hard-line policy that would 'threaten' his regime). It is unclear whether this was bluster, or simply leaked to Lim by the North Koreans in order to 'crank up the pressure' on the US government, or perhaps even to intentionally drive a wedge into the ROK–US alliance, which was undergoing sensitive challenges at the time (some of which continue as of the writing of this chapter).[29] What is clear from an analysis of North Korean statements made during 2004 is that the government in Pyongyang decided to use a strategy seldom utilized in the past – a strategy designed to influence the internal political dynamics within the US and South Korea.

During the first few months of 2004 as it became obvious that John Kerry would be the Democratic party's nominee for President of the US, the North Korean state-run media commented several times on that party's nominee for President, John Kerry, and his criticism of Bush's hard-line policy toward Pyongyang. When this first occurred, most experienced North Korean analysts considered it quite unusual, as traditionally, North Korea's government has not commented on US domestic politics in the past. Based on an analysis of propaganda coming out of North Korea, it appears that Pyongyang was carrying out this unusual activity in the hope that if

---

29 See David W. Shin, 'ROK and the United States 2004–2005: Managing Perception Gaps?', *Asia-Pacific Center for Security Studies Special Assessment* (February 2005), available at <http://www.apcss.org/Publications/SAS/APandtheU.S./ShinROK1.pdf>.

elected, Kerry would again return to the North Korean policies carried out during the final months of the Clinton administration.[30]

The Clinton administration policies included (particularly during the final months of the Clinton administration), an unprecedented visit to North Korea by Secretary of State Madeline Albright. Albright later argued in an interview given with PBS's *Frontline*, that her visit was not appeasement, and that the Bush administration 'has kind of dug its heels in and said anything that we did vis-à-vis North Korea is appeasement. Once you define it that way, it's very hard to unpaint yourself, and I think that's where we are now.'[31] The last months of the Clinton also witnessed a visit to the US by the second highest ranking official in North Korea, Cho Myong-rok – a trip that included calling on the Pentagon, the White House (for a meeting with President Clinton), and the State Department.[32]

While, in the opinion of the author, Kerry would have been unlikely to return US foreign policy with North Korea back to the 'good old days' (primarily because of the brinkmanship and rogue behavior of Pyongyang since the fall of 2002) during the last few months of the Clinton administration, the Democratic party candidate for president remarked publicly on numerous occasions that if he won the presidential election in November of 2004, he would 'find ways' to resume the bilateral talks with North Korea.[33] Kerry stated repeatedly during the election of 2004 (including during the Presidential debates) that George W. Bush has 'failed in his policy on North Korea.'[34]

Perhaps even more disturbing were the frequent and rather clumsy attempts by the North Koreans through their propaganda, to influence the political process in South Korea during 2004. During March of that year, when South Korean President, Roh Moo-hyun, was impeached by what was then a National Assembly with a majority from the opposition Grand National Party, the North Korean state-run press discounted the act for its 'illegality and impudence,' going on to say that 'The US is chiefly to blame for the incident,' and concluding, 'The US egged the South Korean political quacks, obsessed by the greed for power, on to stage such an incident

---

30 Joel Sano, 'Pyongyang Pins False Hopes on Kerry', *Asia Times Online*, March 17, 2004, available at <http://www.atimes.com/atimes/Korea/FC17Dg04.html>.

31 'Interview with Madeline Albright', *Frontline: PBS.ORG*, March 27, 2003, available at <http://www.pbs.org/wgbh/pages/frontline/shows/kim/interviews/albright.html>.

32 'North Korean Envoy Starts Washington Meetings', *Reuters*, October 10, 2000, available at <http://www.nytimes.com/reuters/world/international-korea-n.html>.

33 Soon-taek Kwon, 'Kerry to Resume Bilateral Talks With North Korea When Elected', *Donga Ilbo*, March 17, 2004, available at <http://english.donga.com/srv/service.php3?biid=2004031801718>.

34 See 'Bush Rejects Direct Dialogue With North Korea Over Nuclear Question', *AFP*, April 29, 2004, available at <http://news.yahoo.com/news?tmpl=story&u=/afp/20040429/pl_afp/us_nkorea_dialogue_040429215713>. See also 'Kerry Again Promises Direct Talks With NK On Nuclear Issue', *Chosun Ilbo*, October 21, 2004, available at <http://english.chosun.com/w21data/html/news/200410/200410210014.html>.

in a bid to install ultra-right pro-US regime there.'[35] Many in South Korea were reportedly quite offended by this attempted intrusion into South Korean internal affairs. The reaction from the ROK mainstream press was fairly strong, including one editorial which read in part, 'We do not understand why the North is interfering in the South's domestic affairs. This is a clear violation of the basic principles agreed upon by the two Koreas.'[36]

During the spring of 2004, North Korea's attempts to influence the hotly contested National Assembly elections became obvious. During this time period, Pyongyang's print and broadcast outlets urged voters to put the Left into power with numerous statements and broadcasts. In one such de facto endorsement of Roh Moo-hyun during April of that year, the DPRK urged South Koreans to vote against 'conservative forces' in the elections.[37] During the same week, Pyongyang's press again made statements supporting the left, this time referring to the US, stating in part, 'pro-US conservative forces in South Korea' were plotting to scuttle the National Assembly elections.[38] Pyongyang's attempted intervention in the elections was analyzed by many as a rather clumsy effort (well publicized in both the ROK and American press) to build on the division in ROK society that some have seen as being between older conservatives and younger more liberal voters (again, widely publicized in ROK and American press outlets), who are more sympathetic to North Korea (the younger voters are also widely viewed as being more 'anti-American', another advantage to North Korea). In South Korea, the Uri party was at the time fighting a reputation (brought on by some rather unfortunate statements made by its leaders) that it only wanted to appeal to younger and liberal voters.[39] Whether the polarized political climate in South Korea during the National Assembly elections of 2004 was overplayed in the world press or not, obviously the government in Pyongyang clearly felt that it would be at a distinct advantage with a left-leaning government in power in South Korea – and would have even more to gain if the same situation existed in the US.

---

35 'KCNA Slams Parliamentary Coup in S. Korea', *KCNA*, March 17, 2004, available at <http://www.kcna.co.jp/item/2004/200403/news03/18.htm>.

36 'Editorial: Butt Out, Pyongyang', *Joongang Ilbo*, March 17, 2004, available at <http://joongangdaily.joins.com/200403/17/200403172143276639900090109011.html>.

37 Andrew Ward, 'N Korea Endorses Roh's Party in South's Poll', *Financial Times*, April 7, 2004, available at <http://www.nautilus.org/archives/napsnet/dr/0404/APR07-04.html#item8>.

38 'Pyongyang Warns of Election Plotting', *Joongang Ilbo*, April 9, 2004, available at <http://joongangdaily.joins.com/200404/09/200404090042107109900090309031.html>.

39 See Pak Du-shik, 'Elderly Voters Can Stay Home', *Chosun Ilbo*, April 1, 2004, available at <http://english.chosun.com/w21data/html/news/200404/200404010026.html>. See also Bruce E. Bechtol, Jr, 'The Impact of North Korea's WMD Programs on Regional Security and the ROK–US Alliance, *International Journal of Korean Studies*, vol. 8, no. 1 (Fall/Winter 2004), pp. 142–157.

Stability Issues in Pyongyang and Their Impact on US–DPRK Relations

Since the late 1990s, there has been much debate within the academic and policy communities about how the US should pursue its diplomatic strategy with North Korea. But one issue that there has not been great debate about is whether or not Kim Jong-Il is firmly in charge. During the fall of 2004, several events were reported that, if true, show disturbing trends in the ongoing stability of the Kim regime in North Korea.[40] Because the stability of Kim's regime is important when it comes to a strategy of dealing with North Korea, I will briefly conduct an analysis of these events.

During early November of 2004, unusual reports began to filter out of North Korea that portraits of Kim Jong-Il had been removed from honored spots.[41] During the same time frame, the press in Japan and South Korea reported that North Korea's official media had at least temporarily dropped the glorifying title of 'Dear Leader' when referring to Kim Jong-Il.[42] Later during the fall of 2004, reports surfaced from China that several generals and high-ranking government officials were defecting. Up to 130 generals reportedly defected, and an unknown number of government officials. According to Zhao Huji, one of China's leading North Korean experts and a researcher at the Communist Party School, '… unlike most defectors crossing into China, the high-level defectors and their families did not lack basic necessities. Rather, they were disconcerted with Kim Jong-il's rule.'[43] A North Korean Foreign Ministry official denied the press reports that Kim Jong-Il's pictures had been removed from public offices and schools, citing the reports as 'groundless fabrication.'[44] A North Korean Foreign Ministry spokesman also denied the reports that hundreds of the country's generals had defected to China, stating, 'Never mind the generals, not even a single button of their uniforms has crossed the border.'[45] It is interesting to note,

---

40 'What Do Strange Signs in North Korea Mean?', *Chosun Ilbo*, November 18, 2004, available at <http://english.chosun.com/w21data/html/news/200411/200411180035.html>.

41 James Brooke, 'Monitors of North Korean News Note Dip in Reverence for Kim', *New York Times*, November 18, 2004, available at <http://www.nytimes.com/2004/11/18/international/asia/18korea.html?oref=login&pagewanted=print&position=>.

42 'North Korean Media Drop Kim Jong-il's Dear Leader Title', *Chosun Ilbo*, November 18, 2004, available at <http://english.chosun.com/w21data/html/news/200411/200411180014.html>.

43 'North Korean Generals, Officials Defecting, But Kim Jong-il Still Strong', *AFP*, December 9, 2004, available at <http://story.news.yahoo.com/news?tmpl=story&cid=1530&ncid=2181&e=10&u=/afp/20041209/wl_asia_afp/nkoreachinadefection_041209040849>.

44 'NK Foreign Ministry Denies Removal of Kim Jong-il Portraits', *Chosun Ilbo*, November 19, 2004, available at <http://english.chosun.com/w21data/html/news/200411/200411190019.html>.

45 'North Korea Denies Defection of Generals', *Joongang Ilbo*, December 14, 2004, available at <http://joongangdaily.joins.com/200412/13/200412132234036479900090209021.html>.

that not long after these events were reported, the 'top brass' of the North Korean military pledged their support to Kim Jong-Il publicly at an event in Pyongyang.[46]

Interesting developments have also occurred regarding the power circle that surrounds Kim Jong-Il. Chang Sung-taek, Kim's brother-in-law and a highly placed official within the North Korean government, was reportedly purged sometime during 2004 – perhaps because of succession issues in the government over which he and the 'Dear Leader' disagreed.[47] During 2004, Kim reportedly purged several of his relatives and up to 80 other officials and their families (reportedly for trying to 'seize power', but perhaps over succession issues, as with Chang). Chang's wife (Kim's sister), Kim Kyong-hee was reportedly injured in an auto accident during 2004 – which is assumed to have been a possible attempt on her life.[48] Kim Kyong-hee may have been in deep depression, and is reported to have undergone medical treatment for alcohol addiction in France, possibly during the same time period.[49] Finally, Kim's eldest son Kim Chong-nam reportedly narrowly avoided an assassination attempt while on a trip to Austria. There has also been speculation that this was because of infighting within the inner circle over succession and power issues involving who will wield the reigns of power once Kim Jong-Il is gone.[50]

The issues in the paragraphs above all surfaced during the fall of 2004, yet they may point to two internal concerns for Kim's regime. The first is speculation that the situation in North Korea is now so extreme that high-level party officials and members of the military elite may now be defecting in larger than usual numbers. A video tape recently smuggled into Japan and then South Korea shows extremely bad conditions and rare scenes of North Korean criminal trials that add some credence to this assessment.[51] The second internal concern appears to be regarding who Kim Jong-Il's successor will be in the repressive Pyongyang regime. A South Korean Unification Ministry official remarked during December of 2004, that '… because 2005 is the 60th anniversary of the nation's liberation, the tenth anniversary of the

---

46 'N. Korean Military Leaders Pledge Loyalty to Kim Jong-il', *Yonhap*, February 8, 2005, available at <http://english.yna.co.kr/Engnews/20050208/320000000020050208161124E0.html>.

47 Barbara Demick, 'Kim Ousts Relative, a Potential Rival, From N. Korean Government', *Los Angeles Times*, December 9, 2004, available at <http://www.latimes.com/news/nationworld/la-fg-purge9dec09,0,4477486.story?coll=la-headlines-world>.

48 Jasper Becker, 'Portrait of a Family at War: Kim Jong-il Purges Relatives After Alleged Coup Bid', *The Independent*, December 28, 2004, available at <http://news.independent.co.uk/world/asia/story.jsp?story=596607>.

49 'N. Korean Leader's Younger Sister Alive: Source', *Yonhap*, February 7, 2005, available at <http://english.yna.co.kr/Englishnews/20050207/320000000020050207175052E8.html>.

50 'N.K. Leader's Son Avoids Assassination Plot in Austria', *Chosun Ilbo*, December 19, 2004, available at <http://english.chosun.com/w21data/html/news/200412/200412190013.html>.

51 Lee Young-jong, 'Video Details Life in North Korea', *Joongang Ilbo*, January 2, 2005, available at <http://joongangdaily.joins.com/200501/06/200501062243482113990009 0309031.html>.

birth of Kim Jong-il's military-led Songun politics, and the fifth anniversary of the intra-Korean summit, it is possible that a measure worth remembering might be taken.' According to Chung Sung-jang of the Sejong Institute, this points to the possibility that Kim might have named his successor in 2005.[52] Indeed, in what is widely considered to be the first time Pyongyang has openly addressed the issue of hereditary power succession following the death or 'retirement' of Kim Jong-Il, North Korean official radio during January of 2005 proclaimed, 'Our founder Kim Il-sung when he was alive, emphasized that if he falls short of completing the revolution, it will be continued by his son and grandson.'[53]

An examination of these important issues that have arisen since the fall of 2004 leads one to ask the question, is Kim firmly in control, and how tenuous is the situation in North Korea? According to Hudson Institute Senior Fellow, Michael Horowitz, the regime will implode within a year. But many analysts in Seoul and the US disagree, assessing that North Korea has had hard times in the past and still managed to get through even the toughest of crisis situations.[54] The view that the North Korean regime is near collapse is also not supported by the Russian government according to the Russian ambassador to South Korea, as reported during an interview in January of 2005.[55] China's ambassador to South Korea has also stated that Pyongyang's government was not on the verge of collapse, remarking in part, 'To think that North Korea will collapse is far-fetched speculation …'[56] The view that Kim Jong-Il is in full control is also supported by one of the most well-known defectors from North Korea, Hwang Jang-yup, who said during December of 2004 that reports of a political crisis in North Korea were groundless.[57]

While from an analytical sense it is practical to assume that 'where there is smoke, there is fire,' there is precedent for disruption and large-scale purges within Kim Jong-Il's regime – and the government there being able to handle the challenges presented

---

52 Kwon Kyeong-bok, 'Kim Jong-il May Name Successor in 2005: Scholar', *Chosun Ilbo*, December 31, 2004, available at <http://english.chosun.com/w21data/html/news/200412/200412310032.html>.

53 Lee Young-jong, 'Pyongyang Radio Speaks of Dynasty', *Joongang Ilbo*, January 31, 2005, available at <http://joongangdaily.joins.com/200501/30/200501302204229039900090309031.html>.

54 Joo Sang-min, 'Kim Likely to Maintain Grip on Ailing Regime', *Korea Herald*, January 11, 2005, available at <http://www.koreaherald.co.kr/SITE/data/html_dir/2005/01/11/200501110003.asp>.

55 Bae Myung-bok, 'Russia Sees No Collapse in North', *Joongang Ilbo*, January 17, 2005, available at <http://joongangdaily.joins.com/200501/16/200501162108084879900090309031.html>.

56 You Sang-chul, 'Chinese Envoy Discounts Pyongyang Collapse', *Joongang Ilbo*, January 14, 2005, available at <http://joongangdaily.joins.com/200501/13/200501132254177779900090309031.html>.

57 Kwon Kyung-bok, 'Senior N.K. Defector Says Dear Leader is in Full Control', *Chosun Ilbo*, December 20, 2004, available at <http://english.chosun.com/w21data/html/news/200412/200412200039.html>.

promptly and efficiently without losing control. During 1996, Kim's security service was able to uncover a plot that appears to have been a plan to conduct a coup by high ranking officers within the 6th Army Corps. The plot was unsuccessful, and resulted in large-scale purges among the ranks of the North Korean military and many high-ranking government officials during late 1996 and 1997.[58] Regarding the issue of succession, this is an issue that the DPRK has already successfully addressed once, with the death of Kim Il-sung in 1994, as there was relatively little internal turmoil when Kim Jong-Il assumed power following the passing away of his father. Thus, while it is safe to assume that the internal intrigue within North Korea is disturbing, and that it may have diverted Kim's attention somewhat away from diplomatic dealings with the US during 2004, this intrigue is unlikely to change the current policies and strategies that will be used as the six-party talks (and nuclear brinkmanship) continue.

Differences in the ROK–US Alliance: The Impact on Containment of the DPRK

While the debate within the US has been relatively heated regarding Washington's policy toward the DPRK since 2003, the disagreement over how to deal with North Korea's brinkmanship and nuclear capability has been equally noteworthy during the same time frame between Washington and Seoul. To exacerbate the difficulties in the relationship between these two long-standing allies, 2004 was a year that witnessed extremely difficult negotiations over such alliance issues as the cost of moving US military units away from the Demilitarized Zone (DMZ) and Seoul to south of the Han river, when and how these moves should occur (Seoul has asked that the moves be delayed), how the troops will be used (the Global Posture Review (GPR) in the Pentagon is likely to have an impact on whether or not troops can be deployed off-peninsula in time of crisis elsewhere), the future status of the Combined Forces Command (CFC), and other important issues that impact the security and stability of the Korean peninsula and the region as a whole.[59]

---

58 Andrew Natsios, 'The Politics of Famine in North Korea', *United States Institute of Peace Special Report 51*, August 2, 1999, available at <http://www.usip.org/pubs/specialreports/sr990802.html>.

59 See Park Shin-bon and Brian Lee, 'Seoul Seeking to Reduce Costs of Keeping US', *Joongang Ilbo*, October 24, 2004, available at <http://joongangdaily.joins.com/200410/19/20041019220931983990090309031.html>. See also Kim Min-seok and Ser Myo-ja, 'US Tells Korea Early Force Cuts Won't Change', *Joongang Ilbo*, August 20, 2004, available at <http://joongangdaily.joins.com>. See also 'US Requests Koreans Share in C4I Modernization Costs', *Chosun Ilbo*, October 18, 2004, available at <http://english.chosun.com/w21data/html/news/200410/200410180019.html>. See also Brian Lee, 'US Patrols of Border Come to an End', *Joongang Ilbo*, November 2, 2004, available at <http://joongangdaily.joins.com/200411/01/200411012252431079900090309031.html>. See also Ahn Sung-kyoo, 'Talks To Help Decipher Future US Military Role', Joongang Ilbo, February 3, 2005, available at <http://joongangdaily.joins.com/200502/02/200502022242232879900090309031.html>. See

While the differences in the future of the ROK–US alliance have been an important foreign policy issue for both Washington and Seoul, the differences in policy over how to deal with North Korea have been equally as important. During a trip to the US during the fall of 2004, Roh Moo-hyun called for a 'softer stance' on North Korea by the US, saying that there was some validity to the North's claims that their pursuit of nuclear arms was in self-defense.[60] During the same visit, Roh also remarked that US sanctions against North Korea would be undesirable, stating, 'We can think about a sanctions policy toward North Korea, but it will just prolong unrest and a threat. It is not a desirable solution.' Roh also remarked that the US should look at providing North Korea with the 'security guarantee' it had been asking for since the nuclear confrontation began in the fall of 2002.[61] Roh's remarks were troubling to some on both sides of the Pacific because they appear to be in sharp divergence with the current policy of the US – and because they were made so publicly on US soil. Indeed, as Don Oberdorfer, Adjunct Professor of International Relations at the Johns Hopkins University's Nitze School of Advanced International Studies has stated, 'The inescapable fact is that the US and ROK have been drifting apart as the US and its body politic have moved to the right, and the Korean government and body politic have moved to the left.'[62]

The Roh administration has frequently commented that North Korea should no longer be perceived through a 'Cold War perspective', and some analysts – both in Korea and the US – have interpreted this to mean that conservatives (both those in South Korea and the US) are wrong to view Pyongyang in such a light. In fact, during a speech given at Georgetown University during November of 2005, Dr. Cho Kisuk,

---

also Ho-Won Choi, 'Reduction of US Forces in Korea to be Completed by 2007', *Donga Ilbo*, August 20, available at http://english.donga.com/srv/service.php3?biid=2004082113518>. See also Heo Yong-beom, 'No Reduction in Rank of USFK: Lawless', *Chosun Ilbo*, October 8, 2004, available at <http://english.chosun.com/w21data/html/news/200410/200410088003 1.html>. See also Chae Byung-gun and Brian Lee, 'LaPorte Says US Forces Will Stay in Korea', *Joongang Ilbo*, January 7, 2005, available at <http://joongangdaily.joins.com/200501 /07/200501071553312579900090309031.html>. See also Yoo Yong-won, 'Defense Ministry Releases Cooperative Self-Defense Plan', *Chosun Ilbo*, November 18, 2004, available at <http://english.chosun.com/w21data/html/news/200411/200411180026.html>. See also Ho-Won Choi, 'Future of the Security of the Korean Peninsula and USFK', *Donga Ilbo*, November 3, 2004, available at <http://english.donga.com/srv/service.php3?bicode=050000 &biid=2004110467718>. See also Kang Chan-ho, 'Korea and US Agree on Base Locations, Size', *Joongang Ilbo*, July 23, 2004, available at <http://joongang.daily.joins.com>.

60 Ser Myo-ja, 'Roh Calls for Softer Stance Against North', *Joongang Ilbo*, November 15, 2004, available at <http://joongangdaily.joins.com/200411/14/20041114215713790990000 90309031.html>.

61 Jung-Hun Kim, 'President Roh Says US Sanctions to N. Korea Would Be Undesirable', *Donga Ilbo*, November 14, 2004, available at <http://english.donga.com/srv/service.php3?bii d=2004111590368>.

62 Don Oberdorfer, 'The United States and South Korea: Can This Alliance Last?' *Nautilus Institute Policy Forum Online 05-93A*, November 17, 2005, available at <http://www.nautilus.org/fora/security/0593Oberdorfer.html>.

the Senior Secretary to President Roh for Public Relations remarked (referring to the older, more conservative generation of South Koreans):

> ... I call it one-dimensional vs. multi-dimensional thinking: it is the difference in the way of thinking between young people and the elderly. Older people see North Korea through a Cold War perspective. In other words, they understand international relations as a dichotomy: North Korea threatens our system whereas the US safeguards us. Therefore, friendly attitudes toward North Korea are automatically construed as hostility toward the United States.[63]

Certainly such remarks reflect an interesting spin on attitudes among left of center government officials in the Roh administration toward both the US, and their fellow Koreans who have more conservative views.

In the opinion of the author, North Korea cannot cease to be viewed through a Cold War prism simply because of a policy of active engagement by Seoul (and the US). The Cold War paradigms that existed during the period when the US and her allies were engaged in a face-off with the Soviet Block were highlighted by three very important characteristics. First, the Soviet Union maintained a nuclear arsenal that threatened the US and her allies (as well as the missile platforms to deploy nuclear weapons). Secondly, the Soviet Union maintained a large, forward-deployed array of conventional forces that threatened the US and her allies in Europe. Finally, the Soviet Block refused to join the global capitalist economy, instead surviving through trade that existed only among communist nations under a socialist economic system.[64]

Today, all three of these old Cold War paradigms exist in North Korea. Pyongyang continues to maintain a nuclear arsenal and the missiles to carry these nuclear weapons.[65] North Korea also maintains one of the largest conventional forces (the fifth largest) in the world, forward deployed along the DMZ, with long-range artillery, missiles, and special operations forces that can threaten Seoul and other key areas of South Korea with little or no warning.[66] Finally, North Korea continues to refuse to make any real effort to join the world economy, instead relying on foreign aid, illicit

---

63 Cho Kisuk, 'Understanding Public Opinion in Korea', Keynote speech presented at Georgetown University, Washington DC, November 4, 2005, at Georgetown University's School of Foreign Service and Korea's Sejong Institute co-sponsored conference entitled, 'New Era: New Alliance', available at <http://www.kois.go.kr/news/news/newsView.asp?serial_no=20051104015&part=111&SearchDay=>.

64 See, 'At Cold War's End: US Intelligence on the Soviet Union and Eastern Europe, 1989-1991', History Staff, Center for the Study of Intelligence, Central Intelligence Agency, available at <http://www.cia.gov/csi/books/19335/art-1.html>.

65 See 'Special Report on the North Korean Nuclear Weapons Statement', Center for Nonproliferation Studies, Monterey Institute of International Studies, February 11, 2005, available at < <http://cns.miis.edu/pubs/week/050211.htm>.

66 Donald Macintyre, 'Kim's War Machine', *Time Asia*, February 17, 2003, available at <http://www.time.com/time/asia/covers/ 501030224/army.html >.

activities, and small economic endeavors to 'skate by.'⁶⁷ Thus, North Korea has maintained a 'Cold War in Miniature' on the Korean peninsula, even as the rest of the world has moved on.⁶⁸ While it would be convenient to assume such a condition no longer exists, like the US during the days of tension with the Soviet Union, even as engagement occurs, Cold War tensions and paradigms will continue to exist on the Korean peninsula until North Korea makes significant policy changes.

There have been other issues that have caused controversy between the governments in Seoul and Washington since mid-2004. President Bush signed the North Korean Human Rights Act into law during the fall of 2004, which will allow Washington to provide up to 24 million dollars a year to support programs promoting human rights and democracy in the North. Reportedly, concerns mounted in South Korea that the new law might trigger a mass exodus from the North.⁶⁹ The signing of the law caused some discord in South Korea, mostly among the Roh-supporting Uri party. While the Blue House remained silent at the time of the bill signing, several Uri party members in the South Korean National Assembly were highly critical of the bill, criticizing it as 'interference in North Korea's internal affairs.'⁷⁰ Another key 'misunderstanding' arose when US officials remarked during December of 2004, that North Korea needed to undergo 'Regime Transformation.'⁷¹ Commenting on the remarks made by US officials, South Korean Unification Minister Chung Dong-young stated, 'We do not oppose North Korea's regime transformation. Yet, the difference between the Korean and the US governments is the methodology', further stating, '… What is sure is that external pressures have no effect on North Korea's regime.'⁷²

Based on the examples of recent policy differences between Washington and Seoul, it is clear that the approaches these two allies have been taking to dealing with

---

67 See Marcus Noland, 'North Korea and the South Korean Economy', paper presented to Roh government transition team, Seoul Korea, February 24, 2003, available at <http://www.iie.com/publications/papers/paper.cfm?ResearchID=242>.

68 David L. Asher, 'The North Korean Criminal State, its Ties to Organized Crime, and the Possibility of WMD Proliferation', remarks presented to the Counter-Proliferation Strategy Group, Woodrow Wilson Center, Washington DC, October 21, 2005, available at <http://www.nautilus.org/fora/security/0502Asher.html>.

69 'Bush Signs North Korean Human Rights Act of 2004', *Chosun Ilbo*, October 19, 2004, available at <http://english.chosun.com/w21data/html/news/200410/200410190009.html>.

70 'What Do the Government, Uri Party Think About the Passing of the NK Human Rights Act?' *Chosun Ilbo*, September 29, 2004, available at <http://english.chosun.com/w21data/html/news/200409/200409290033.html>.

71 Seung-Ryun Kim, 'The US to 'Induce Transformation of North Korea', *Donga Ilbo*, December 8, 2004, available at <http://english.donga.com/srv/service.php3?bicode=060000&biid=2004120985558>.

72 Hyong-gwon Pu, 'North Korea Should Transform Its Regime By Itself', *Donga Ilbo*, December 24, 2004, available at <http://english.donga.com/srv/service.php3?bicode=050000&biid=2004122596218>.

North Korea have often been polarized from both an ideological and a methodological perspective. To their credit, both governments have spent a great deal of time and effort to resolve their differences, in both their foreign policies toward North Korea, and the military alliance issues discussed earlier. Nevertheless, there can be no doubt that these differences, sometimes very intense differences since mid-2004, have had an effect on the way the US has been able to deal diplomatically with North Korea regarding the nuclear issue.

Breakthrough's in the Six-Party Talks: Challenges for the Road Ahead

On September 19, 2005, a 'breakthrough' appeared to occur in the six-party talks. North Korea agreed to abandon its nuclear weapons and programs in exchange for economic assistance, security pledges from the US, and more 'international respectability.' The deal will reportedly involve the US eventually building a light-water reactor for North Korea in exchange for complete dismantlement of its nuclear program.[73] According to South Korean Unification Minister Chung Dong-young, it was his active efforts in September, several meetings between key US officials and South Korean officials, and active engagement with Kim Jong-Il that led to what eventually would be a major breakthrough.[74] While no specific time frame was adapted at the time, the agreement reached certainly was the most hopeful since the nuclear confrontation began during the fall of 2002.

While the agreement certainly indicated that the six-party talks were moving in the right direction, major challenges continue to exist. The largest challenge will, of course, be the transparent dismantlement of an HEU program that remains highly controversial. On 19 September when a South Korean government official was asked by a reporter if 'enriched uranium will be included in the nuclear programs to be scrapped by North Korea', the senior government officials replied, 'It says all nuclear weapons and existing nuclear programs in the agreement.'[75]

Indeed, verification of the dismantlement of the HEU and other programs will be extremely important in carrying out the agreement with the US, as Chief US Negotiator Christopher Hill stated (on September 20, 2005, immediately following the talks), 'verification is the key element of this agreement.'[76] This statement was

---

73 Brian Lee, 'North Agrees to Give Up its Nuclear Works, *Joongang Ilbo*, September 20, 2005, available at <http://joongangdaily.joins.com/200509/19/200509192255503579900 090209021.html >.

74 'Chung Broke Deadlock in North's Nuclear Crisis', *Joongang Ilbo*, October 4, 2005, available at <http://service.joins.com/asp/print_article_english.asp?aid=2625262&esectcode =e_special&title=Chung+broke+deadlock+in+North's+nuclear+crisis >.

75 'Seoul Saved Six-Party Talks: Unification Minister', *Chosun Ilbo*, September 19, 2005, available at <http://english.chosun.com/w21data/html/news/200509/200509190024. html>.

76 Brian Lee, 'Details Could Stir Controversies', *Joongang Ilbo*, September 20, 2005, available at <http://service.joins.com/asp/>.

further re-enforced by another senior US official on 5 October 2005, when Assistant Secretary of State for Arms Control Stephen G. Rademaker said North Korea would need to scrap both its plutonium and uranium nuclear programs to meet its obligations under the accord signed with the US at the six-party talks in Beijing.[77] As Henry Sokolski, Executive Director of the Nonproliferation Policy Education Center, and former Deputy for Nonproliferation Policy in the Office of the Secretary of Defense (from 1989–93) has said, 'There's no good way to locate Kim's nukes using special technology. Inspectors will have to ask the regime to learn more, and Kim is sure to demand that the US make concessions for every answer. In this game, Pyongyang's deck will always be larger than ours.'[78]

More challenges were encountered in the six-party talks when they again resumed during November of 2005. North Korean officials demanded that the US release frozen assets of firms suspected of weapons proliferation and stop accusing Pyongyang of counterfeiting US money. The accusation referred to sanctions imposed by Washington on eight North Korean companies accused of being fronts for the sale of missiles and WMD. The companies are barred from doing business with US citizens or companies, and any of their assets under US jurisdiction are frozen. Washington has also formally accused the North Koreans of large-scale counterfeiting of $100 bills.[79]

The concerns of the US regarding Pyongyang's illicit activities are not new, and they appear to be legitimate. North Korea's illegal activities include not only counterfeiting and proliferation, but a highly lucrative heroin and methamphetamine drug trade that Japanese officials estimated in 2003 accounted for 43 percent of the Japanese 'meth' market.[80] Revenues from illegal drugs are estimated to be as high as $1 billion annually.[81] During the fall of 2005, the US Department of the Treasury designated Banco Delta Asia in Macao as a 'primary money laundering concern', citing several illegal activities such as counterfeit currency, counterfeit tobacco products, and international drug trafficking.[82] These illegal activities appear to

---

77 'US Aide Says North Must Scrap Uranium', *Joongang Ilbo*, October 5, 2005, available at <http://joongangdaily.joins.com/200510/04/200510042254161839900090209021.html>.

78 Henry Sokolski, 'Hide and Seek With Kim Jong-Il', *Nautilus Institute Policy Forum Online 05-80A*, September 29, 2005, available at <http://www.nautilus.org/fora/security/0580Sokolski.html>.

79 Kwang-tae Kim, 'N. Korea Claims US Undermine Nuke Talks', *Associated Press*, November 10, 2005, available at <http://www.adelphia.net/news/read.php?ps=1012&id=12340267>.

80 Nick Green, 'Dealing Drugs: North Korean Narcotics Trafficking', *Harvard International Review*, vol. 26, no. 1 (Spring 2004), available at <http://hir.harvard.edu/articles/1201>.

81 Ah-Young Kim, 'Targeting Pyongyang's Drug Trade Addiction', *Asia Times*, June 18, 2003, available at <http://www.atimes.com/atimes/Korea/EF19Dg04.html>.

82 'Treasury Designates Banco Delta Asia as Primary Money Laundering Concern under USA PATRIOT Act', *United States Department of Treasury Press Release*, September 15, 2005, available at <http://www.treas.gov/press/releases/js2720.htm>.

actually be generating close to the same amount of currency (or more) for Pyongyang as legal trade. Perhaps even more disturbing is evidence that money generated from these illegal activities is possibly being used to help fund North Korea's nuclear and missile programs.[83] Because of the fact that the US concern and reaction to these activities is not new, one wonders, was North Korea merely using this as an excuse for bluster and delay at the six-party talks?

Despite the fact that during November of 2005, North Korea once again raised issues that will bring about challenges to resolving its nuclear program in the six-party talks, the US now appears eager to address all of the issues necessary to bring about a successful conclusion to this problem. In fact, according to sources in the Japanese press, the US may even consider eventually discussing a peace treaty that would replace the armistice in place since the end of the Korean War in 1953.[84] In fact, as Special Envoy Joseph DeTrani stated during November of 2005, the US is ready to match North Korea 'word for word and action for action.' He also remarked that 'nobody was asking North Korea to give up its nuclear programs before the US gives up anything.'[85] Following the round of six-party talks in November, Assistant South Korean Secretary of Foreign Affairs and Trade Song, remarked, 'Stopping the operation of the Yongbyon reactor, the most visible sign of North Korea's nuclear activities, can be a symbolic gesture, and measures (compensation) that match it, should follow.' US Assistant Secretary of State Christopher Hill also emphasized 'the sooner the better for the halt of the Yongbyon nuclear reactor.'[86]

As of the writing of this chapter, while there is hope on the horizon, many major challenges (as articulated above) remain in the six-party talks. Key among the challenges is, of course, North Korea's demand that the US build a light-water civilian reactor before all of Pyongyang's nuclear programs have been verifiably dismantled. On November 17, 2005, President George Bush remarked, 'We'll consider the light-water reactor at the appropriate time – the appropriate time is after they have verifiably given up their nuclear weapons and/or programs.' President Roh supported this statement by saying, 'that a nuclear-armed North Korea will not be tolerated', adding that, 'we have no disagreement at all that this issue must be resolved.'[87] Thus, while the statement issued during the six-party talks of September of 2005 articulated in principle that North Korea would abandon its nuclear weapons – all of its nuclear

---

83 See Raphael F. Perl, 'Drug Trafficking and North Korea: Issues for US Policy', *CRS Report for Congress*, Congressional Research Service, Washington, DC, December 5, 2003, available at <http://www.fas.org/sgp/crs/row/RL32167.pdf>.

84 'US Mulls Team to Discuss Korea Peace Treaty', *Chosun Ilbo*, November 2, 2005, available at <http://english.chosun.com/w21data/html/news/200511/200511020027.html>.

85 'US Vows to Match N. Korea Action for Action', *Chosun Ilbo*, November 3, 2005, available at <http://english.chosun.com/w21data/html/news/200511/200511030015.html>.

86 Young-Gun Lee, 'Outlook Uncertain as Six-Party Talks End', *Donga Ilbo*, November 12, 2005, available at <http://english.donga.com/srv/service.php3?bicode=050000&biid=2005111283758>.

87 Peter Baker and Anthony Faille, 'US, S. Korea Find Unity against North's Nuclear Arms Program', *Washington Post*, November 17, 2005.

weapons – in return for economic incentives and security guarantees, 'the devil is in the details,' details that will have to address how verification of dismantlement will occur, exactly what the security guarantees and economic incentives will be, and how 'each step will match each step.' In addition, North Korea's newly raised issue of US economic sanctions must be resolved in a way that is satisfactory for both Washington and Seoul. These are all daunting and large-scale challenges, but as of the writing of this chapter, they do appear to be surmountable.

Washington's Answer to the Nuclear Confrontation 2002–2005: How Successful?

Before examining the current policy in Washington regarding Pyongyang's nuclear program, it is important to understand the reasons why there are such concerns regarding its existence. There are three things that the North Koreans can do which will cause both regional instability and pose a national security threat to the US. First, Pyongyang could test a nuclear weapon. Eric Heginbotham, the North Korea Project Director at the Council on Foreign Relations stated during February of 2005, that if Pyongyang did this, '… it would strengthen the hand of hardliners here in the US, and would really bring a lot of pressure on China and South Korea, perhaps, to bring North Korea, at a minimum, to bring them to the UN Security Council.'[88] The second important fear is, of course, that North Korea would in the near future be able to weaponize an HEU warhead on a missile capable of hitting US forces or allies in the region (a missile such as the No Dong).[89] Third, and perhaps most importantly, is the very real fear that North Korea would proliferate nuclear weapons and/or technology to rogue states or terrorists. Pyongyang already has a track record of proliferation of missiles to rogue states.[90] In fact, reports surfaced during 2004 that Iran had dispatched three groups to North Korea for the purpose of acquiring 'nuclear knowledge.'[91]

To date, the primary US foreign policy initiative to deal with the 'testing of nukes' issue has been to use the six-party talks in attempting to bring about 'CVID.' Some

---

88 Eleanor Hall, 'Interview: Expert Says North Korea Statement Should Not Be Taken at Face Value', *ABC Online*, February 11, 2005, available at <http://www.abc.net.au/worldtoday/content/2005/s1300969.htm>.

89 Randall Parker, 'Pakistan Buys North Korean Missiles', *ParaPundit.com*, March 31, 2003, available at <http://www.parapundit.com/archives/001086.html>.

90 See Joby Warrick, 'North Korea Shops Stealthily for Nuclear Arms Gear', *Washington Post*, August 15, 2003, available at <http://www.washingtonpost.com/ac2/wp-dyn?pagename=article&node=&contentID>. See also: Joby Warrick, 'On North Korean Freighter, a Hidden Missile Factory', *Washington Post*, August 13, 2003. See also 'Syrians With Secret CBW Material on Train that Exploded?', *IMRA.com*, May 15, 2004, available at <http://www/imra.org.il/story.php3?id=20828>. See also 'Source Notes Syrian Technicians Killed in Yongch'on Train Explosion', *Tokyo Sankei Shimbum*, May 7, 2004.

91 Soon-Taek Kwon, 'Iran Visited North Korea and Learned Nuclear Technology', *Donga Ilbo*, August 11, 2004, available at <http://english.donga.com/srv/service.php3?biid=2004081295858>.

have said this was very dangerous, as it prolongs the time during which Pyongyang can develop more weapons. Kenneth Quinones, the director of the Korea Program at the International Center in Washington remarked on this during a 2003 *PBS Forum* saying, 'I think the problem here is that the Bush administration's strategy is essentially both allowing the North Koreans to continue development of their weapons, while on the other hand, the heated rhetoric that comes out of Washington tends to play into the hands of North Korea's hard-line advisors...' During the same forum, North Korean expert and former Georgetown professor Victor Cha commented on why the US should pursue a more hard-line strategy in dealing with Pyongyang, stating in part, 'I would argue that that was once tried before, in 1994. And apparently was not the case that the North Koreans wanted to stay nuclear free.'[92] The ramifications of the six-party talks also have relevance to the second key concern Washington has regarding North Korea's nuclear program – arming a missile that can threaten the region. While it is true that development can occur while the talks remain bogged down, I believe a legitimate argument can also be made that, because of the regional arms race that the arming of such a missile would probably create, it is extremely important to ensure that the nuclear/missile program be transparently dismantled – otherwise, it could be used for the brinkmanship that past precedent has shown North Korea is more than willing to use as a tool of foreign policy.

Getting to the third key concern regarding North Korea's nuclear program, proliferation, Washington has made steps with key allies during 2004 to counter such a threat. The US-led Proliferation Security Initiative (PSI) is a program that Washington is now actively involved in with several allies (including Japan and Australia) in the region. PSI is set up to deny the trafficking of WMD, primarily through maritime means. During October of 2004, a large exercise was conducted (and televised by several news groups) in Japan, code named 'Team Samurai.' Though North Korea was never explicitly mentioned during the exercise, it was clear that they remain the primary threat when it comes to proliferation of WMD, and the main target.[93] While the PSI is certainly not perfect, it does take an important step in seeking to keep North Korea from proliferating nuclear weapons or technology. It also sends a clear message to Pyongyang that the US and her allies will continue to take active measures to eliminate proliferation of WMD – even as Pyongyang moves to take measures to eliminate the North Korean nuclear program.

---

92 'Nuclear Challenge: A News Hour With Jim Lehrer Transcript', *PBS Online News Hour*, August 29, 2003, available at <http://www.pbs.org/newshour/bb/asia/july-dec03/nkorea_8-29.html>.

93 James Brooke, 'US-Led Naval Exercise Sends Clear Message to North Korea', *New York Times*, October 27, 2004, available at <http://www.nytimes.com/2004/10/27/international/asia/27bolton.html?8bl>.

Conclusion

Despite much of the rhetoric that is often reflected in the press, it is clear that the North Korean nuclear confrontation can only be solved through diplomacy. Despite the paranoid behavior in Pyongyang, the current administration in Washington has stated on numerous occasions that the US has no intention of attacking or invading North Korea.[94] Indeed, while there have been disagreements between Washington and Seoul regarding the methodology and politics of dealing with North Korea, both sides agree that peaceful negotiation through the six-party process is currently the best way to convince Pyongyang that its nuclear program is bad for the Korean peninsula and the region. The Presidents of South Korea and the US both reaffirmed this in a telephone conversation during February of 2005.[95]

The recent February 2005 disclosure regarding nuclear weapons, and the 'chest pounding' by Pyongyang in state-run media during the six-party talks of November 2005, points to the fact that resolving the nuclear issue is a slow, difficult process that is exacerbated by the fact that Washington is dealing with one of the most paranoid and unique rogue states in the world. As North Korea begins to dismantle its nuclear program programs, other challenges are likely to emerge that have not even yet been discussed as of the writing of this chapter. What is clear from past precedent is that North Korea has a track record of behavior that has not led to an atmosphere of trust when it comes to negotiations. Only through a transparent initiative that leads to complete, verifiable dismantlement of its nuclear program, will North Korea be able to ease the current environment of tension that exists in the region.

Once all nuclear programs are dismantled in a transparent manner, other issues will need to be resolved before the Korean peninsula and the region can truly exist in an environment of peace and stability. North Korea will need to halt production and proliferation of its long-range missiles. Pyongyang will need to take steps to eliminate its illicit money-making activities such as manufacture and distribution of heroin and methamphetamines, as well as the distribution of counterfeit US dollars and cigarettes. And, of course, North Korea will eventually need to address the issue of what to do about its large, forward-deployed conventional military forces, arrayed in formations that are prepared to wreck havoc and destruction on Seoul and other key areas in South Korea. As these issues are resolved, the Korean peninsula can look to a future of peace, prosperity, and eventual peaceful unification.

---

94 Kang In-sun, 'Powell Refutes US Has Hostile Intent Toward North Korea', *Chosun Ilbo*, December 19, 2004, available at <http://english.chosun.com/w21data/html/news/200412/200412190032.html>.

95 Choi Hoon and Park Shin-hong, 'Bush, Roh Agree to Push Six-Party Talks', *Joongang Ilbo*, February 7, 2005, available at <http://joongangdaily.joins.com/200502/06/200502062137351679900090309031.html>.

Chapter 7

US–DPRK Relations: The Nuclear Issue

Edward A. Olsen

The US and North Korea have had a troubled relationship since the creation of the Democratic People's Republic of Korea (DPRK) September 9, 1948, in the wake of the US-backed creation of the Republic of Korea (ROK) on August 15, 1948 and three preceding years of increasing tensions within the Korean nation divided into two post-World War II occupation zones. Since the 1948 turning point US–DPRK relations were worsened in the course of the bitter Korean War, the divided peninsula's front line role throughout the Cold War, and North Korea's pursuit of an assertive geo-political agenda that made the DPRK an anachronistic remnant of the Cold War in the post-Cold War era.[1] For the US the DPRK was one of many strategic adversaries, but a particularly nasty one because of its hostile attitude, dictatorial rigidity, and opaque qualities that made it difficult to understand and deal with. From North Korea's Marxist perspective in principle the US epitomized an imperial threat to everything the DPRK represented and in practice posed a tangible military threat to the DPRK's very existence.

The United States and the Two Koreas

In this sense the adversarial nature of US–DPRK relations was distinctly imbalanced. While North Korea was part of an international milieu of threats posed to US national interests that had to be taken very seriously by Washington, it was not a threat to the US's literal existence. On the other hand, the US's adversarial threats to North Korea were far more profound, causing genuine fear and hatred of Americans who shaped US policy and who served in the US armed forces, and focusing North Korean animosity toward the US in a very harsh manner.[2] To be sure both the US and North Korea were reacting to each other's geo-political posture. This accounts for the imbalance in that the US's position was at the center of the non-communist camp of the Cold War and well beyond the military reach of North Korea. Conversely

---

1   The author assessed the nature and consequences of the Korean nation's division in depth in *Korea, The Divided Nation* (Westport, CT: Greenwood/Praeger Publishers, 2005).
2   The author examined the roots of North Korea's foreign policy in the inaugural issue of the first US scholarly journal focusing on North Korea in 'US–North Korea: Foreign Policy Dilemmas', *North Korea Review*, vol. 1, no. 1 (Fall 2005), pp. 63–75.

North Korea was on the margins of the Communist camp's military power base and was very vulnerable to the US's ability to project ground, naval, and air power. This caused North Korea to pay far more attention to the threats posed to it by the US than the US had to do regarding North Korea. Over time this set of circumstances led North Korea to escalate the tense relations by raising its nuclear agenda and by trying to inculcate anxiety about the North Korean threat potential among US leaders which could be used by the DPRK to strengthen its diplomatic arsenal by inculcating US anxieties through concern about the sanity of North Korean leaders. At the base of this North Korean reactive approach was its understanding of the value of 'calculated irrationality' within its diplomatic brinkmanship designed to utilize US anxieties as an instrument to induce mediation in order to avoid irrationally reckless acts.[3] Against this background, North Korea's expanded experimentation with its nuclear weapons option in the post-Cold War years, knowing full well that the US had blocked the ROK from pursuing that option during the Park Chung-Hee administration,[4] caused a pronounced intensification of US–DPRK frictions.[5]

From a US perspective, tensions surrounding North Korea escalate unpredictably on an almost daily basis. Much of this volatile situation can be ascribed to Pyongyang's willingness to engage in a reckless combination of provocative acts and rhetorical tirades that constitute its infamous diplomatic brinkmanship. North Korea's willingness to make pointed use of its nuclear option in a high-level US–DPRK diplomatic meeting in October 2002 seems to have been motivated by a desire to reinforce its peculiar brand of strategic and psychological deterrence.[6] The Kim Jong-Il government was further emboldened in subsequent months by the combination of two sets of circumstances. First, there were favorable political developments in South Korea – in the form of the December 2002 election of President Roh Moo-

---

3   The author explored the motives of calculated irrationality and its goal of mediation in 'The Goal of North Korean Brinkmanship: Mediation', *Strategic Insights*, vol. 3, no. 3 (March 2004), available online at <www.ccc.nps.navy.mil>.

4   For background on the US's role in blocking South Korea's nuclear option, see Selig Harrison, Chapter 20, 'South Korea and Nuclear Weapons', *Korean Endgame: A Strategy for Reunification and US Disengagement* (Princeton, NJ: Princeton University Press, 2002).

5   These frictions have been assessed in a diverse spectrum of analyses, see Michael J. Mazarr, *North Korea and the Bomb: A Case Study in Nonproliferation* (New York: St. Martins, 1995); Young-whan Kihl and Peter Hayes, eds, *Peace and Security in Northeast Asia: The Nuclear Issue and the Korean Peninsula* (Armonk, NY: M.E. Sharpe, 1997); Leon V. Segal, *Disarming Strangers: Nuclear Diplomacy with North Korea* (Princeton, NJ: Princeton University Press, 1998); James Clay Moltz and Alexandre Mansourov, eds, *The North Korean Nuclear Program* (New York: Routledge, 2000); Victor D. Cha and David C. Kang, *Nuclear North Korea: A Debate of Engagement Strategies* (New York: Columbia University Press, 2003); and Jasper Becker, *Rogue Regime: Kim Jong Il and the Looming Threat of North Korea* (Oxford: Oxford University Press, 2005).

6   For coverage of that meeting, see Doug Struck, 'US Plays Down Talks with N. Korean Officials', *Washington Post*, October 6, 2002; and Howard W. French, 'US Envoy Angers North Korea', *New York Times*, October 8, 2002.

Hyun, who strongly favors ROK engagement of the DPRK and took office riding a wave of strident anti-Americanism.[7] Those attitudes have complex roots. Anti-US sentiments have surfaced in the past as a result of popular reactions to periodic incidents involving the behavior of US forces in Korea causing the US–ROK alliance's legal provisions to be adjusted occasionally. Past US policy toward South Korean human rights standards and economic protectionism, which contributed to ROK political and market reforms, also exacerbated anti-US attitudes. While most of those critical attitudes were spontaneous, reflecting a cultural gap in US–ROK relations, there also were instances in which the ROK government manipulated anti-US sentiments for its own purposes. Against that historical background, in the more contemporary era, South Korean society's attitudes toward the US were influenced by generational change in which younger South Koreans who lacked first hand adult experiences with either the Korean War or the Cold War proved to be far more critical of the current Bush administration's hawkish post-9/11 worldview. In turn, this set the stage for Roh Moo-Hyun's political campaign for ROK president that appealed to that younger generation as its base. The second circumstances were the US's commitments within its war on terrorism and related tensions in the Middle East that stretched US strategic resources. South Koreans and other allies became increasingly anxious about the ability of the US to deliver on multiple strategic commitments simultaneously. Against this political and geo-political background, North Korea saw an opportunity.

Pyongyang proceeded to do its utmost to make the international community, with the US in the forefront as the sole superpower, pay more attention to North Korea's dire economic straits by taking its geo-political posture more seriously. The DPRK has been in bad shape for years, causing many foreign observers to anticipate its collapse[8] – even as more hopeful South Koreans viewed these conditions as an opportunity to reach out to their fellow Koreans in an attempt to induce inter-Korean reconciliation through the provision of economic assistance that would, in turn, lead to the transformation of Pyongyang's policies. This was the basis of President Kim

---

7   For coverage of that wave, see Choong-nam Kim, 'Bush's America is Getting a Bad Name', *International Herald Tribune*, September 26, 2002; Robert Marquand, 'Anti-US Voices Surge in Streets of a Major Asian Ally', *Christian Science Monitor*, December 16, 2002; and Peter S. Goodman and Joo hee Cho, 'Anti-US Sentiment Deepens in S. Korea', *Washington Post*, January 9, 2003.

8   For journalistic assessments of North Korean socio-economic problems and North Korean efforts to rectify them, see Jim Mann, 'US Watches North Korea for Signs of Collapse', *Los Angeles Times*, February 12, 1996; and John Pomfret, 'Reforms Turn Disastrous for North Korea', *Washington Post*, January 27, 2003. For scholarly assessments of that issue, see Nicholas Eberstadt, *The End of North Korea* (Washington, DC: The AEI Press, 1999); Marcus Noland, *Avoiding the Apocalypse: The Future of the Two Koreas* (Washington, DC: Institute for International Economics, 2000); and Marcus Noland, *Korea After Kim Jong Il* (Washington, DC: Institute for International Economics, January 2004).

Dae-Jung's innovative 'sunshine policy' approach to inter-Korean issues.[9] Despite some sporadic inter-Korean accomplishments, not much of genuine substance was being done to reduce US–DPRK tensions on the nuclear front drawing on the legacy of the Clinton administration's negotiations with North Korea. Given the Kim Jong-Il regime's odd world view based on its *juche* ideology,[10] Pyongyang decided to maximize its leverage amidst the multiple pressures upon its US foes by upping the ante in the form of several cage rattling endeavors.

From late 2002 through early 2003, North Korea consciously pushed the envelope. With one eye on the US's decision to withdraw from the ABM treaty, Pyongyang announced its plans to withdraw from the Nuclear Non-proliferation Treaty, inflaming tensions surrounding its violations of the 1994 Geneva Agreed Framework.[11] Those tensions were exacerbated by the DPRK's ability to make a credible case that the US also had opted to delay its reciprocal commitments to supply fuel oil and light-water reactors.[12] Then, with an eye on the Bush administration's development of a controversial post-9/11 preemptive strategic doctrine that diminishes the US's reliance on the principles of deterrence, Pyongyang, as noted below, claimed the same prerogative. Also, knowing full well that the armistice that had halted the Korean War had an ambiguous legacy in South Korea and that South Koreans were still hopeful that an ROK–DPRK 'Agreement on Reconciliation, *Non-aggression*, Exchanges & Cooperation' [emphasis added] that went into effect in 1992 is fully viable,[13] Pyongyang pushed the non-aggression pact theme vis-à-vis the US. North Korean elites had to know this idea would resonate positively among South Korea's progressive leaders. Given the long-standing US aversion to unenforceable international agreements to outlaw war that skeptics in the US consider to be utopian, Pyongyang presumably knew this option was a non-starter for the United States, but pushed it in order to embarrass Washington conservative decision makers and complicate US relations with Seoul's more idealistic liberal leaders. This was a plausible approach for North Korea because the US aversion to non-aggression

---

9 For contextual background on this policy, see Moon Chung-in and David I. Steinberg, eds, *Kim Dae-Jung Government and Sunshine Policy: Promises and Challenges* (Washington, DC and Seoul: Georgetown University Press and Yonsei University Press, 1999); and Norman D. Levin and Yong-sup Han, *Sunshine in Korea; The South Korean Debate over Policies toward North Korea* (Santa Monica, CA: RAND, 2002).

10 For a solid appraisal of that ideology, see Han S. Park, 'The Nature and Evolution of *Juche Ideology*', in Han S. Park, ed., *North Korea: Ideology, Politics, Economy* (Englewood Cliffs, NJ: Prentice-Hall, 1996).

11 For coverage of North Korea's actions, see Seth Mydans, 'North Korea Says It Is Withdrawing from Arms Treaty', *New York Times*, January 10, 2003; and 'North Korea Announces to Withdraw from NPT', *Korean Unification Bulletin*, February 2003.

12 For coverage of North Korea's responses, see Paul Shin, 'N. Korea Threatens to Break Nuclear Deal', *Washington Post*, August 14, 2002; and Doug Struck, 'For North Korea, US Is Violator of Accords', *Washington Post*, October 21, 2002.

13 For background on that 'agreement', see Don Oberdorfer, *The Two Koreas, A Contemporary History* (Reading: Addison-Wesley, 1997).

agreements tends to arouse suspicions throughout the international community where such agreements are perceived positively. Moreover, if the US eventually moves toward normalizing its bilateral relations with North Korea or toward overall engagement with the DPRK as part of US support for Korean reunification, a non-aggression agreement is likely to be essential in ways that are encouraged by South Korea's policies.

Escalating Tensions

All of these maneuvers were compounded by a series of North Korean military provocations – including violations of the Demilitarized Zone (DMZ) air space, missile tests into the East Sea, and pursuit of a US reconnaissance plane in international air space.[14] While such provocations are not surprising and can be perceived as part of North Korea's assertive approach to defense, they nonetheless intensify the tensions. Most observers of North Korea anticipate these types of military provocation will continue and may well be escalated. While it is clear that North Korea's approach to international affairs is motivated by its economic vulnerabilities[15] that are undermining its strategic assets, those weaknesses do not prevent it from being a major threat to stability in Asia via such brinkmanship. As such it poses an enormous challenge to US policy in the region.

Arguably the greatest evolving danger is North Korea's perception that contemporary US strategic policy is substantially in the hands of neo-conservatives who intend to deal with North Korea after achieving 'regime change' in Iraq – either by toppling the DPRK via sanctions or via preemptive military strikes aimed at eliminating its nuclear capabilities. The accuracy of this perception is debatable, but North Korean analysts who follow the US policy debate in the major media will have found prominent examples of US neo-conservatives advocating a more assertive US policy toward North Korea.[16] North Korean analysts of US policy making, who

---

14 The US's responses to a series of North Korean actions was tempered, see Howard LaFranchi, 'Why US Is Reacting Quietly to N. Korea's Provocations', *Christian Science Monitor*, March 5, 2003. That included responses to the act most pointedly targeted at the United States: Bradley Graham and Glenn Kessler, 'N. Korea Tails US Spy Plane', *Washington Post*, March 4, 2003; and Eric Schmitt, 'North Korea's MIGs Intercept US Jet on Spying Mission', *New York Times*, March 4, 2003.

15 The author assessed North Korea's evolving socio-economic status in the Bertelsmann Transformation Index 2005, online at <www.bertelsmann-transformation-index.de>.

16 For a cross-section of such perspectives during a formative phase of US–ROK policy making, see Ju Yong-jung, 'US Hawk [Richard Perle] Warns Not to Rule Out Military Option', *Chosun Ilbo*, December 18, 2002; Max Boot, 'Korean Crisis Reveals US War Flaws', *USA Today*, January 8, 2003; Charles Krauthammer, 'Korea Follies', *Washington Post*, January 17, 2003; and William Kristol and Robert Kagan, 'North Korea Goes South', *The Weekly Standard*, January 20, 2003. For a more authentic conservative's view of that option, see Henry S. Rowen, 'Kim Jong il Must Go', *Policy Review* (Hoover Institution) (October–November 2003).

inform the views of their leaders in Pyongyang, cannot have missed the US media's extensive coverage of neo-conservatives' impact upon US strategy toward Iraq.[17] North Korean anxieties in that regard were unlikely to have been calmed by repeated reassurances from the White House that the US 'has no intention of invading North Korea.' The more a ground force conventionally armed 'invasion' is disavowed, the more the North Koreans seem to be convinced the US has other military plans for a preemptive attack. The ways US officials state what the US will not do tends to underscore by implication to North Koreans what the DPRK fears the US may do and motivates DPRK leaders to suggest reciprocal threats. Although the details of this North Korean perspective have not received much attention in the United States, they have appeared in the press. The DPRK Foreign Ministry's Deputy Director, Ri Pyong-gap said – using the phrase noted above – 'The United States says that after Iraq, we are next, but we have our own countermeasures. Preemptive attacks are not the exclusive right of the United States.'[18] And the KCNA, North Korea's news agency, noted 'the US intention to make a preemptive strike at [North Korea's] nuclear facilities.'[19] North Korea's perceptions of US motives clearly are open to serious question, but that does not diminish their salience for the Northeast Asian threat environment.

North Korea's perceptions of US motivations and the strategic intentions of US policy makers toward the DPRK also should be taken more seriously because of the apparent impact they have had among South Koreans as a result of Pyongyang's appeals to pan-Korean solidarity. Although South Korean officials are well aware that North Korea long has sought to drive wedges between Washington and Seoul that will disrupt the US–ROK alliance's cohesiveness, and routinely discount such efforts, Pyongyang's appeals seem to be reaching a more amenable South Korean audience. Partly because of sporadic South Korean anti-American sentiments that feed ambiguity about US interests regarding Korea, and partly because of South Korean unease about the Bush administration's usage of the 'axis of evil' metaphor with attendant fears that the US will successively pursue 'regime change' in each member of the axis,[20] North Korea's message is effective among a sizable proportion of South Koreans. This does not mean that North Korea has developed an independent ability to disrupt US–ROK relations, but the DPRK has become more adept at making

---

17 For scholarly analyses of that issue, see Gary Dorrien, *Imperial Designs: Neoconservatism and the New Pax Americana* (New York: Routledge, 2004); James Mann, *The Rise of The Vulcans: The History of Bush's War Cabinet* (New York: Viking Penguin, 2004); and Jon Western, *Selling Intervention and War: The Presidency, the Media, and the American Public* (Baltimore: Johns Hopkins University Press, 2005).

18 Quoted in Jonathan Watts, 'N Korea Threatens US with First Strike', *The Guardian*, February 6, 2003.

19 Quoted in Simon Jeffery, 'North Korea: US Intends to Attack Us', *The Guardian*, March 7, 2003.

20 The author examined that aspect of US–Korea relations in detail in '"Axis of Evil": Impact on US–Korean Relations', *Korea and World Affairs*, vol. 26, no. 2 (Summer 2002), pp. 184–197.

use of South Korean reactions to aspects of US policy that many South Koreans reject as not being in Korean national interests for the entire Korean nation. Because of South Korean fears about the impact US military action against North Korea almost certainly would have on South Korea, South Koreans have become more critical of what is perceived as a US tendency toward unilateralism. Against this background, South Korea's new president, Roh Moo-Hyun, shortly before taking office observed 'Koreans should stand together, although things will get difficult when the United States bosses us around.'[21] And, after he took office, President Roh, as part of a campaign to encourage the US to pursue a bilateral dialogue process with North Korea, urged the US 'not to go too far' in its pressures to resolve the nuclear problem.[22] His first Unification Minister, Jeong Se-hyun, elaborated on that approach when he asked, 'How could the United States ignore South Korea's position and contradict it while pursuing its North Korean policy?'[23] The consequences of President Roh's approach to US–ROK alliance relations in a regional context shall be assessed below.

Because of such North Korean anxieties, and their ability to disrupt US–ROK harmony, there is great risk that North Korea will try to take advantage of the US being stretched thin as a result of the pressures created by the war in Iraq, through escalating its brinkmanship. Contemplating a provocative military step that could lead to a second front war may well be seen by Pyongyang as a way to compel the US to negotiate bilaterally on North Korea's terms. The point here is not that North Korea is seriously poised to launch a war on South Korea because the US is stretched too thin elsewhere, but that encouraging US observers of North Korean policy to think that North Korean leaders might be irrational enough to consider such an option will help the DPRK's diplomatic brinkmanship and motivate the US to pursue creative diplomacy designed to prevent such a disastrous scenario. Such circumstances, if not managed skillfully, could easily get out of control – escalating to a full-scale war that could be far more daunting than the situation in Iraq. Pyongyang will not necessarily wait until the US wraps things up in Iraq and can turn its full attention – diplomatically or militarily – to North Korea. Although the US seems poised to cope with more North Korean reckless brinkmanship in the heat of war with Iraq, Pyongyang – if diplomatic efforts do not prevail and the DPRK fears proactive US efforts for regime change – might take advantage of the US being stretched thin to use its own preemptive preemption strategy. In this sense, for many people on

---

21 Quoted in Howard W. French, 'North Korea Crisis Straining Washington's Asian Alliances', *International Herald Tribune*, February 25, 2003.

22 Quoted in Hong Soon-il, 'Pawn of Saber Rattling', *Korea Times*, March 12, 2003.

23 Quoted in Seo Hyun-jin, 'US–N.K. Tension Unlikely to Lead to War, Experts Say', *Korea Herald*, March 6, 2003. Jeong's critical statement also was quoted as, 'How can the US ignore South Korea and go against our will in pursuing its North Korean policy?' in Reuters, 'Roh's Words Reveal Gulf With Washington', *Taipei Times*, March 6, 2003.

various levels of US society, North Korea represents a profoundly dangerous threat to world peace that has stirred a serious debate within the US.[24]

One way out of this potential disaster would be for the US to recognize and accept the ways Pyongyang's bid for a bilateral dialogue process with Washington meshes with Seoul's objectives. South Korea's long-standing aspirations for regional multilateralism aimed at Korean reconciliation and reunification is predicated on providing North Korea with the same level of bilateral connections that South Korea has had for years as a result of the success of the ROK's late Cold War *nordpolitik* 'cross recognition' plan. This enabled Seoul to use its newly established bilateral ties with China and Russia to reinforce its existing ties with the US and Japan in order to strengthen multilateralism designed to induce moderation in North Korea.[25]

The origins of this conceptual framework are especially significant for the current US administration. This South Korean paradigm's roots are partially in the approach the previous (G.H.W.) Bush administration took toward post-Cold War limited multilateralism based on a foundation of bilateralism. That approach is what caused so much consternation for the Kim Dae-Jung government when Henry Kissinger, in a March 2001 *Washington Post* column, advised the current Bush administration 'Pyongyang must be convinced that the road to Washington leads through Seoul and not the other way around.'[26] Kissinger's recommendation was in keeping with past US policies of reassuring the ROK that Washington would not ignore Seoul in the US's overall Korea policies, but the way it was phrased was out of step with what Kim Dae-Jung was encouraging the US and the DPRK to do bilaterally in order to strengthen multilateralism in a manner consistent with the previous Bush administration's approach. The US approach advocated by Kissinger is contrary to how former President Kim and current President Roh Moo-Hyun visualize achieving a positive US–North Korea dialogue process intended to reduce tensions and encourage the DPRK to join in a multilateral engagement process designed to facilitate inter-Korean peaceful reconciliation. In short, a genuine solution may be 'the other way around', with improved US–DPRK relations on the nuclear front acting as a catalyst for ROK–DPRK progress on the unification front.

US–North Korea bilateral negotiations focusing on resolving the nuclear problem can be integral to broader multilateral talks fostering tension reduction and inter-

---

24 For a sense of that debate, see Selig S. Harrison, 'Did North Korea Cheat?', *Foreign Affairs*, (January/February 2005), pp. 99–110; Mitchell B. Reiss and Robert L. Gallucci, 'Red-Handed; The Truth about North Korea's Weapons Programs/Dead to Right', *Foreign Affairs*, (January/February 2005), pp. 142–145, Richard L. Garwin, 'HEU Done It', *Foreign Affairs* (March/April 2005), pp. 145–146; Selig Harrison, 'Harrison Replies', *Foreign Affairs* (March/April 2005), 146–148. For a survey of the debate's context, see Colonel David J. Bishop, 'Dismantling North Korea's Nuclear Weapons Program', *Carlisle Papers in Security Strategy* (Carlisle, PA: Strategic Studies Institute, US Army War College, April 2005).

25 The viability of the US using South Korea's approach to North Korea was assessed by the author in 'A Korean Solution to the United States' Korean Problems', *The Journal of East Asian Affairs*, vol. 17, no. 2 (Fall/Winter 2003), pp. 215–240.

26 Henry Kissinger, 'A Road through Seoul', *Washington Post*, March 6, 2000.

Korean reconciliation. North Korea continues to press for a non-aggression pact from the US, despite its 'poison pill' qualities among the intended US policy-making audience.[27] Over the longer term, North Korea hopes such a pact could yield a peace treaty to formally end the Korean War. Nonetheless, if one juxtaposes North Korea's desires for ousting a US armed presence from Korea and desires on the part of US policy makers for eliminating North Korea's threat potentials – especially its weapons of mass destruction – these desires could be grounds for a consensus providing a de facto security guarantee. In exchange for verifiable North Korean demobilization of a significant proportion of its conventional forces and elimination of its weapons of mass destruction (WMDs), the US can offer reciprocal removal of *all* US forces from Korea, enabling both sides to get what they want from each other.[28] As the US experiments with its transformation of the US armed forces in ways that will lead to cuts in US force levels in South Korea, the Bush administration should consider using such cuts as part of the US–DPRK tension reduction process aimed at resolving the nuclear issue by reducing the potentials on each side for aggression against the other side. To be sure, the North Koreans would be well aware of the US's global military power and its regional strategic presence beyond the Korean peninsula, notably in Japan, but such US force reductions in Korea would nonetheless be useful for inter-Korean negotiations and help induce better US–DPRK relations. Equally important, such a bilateral exchange will incite mutual confidence building, facilitating North Korea's regime transformation within a multilateral effort to bring North and South Korea closer together en route to national unification.

Instead of running the risks so apparent in the current environment, it would be much more prudent for the US to innovatively utilize South Korea's approach to coping with North Korea. Rather than impeding our South Korean ally's diplomatic agenda in ways that aggravate anti-Americanism among South Koreans and have contributed to a rift in US–ROK relations,[29] it would be far better if Washington adopted Seoul's approach to defusing the current round of nuclear crises and treated US–North Korean bilateral negotiations as part of the foundation for multilateralism intended to mitigate North Korea's threat potentials and be a catalyst for it to live in harmony with its neighbors.

---

27 The author explored the nuances of the 'poison pill' metaphor and US expectations about Korean failure in *Toward Normalizing US–Korea Relations, In Due Course?* (Boulder, CO: Lynne Rienner, 2002); and its expanded Korean translation: *Hanmi kwangae ui sae jipyung* [New Horizons of US–Korea Relations] (Seoul: Ingansarang Publishers, 2003).

28 As explained in a previous article that explored this option, 'A Korean Solution to the United States' Korean Problems' (op. cit.), this 'bargaining chip' approach was first raised by Kwak Tae-hwan in 'US Military-Security Policy Toward the Korean Peninsula in the 1990s', *Korean Journal of Defense Analysis*, vol. 7, no. 2 (Winter 1995), pp. 237–262.

29 For background on South Korea's discontent regarding US policy toward both Koreas, see Eric V. Larson, Norman D. Levin, Seonhae Baik and Bogdan Savych, *Ambivalent Allies? A Study of South Korean Attitudes Toward the US* (Santa Monica, CA: RAND, 2004); and David Steinberg, ed., *Korean Attitudes Toward the United States: Changing Dynamics* (Armonk, NY: M.E. Sharpe, 2005).

Sino-Korean Factors

To achieve these goals it would be useful for those who shape US policy toward North Korea's nuclear agenda to grasp the nuances behind Pyongyang's approach to brinkmanship. North Korean policy toward its nuclear option since the early 1990s has been notorious for its brinkmanship approach – using provocative acts and inflammatory rhetoric to escalate tensions in ways that either enhance Pyongyang's power or its diplomatic leverage. The August 2003 six-party talks in Beijing where North Korea's representatives overtly announced its intention to conduct a nuclear test illustrated Pyongyang's brinkmanship style. The round of talks that were revived in February 2004 raised questions about the prospects for North Korean brinkmanship. North Korea's rapid withdrawal from that round of talks and prolonged manipulation of the conditions surrounding the DPRK's re-entry into the talks exacerbated concerns about Pyongyang's use of brinkmanship.[30] This is consistent with North Korea's use of brinkmanship and may well be repeated intermittently as Pyongyang's way of using pressure to counteract US pressures. The revived six-party talks achieved conditional progress in September 2005, which permitted both Pyongyang and Washington to be confident that DPRK brinkmanship and US pressures were effective. After prolonged negotiations a 'joint statement' of the sixparties was issued on September 19.[31] As the major media's skeptical coverage in the US indicated, the agreement portended serious progress in principle on the nuclear issue for the US and on economic and energy improvement for North Korea, but it was tenuous in terms of the specific details being subject to future open-ended negotiations.[32] It also was increasingly apparent to the US media that China was playing a significant role in the six-party talks in ways that should be heeded by US officials.[33] How the 'joint statement' might be followed up in subsequent

---

30 For background on North Korea's motives to manipulate the criteria for returning to the six-party talks, see 'DPRK FM [Foreign Minister] on its Stand to Suspend its Participation in Six-party Talks for Indefinite Period', February 10, 2005, available at <http://www.kcna.co.jp>; Gordon Fairclough, 'Seoul Tries to Lure North Korea Back To Nuclear Talks', *Wall Street Journal*, May 17, 2005; Donald Kirk, 'N. Korea Plays Waiting Game on Nuclear Talks', *Christian Science Monitor*, May 20, 2005; and David E. Sanger and Thom Shanker, 'North Korea Is Reported to Hint at Nuclear Talks', *New York Times*, June 6, 2005.

31 For the text of the joint statement, see 'A 6-party Statement: The Deal and Details', (AP) *International Herald Tribune*, September 19, 2005.

32 For representative examples of that coverage, see Mark Magnier and Barbara Demick, 'N. Korea Waives Nuclear Programs', *Los Angeles Times*, September 19, 2005; Gordon Fairclough and Carla Anne Robbins, 'North Korea Vows to Give up Nuclear Programs', *Wall Street Journal*, September 20, 2005; Donald Kirk and Howard LaFranchi, 'North Korea's Agreement to Scrap its Nukes', *Christian Science Monitor*, September 20, 2005; and Thomas Omestad, 'Decoding the Pyongyang Shuffle', *US News & World Report*, October 3, 2005.

33 For example, see Michael Hirsh and Melinda Liu, 'North Korea Hold 'Em', *Newsweek*, October 3, 2005; and Peter Baker and Glenn Kessler, 'US to Push Koreans on Nuclear Program', *Washington Post*, October 5, 2005.

talks remained uncertain, but North Korea's willingness to pursue this approach demonstrated what is probably the real purpose behind DPRK brinkmanship.

While many fear North Korea's use of brinkmanship techniques is part of an aggressive stance that will lead to war, that perception is doubtful. North Korea's frequent redefinition of a nuclear brink's demarcation has another viable purpose. Pyongyang's goal is not to go over the brink, but to be pulled back from the brink. Many wonder why North Korea, given its dismal societal condition and famines that seem to augur regime collapse, behaves in a reckless manner that encourages US hard liners to contemplate regime change in this member of the 'axis of evil.' Often the conclusion reached is that this behavior is calculated to induce the US to acquiesce to North Korean blackmail: Rescue us on our terms, or else! In other words, if you do not come to your senses and do whatever is necessary to help us North Koreans recover from our failed economic policies and facilitate our participation in the international economic system in ways that will enable the DPRK to close the gap with the ROK and deal with both South Korea and China on a level of greater parity, we North Koreans will fulfill your nightmare scenarios about our geo-political insanity. In short, we North Koreans are prepared to go over the brink in ways you people in the US should do your utmost to avoid. Although that contention is plausible, and it must be factored into US calculations to the extent it draws upon South Korea's unification policy agenda, it is more likely that North Korea is motivated by a more sophisticated model of an external rescue that may pose additional problems for US policy toward all of Korea.

Pyongyang's brinkmanship does not seem to be simply a distracting tactic in a larger war-fighting strategy. Instead, it is an essential element of a strategy designed to create two results. The first result is a form of interim deterrence versus what the North Koreans perceive as US brinkmanship – the world's sole superpower applying a preemptive doctrine toward a cluster of rogue states and terrorists. This aspect of its brinkmanship is designed to compensate for North Korea's manifest weaknesses and to keep US military capabilities which have been stretched thin by over commitments[34] as off balance as possible. A plausible case can be made that North Korea has succeeded in that regard. The second result is more important for Pyongyang's view of North Korean survival, namely bringing about eventual third-party intervention. Pyongyang's goal seems to be to set the stage for external diplomatic and economic intervention that will pull the confrontational US–North Korea parties away from the brink and act as a catalyst for resolving the North–South Korean national division en route to negotiated reunification. Increasingly,

---

34 North Korean analysts who follow the evolution of US security policy and the criticism it has generated within the US are presumably familiar with analyses such as: Paul Kennedy, *The Rise and Fall of Great Powers: Economic Change and Military Conflict from 1500 to 2000* (New York: Random House, 1987); Chalmers Johnson, *Blowback: The Costs and Consequences of American Empire* (New York: Owl Books/Henry Holt, 2000); and Clyde Prestowitz, *Rogue Nation: American Unilateralism and the Failure of Good Intentions* (New York: Basic Books, 2003).

the most likely candidate to fill that international role is China because of its ties to both Koreas, its ability to play such a role in Asian regional affairs, and – under certain circumstances – its means to persuade US policy makers that this would be in the US's best interests. While a strong case can and should be made regarding US policy options that the US should try to play the major role as the facilitator of Korean reconciliation and unification as the means to resolve the nuclear dilemma as part of the peaceful negotiations process,[35] because the US today is unwilling and unprepared to play that role it should be more innovative in how it might utilize another country in that role – namely China.

North Korea's use of brinkmanship is a perverse way of facilitating an amicable negotiated resolution of North Korea's myriad problems as part of an inter-Korean confidence-building process that will lead to coexistence and incremental reunification. North Koreans are well aware that the younger generation of their fellow Koreans in South Korea is avid supporters of such peaceful reconciliation processes. What both Koreas require is a mutual benefactor that is not perceived as currently tilting toward either Korea geo-politically. Despite China's Cold War ties to North Korea, today the People's Republic of China (PRC) fits that balanced bill more than any other country – including the US.

This was well illustrated by the visit of one of the PRC's top leaders, Wu Bangguo, to Pyongyang in October 2003 where he conducted negotiations with Kim Jong-Il to support reviving the six-party talks.[36] The later announcement of rescheduled multilateral talks in Beijing was welcomed by Seoul. Not many South Koreans think a comparably high-level US official would be tasked with such a mission. That perception is reinforced by South Korean understanding of the sometimes ambiguous relations between North Korea and the PRC, due to ROK–PRC ties, that can be advantageous to Beijing, but also used by Pyongyang on occasion.[37] The PRC's inter-Korean leverage also is demonstrated by China's rise to the status of the ROK's largest economic partner, South Korea's ranking as the PRC's second-ranking foreign economic partner, and by China's encouragement of the DPRK to emulate the brand of capitalist reforms that Chinese communists have so successfully embraced. China's emergence as a major player in the overall economy of the Asia region strengthens its role vis-à-vis both Koreas and puts China back into its traditional hierarchical role regarding Korea. This stature reflects the entire world's interest in the rapid rise of China.[38] As positive as this can be, it also raises Korean

---

35 The author explores that option more extensively in several analyses cited elsewhere in this chapter.

36 Anthony Faiola, 'N. Korea Agrees to Resume Nuclear Talks', *Washington Post*, October 31, 2003.

37 For background on the PRC–DPRK peculiar relationship, see Andrew Scobell, *China and North Korea: From Comrades-In-Arms To Allies At Arm's Length* (Carlisle, PA: Strategic Studies Institute, US Army War College, 2004).

38 For analyses of China's growing role regarding Korea, see Quangsheng Zhao, 'China and the Korean Peace Process', in Tae-hwan Kwak and Seung-ho Joo, eds, *The Korean Peace Process and the Four Powers* (Aldershot: Ashgate Publishing, 2003); Victor D. Cha and

concerns in both Koreas that a resurgent Chinese 'big brother' may try to throw its weight around at Korea's expense. Such Korean concerns became very evident when China used its position on the legacy of the ancient Goguryeo kingdom's Chinese versus Korean roots as a way to send a signal to both Koreas about who ranks where in Sino-Korean relations.[39] Nonetheless, China is in an excellent position to mentor North Korean reforms, be a catalyst for inter-Korean reconciliation, and do many things to or for Korea that the US is either unwilling or unable to do.

Japan–Korea Factors

China's position vis-à-vis both Koreas is strengthened further by its relations with Japan and the US, and their alliance. From Korean vantage points (North and South) Sino-Japanese relations loom largest because of Japan's proximity, their history, and Japan's perceived influence over US policy toward Asia. With that relationship in the background, Koreans have tried to make the best of Japan's policies toward each Korea.[40] On balance, South Korean relations with Japan have been, and are, better than North Korea's, which have been made worse since the end of the Cold War by Japan's fears of the DPRK's nuclear and missile potentials and Tokyo's readiness to cooperate with Washington in constraining North Korea.[41] As Japan's role in US–Japan policies toward North Korea underscored China's constructive intermediary role between the two Koreas, it also called attention to the parallels between Sino-

---

David C. Kang, 'The Korea Crisis', *Foreign Policy* (May–June 2003); and Lee Guen, 'The Rise of China and Korea's China Policy', in Kokubun Ryosei and Wang Jisi, eds, *The Rise of China and a Changing East Asia Order* (Tokyo: Japan Center for International Exchange, 2004). For broader perspectives on China's growing stature, see Ross Terrill, *The New Chinese Empire: And What It Means for the United States* (New York: Basic Books, 2003); and Clyde Prestowitz, *Three Billion New Capitalists :The Great Shift of Wealth and Power to the East* (New York: Basic Books, 2005).

39 For examples of Korean reactions to China's stance on Goguryeo, see Seo Hyun-jin, 'Seoul Claims Firm Stance on Goguryeo', *Korea Herald*, January 29, 2004; Kim Tong-hyung, 'Culture Minister Warns against Goguryeo Frenzy', *KOREA Now*, January 24, 2004; and Choe Kwang-sik, 'What Lies behind China's "Northeast Project"?', *KOREA Now*, February 7, 2004.

40 For background on each relationship, see Seongho Sheen, 'Japan–South Korea Relations: Slowly Lifting the Burden of History?', Honolulu: Occasional Paper Series, Asia-Pacific Center for Security Studies, October 2003; and David Fouse, 'Japan's Post-Cold War North Korea Policy: Hedging Toward Autonomy?', Honolulu: Occasional Paper Series, Asia-Pacific Center for Security Studies, February 2004.

41 For assessments of Japan's increasingly hard-line posture toward North Korea, see 'Japan and North Korea; Not Yet Friends', *Economist*, September 21, 2002; Kaneko Takahara, 'Diet Clears Bill to Hit North Korea with Sanctions', *Japan Times*, February 10, 2004; Sebastian Moffett, 'Japan's Tough North Korea Stance Bears Fruit', *Wall Street Journal*, May 24, 2004; Barbara Demick, 'N. Korea Issues Threat to Japan', *Los Angeles Times*, September 24, 2004; and 'Japan and North Korea; Insult and Injury', *Economist*, December 18, 2004.

Japanese historical and territorial frictions[42] and similar frictions between Japan and South Korea.[43] Because Japan–ROK frictions over textbook issues and the Dokdo/Takeshima islands raised uncomfortable questions for Seoul about the interaction of the US–ROK and US–Japan alliances' roles in preserving East Asian stability in the face of North Korean brinkmanship, South Korea indirectly benefited from the global attention to Sino-Japanese tensions that deflected attention from Japan–Korea frictions.[44] This enabled Seoul to work more closely with Beijing in putting pressure on Tokyo, but that closeness also bolstered the PRC's role as an intermediary in inter-Korean affairs.[45]

South Korea's relations with China's role in inter-Korean affairs have been reinforced by the ROK's problems within the triangular security ties between the US and its two Northeast Asian allies. The closest the US and its two regional allies came to having a genuine trilateral entity to deal with North Korea's nuclear agenda was the creation in April 1999 of the Trilateral Coordination and Oversight Group (TCOG)[46] that has held periodic meetings since its founding. Its activities are documented on the US Department of State's web site (http://www.state.gov). Although some analysts have had fairly high expectations about TCOG's potentials for becoming the foundation for a truly effective trilateral decision-making organization,[47] it is far more likely to remain a forum for discussions rather than decisions, much less implementation of policies. TCOG represents a paradigm for the difficulties the three partners have confronted in terms of creating a cohesive trilateral organization able to cope with North Korea. Each of the partners has brought its own set of

---

42 For analysis of China's disputes with Japan, see 'China and Japan, So Hard to be Friends', *Economist*, March 26, 2005; and Bennett Richardson, 'No Apologies As Anti-Japan Riots Continue', *Christian Science Monitor*, April 18, 2005.

43 For coverage of those frictions, see Robert Marquand, 'Korea–Japan Dispute Strains Longstanding Alliances', *Christian Science Monitor*, March 25, 2005; and 'South Korea and Japan, Rocky Relations', *Economist*, March 26, 2005.

44 Lee Joo-hee, 'Intensifying China–Japan Row Takes Spotlight Off Korea', *Korea Herald*, April 19, 2005.

45 Sebastian Moffett, Gordon Fairclough, and Charles Hutzler, 'Japan Takes Heat amid Shift in Asia', *Wall Street Journal*, April 7, 2005; and Takeshi Kamiya, 'China, S. Korea: Japan Needs "Correct" View of History', *Asahi Shimbun*, May 10, 2005, available at <http://www.asahi.com/english>.

46 For coverage of a preliminary agreement, see Chon Shi-yong, 'Korea, US, Japan Agree to Consult on N. Korea Policy', *Korea Herald*, November 18, 1995; and for coverage of TCOG's founding, see Shin Yong-bae, 'South Korea, US, Japan to Establish Trilateral Group on North Korea Policy', *Korea Herald*, April 27, 1999.

47 For optimistic evaluations of TCOG's prospects, see Ralph Cossa, 'US–Japan–Korea: Creating a "Virtual Alliance"', Pacific Forum CSIS *PacNet Newsletter* 47, December 3, 1999; and James L. Schoff, 'Building on the Trilateral Coordination and Oversight Group, Exploring the Prospects for Expanding the TCOG Process as a Key US–South Korea and US–Japan Alliance Management Tool', (undated) and 'WMD Challenges on the Korean Peninsula: A Trilateral Dialogue Report', June 9, 2003 – both from The Institute for Foreign Policy Analysis, available at <http://www.ifpa.org>.

troubling parameters to the table which have not helped them reach any meaningful policy accords regarding North Korea. Beyond those issues, each partner's approach to the consultation process has not helped them cooperate with each other. The US long has had a reputation for being heavy handed in its leadership of international groups. With both Japan and South Korea, the US has earned a reputation for using its consultations with each to confirm decisions Washington has already decided upon rather than an open dialogue over policy options. Moreover, US representatives the South Koreans and Japanese have to consult with usually do not relate well with the two US allies' approaches to building a consensus about policies that are rooted in the Confucian traditions of each. All this has been exacerbated by the US's well-deserved reputation for heightened unilateralism in the wake of the 9/11 terrorist attacks. This entire situation was not helped by South Korean overall perceptions of Japan shifting closer to a hard-line position more in tune with US hawks. This was reinforced in June of 2003 when Japan indicated its readiness to go along with a US-led de facto blockade of North Korea, called the 'Proliferation Security Initiative',[48] compelling North Korea to halt Japan–DPRK ferry traffic and detaining North Korean ships in Japanese ports.[49]

The pressures on the US, South Korea, and Japan to present themselves in a more coordinated fashion at the ongoing series of six-party talks have been useful in terms of nudging the three members of the de facto trilateral alliance somewhat closer to a shared stance. If that were occurring because their desires regarding North Korea were authentically overlapping, that would be a very positive development. On the US–Japan (Bush–Koizumi) leg of the triangle, the overlap does seem to be growing, but each leg of the triangle connecting to the ROK and President Roh does not meet genuine overlap criteria. ROK–PRC views are closer in ways that exacerbate the flaws in the triangular relationship, but compel the three members to put up a facade of greater harmony at the six-party sessions – partly for the sake of appearances, and partly because they are being held in Beijing. On balance, therefore, the track record of past and contemporary trilateral cooperation leaves much to be desired.

Taiwan Factors

In an ironic way, the rise of the PRC as an Asian power economically and militarily, that contributed to more tensions between China and Taiwan due to Taipei's

---

48 For background on the initiative and why its backers do not want it to be considered an actual blockade, see Jay Solomon and Murray Hiebert, 'Some Speak of Pyongyang Blockade', *Wall Street Journal*, May 5, 2003; and Andrew Ward and David Pilling, 'US Considers Blockade To Put Pressure of N. Korea', *London Financial Times*, May 23, 2003; and David Lague and Murray Hiebert, 'North Korea, Pressure Politics', *Far Eastern Economic Review*, July 17, 2003.

49 James Brooke, 'North Korea Suspends Its Passenger Ferry Link With Japan', *New York Times*, June 9, 2003; and James Brooke, 'Japan Detains 2 North Korean Ships, Part of Pressure Strategy', *New York Times*, June 11, 2003.

exploration of the possibility of pursuing national independence,⁵⁰ had an impact on South Korea's relationships with Japan and the US. This issue became more salient to South Korea's position on overall US policy toward Asia when Japan dropped its relatively ambiguous stance on whether it would help the US defend Taiwan in the event of a PRC attack on Taiwan and in early 2005 overtly pledged to support the US commitment to defend Taiwan.⁵¹ In part, Japan's change of course reflected Japanese concerns about the rise of Chinese power that it shared with the Bush administration. Against that background, coupled with China's commitment to bolstering inter-Korean relations, South Korean leaders became concerned that the US's other Northeast Asian ally's change of course regarding Taiwan would end up putting pressure on the ROK to do the same thing – compelling Seoul to have to take sides between the US and China, which it did not want to do.⁵²

Yet another China-related factor in the evolution of inter-Korean affairs is the way North Korea seems to have learned a perverse lesson from the US's earlier policy of strategic ambiguity regarding support of Taiwan in its relationship with the PRC. Just as the US tried to have its cake and eat it too in its relations with China and Taiwan via a simultaneous 'one China' policy, its Taiwan Relations Act-based security commitment to Taiwan, and expectations that the US's two Northeast Asia allies (Japan and South Korea) will be supportive of US commitments to Taiwan despite the lack of any formal commitment by either of them to do so until Japan's policy shift noted above, North Korea seems to have learned from this model. Pyongyang uses a creative version of strategic ambiguity in its relations with both Seoul and Tokyo that takes advantage of the differences in South Korean and Japanese policies toward North Korea in a manner that enhances the DPRK's form of diplomatic deterrence versus the US because of the ways the US tries to overcome these differences. This gap between the US's two allies underscores how the US has become much closer to its Japanese ally than to its South Korean ally in terms of the position of each toward North Korea and how that disparity makes China's role increasingly important to the ROK.⁵³ North Korea's creation of this brand of

---

50 For coverage of PRC–Taiwan frictions at the same time as US concerns about North Korean brinkmanship were mounting, see Lawrence E. Grinter, 'Chinese Military Scenarios against Taiwan; Premises, Options, Implications', Counterproliferation Series, No. 19, December 2002, Maxwell Air Force Base, AL, Air University; Glenn Kessler, 'US Cautions Taiwan on Independence', *Washington Post*, April 22, 2004; Michael Sheridan, 'China Rattles Taiwan Sabre', *London Sunday Times*, August 15, 2004; Philip P. Pan, 'Chinese Premier Pledges To Hold On To Taiwan', *Washington Post*, March 6, 2005; and Philip P. Pan, 'China Puts Threat to Taiwan into Law', *Washington Post*, March 14, 2005.

51 Anthony Faiola, 'Japan to Join US Policy on Taiwan', *Washington Post*, February 18, 2005.

52 'China, Japan, and America; Keeping their Balance', *Economist*, February 26, 2005; and Robert Marquand, 'As China Rises, US Taps Japan as Key Asia Ally', *Christian Science Monitor*, March 21, 2005.

53 Those South Korean perceptions were reinforced in mid-May 2005 when a Japanese deputy foreign minister told ROK officials that Japan could share some intelligence about

strategy ambiguity is useful to Pyongyang's brinkmanship bargaining position on the US–DPRK nuclear front.

Northeast Asian Regional Balance

North Korea's escalating nuclear brinkmanship created an awkward dilemma for the Bush administration as it tried to deal with the DPRK in a creative manner. A truly rogue member of the so-called 'axis of evil' was reacting as though the trilateral axis was actually genuine, despite US recognition that it was a loose metaphor lacking any Middle East–Northeast Asian connections, thereby causing Washington to contemplate multi-front warfare – a war on terrorism, a war in Iraq, and a war in Korea. The US has been scrambling to defuse the latter prospect. One of the means Washington used was to try to draw China into multilateral six-party diplomacy focused on North Korea that opened the door to the developments just described. In short, the US was trying to make use of overlapping US–PRC national interests to use China as means to achieve goals the US desired. This US effort raises interesting possibilities for China.

While it is possible that the PRC will cooperate on US terms, this seems unlikely. China has no incentive to be seen as doing the US's bidding regarding North Korea – conveying an image of being an instrument of US policy. Being deferential to US hegemony is not at all consistent with Beijing's world view. Moreover, the rise of China as a global economic power and its commitment to modernizing and expanding its armed forces which has attracted so much attention regionally and globally has caused concern in US leadership circles. In early June 2005, at a major security conference in Singapore, US Secretary of Defense Donald Rumsfeld sharply criticized the PRC's arms build up as unnecessary and a threat to Asian stability.[54] Equally important, the vantage point reflected in China's world view is identical to Pyongyang's perception of the US and increasingly is a factor in South Korean thinking – as demonstrated in the demeanor of the ROK's president, Roh Moo-Hyun. During Roh's presidential campaign, he pointedly refused to 'kowtow' to US leadership.[55] That refusal was significant in its substance as well as the Chinese expression he used to signal what Korea would not do. Early in his administration, Roh resisted US hard-line 'tailored containment' of North Korea,[56] leading some to

---

North Korea with Seoul because the US government 'does not trust South Korea as much as Japan.' 'South Korea and Japan, America Loves One of them More', *Economist*, June 11, 2005.

54 Thom Shanker, 'Rumsfeld Issues a Sharp Rebuke to China on Arms', *New York Times*, June 4, 2005; and Mark Mazzetti, 'Chinese Arms Threaten Asia, Rumsfeld Says', *Los Angeles Times*, June 4, 2005.

55 Roh's posture was assessed in Aidan Foster-Carter, 'Spleen Versus Sense in Seoul', *Far Eastern Economic Review*, December 19, 2002.

56 That approach was exposed in Michael R. Gordon, 'US Readies Plan to Raise Pressure on North Korea', *New York Times*, December 29, 2002.

fear a budding rift in the US–ROK alliance. Although such a rift has been regularly disavowed by Seoul and Washington, there have been growing indications that South Korea's policies toward North Korea, China, and the US's role in the region differ significantly from US policies. Some of the roots of these differences stem from the Bush administration's attitudes toward Roh Moo-Hyun's candidacy and victory[57] and other roots stem from deviating perspectives in the post-9/11 strategic environment.[58]

In that context, President Roh has been very forthright in articulating a more independent role for the ROK relative to its US ally. Although South Korean officials – led by President Roh – regularly emphasize the continued salience of the US–ROK alliance,[59] his policy positions often send dissenting signals linked to South Korean perceptions of how US policy toward North Korea and China do not mesh well with South Korean perceptions of what should be done. Clear examples of this were evident in President Roh's speeches at the ROK Air Force Academy on March 8, 2005 and the ROK Military Academy on March 22, 2005 in which he outlined South Korea's aspirations to be a strategic balancer between the US and China and between the US and North Korea, and envisaged the ROK within ten years taking over wartime control of ROK forces from the US as the alliance currently specifies.[60] Roh's comments at the Air Force Academy were especially pointed. He said, 'I clearly state that the US Forces Korea should not be involved in disputes in Northeast Asia without our consent,' and, 'Our people will not get entangled in regional disputes against our will in the future.'[61] Although Roh's call for a 'balancer' function was controversial among his domestic conservative opponents and the Bush administration, two South Korean polls indicated about 70 per cent support for the balancer notion.[62] This policy vision, when coupled with some South Korean resistance to US plans for militarily dealing with North Korea in the event of a crisis called greater attention to the emerging gap between the US–ROK alliance

---

57 In addition to the prior citations on the election, see Bruce Cumings' description of a post-election 'lecture' to Roh by an unnamed US official who 'hulked menacingly over the table, his face red and seemingly angered' about Roh's position regarding North Korea. Bruce Cumings, 'Rising Danger in Korea', *The Nation*, March 24, 2003.

58 Norman Levin, *Do The Ties Still Bind? The US–ROK Security Relationship After 9/11* (Santa Monica, CA: RAND, 2004).

59 For examples of President Roh's public focus on the alliance, see Shim Jae-yu, 'Roh Emphasizes Alliance With US', *Korea Times*, February 26, 2005; and Shim Jae-yun, 'S. Korea–US Alliance Is Solid', *Korea Times*, May 21, 2005.

60 For coverage of the speeches and reactions to them, see Joo Sang-min, 'Seoul Preparing for Wartime Troop Control', *Korea Herald*, March 25, 2005; and Burt Herman, 'S. Korea to Play Neutral Role in Asia', *Newsday*, April 10, 2005, available at <http://www.newsday.com>.

61 'Roh Tells US to Stay out of Regional Affairs', UPI (United Press International) *Washington Times*, March 11, 2005.

62 Lee Joo-hee, 'Majority of Public Backs Korea "Balancer" Role', *Korea Herald*, April 11, 2005.

partners.⁶³ When some South Korean conservative politicians criticized President Roh's vision, he retaliated by accusing them of being excessively 'pro-American',⁶⁴ thereby reinforcing the sense that there is a growing gap in the alliance. Although South Korean officials regularly denied that such a gap exists, the fact they worked assiduously to resolve issues that symbolize the 'gap' suggests its reality. President Roh's June 2005 summit with President Bush in Washington exemplifies that reality. Although the press coverage of the summit was positive,⁶⁵ there is ample reason to believe that the gap is real and will persist until one or the other shifts positions.⁶⁶

In the context of these strained US–ROK ties, China has a chance to take the lead on Korean issues. China can draw on its Confucian legacy that strongly influences both Koreas' perceptions of China. The PRC also shares a geo-political bond with North Korea rooted in North Korean backing for the PRC's creation and China's intervention in the Korean War. Less known to most people in the US, in recent years China has become South Korea's primary economic partner and frequent diplomatic asset regarding the inter-Korean relationship. In short, the PRC is in an excellent position to be an intermediary – which is why Washington seeks to utilize China's abilities to restrain North Korean recklessness, but does so in a manner that is not well received in Beijing.

Unlike the US, however, China is culturally more attuned to perceive the budding multifaceted crisis in Korea as an opportunity because of the way the Chinese written character for the word crisis (pronounced *weiji*), that also is used in the Korean language (where it is pronounced *wigi*), is comprised of the ideographs for danger and opportunity. Chinese and Koreans can relate to this nuanced concept in ways that escape the attention of most people in the US. From a Chinese vantage point, the PRC can seize the moment and do what the US is either unable or unwilling to do.

For the short run, China could take the lead in persuading the North Koreans to comply beyond the terms of the September 2005 'joint statement' with past UN sanctioned nuclear agreements in exchange for engagement incentives. As part of such a prospective deal, China's growing economic clout in Asia can offer North Korea the economic means it requires to avoid collapse. South Korea is certain to join such a deal because it is central to Seoul's engagement strategy. And Japan is

---

63 Jung Sung-ki, 'Korea–US Military Alliance Turns Sour', *Korea Times*, April 12, 2005; and Barbara Demick, 'S. Korea Rejected US Plan on North', *Los Angeles Times*, April 16, 2005.

64 Lee Joo-hee, 'Opposition Lawmakers Prod Roh on "Pro-American" Remarks'", *Korea Herald*, April 20, 2005.

65 Gordon Fairclough, 'South Korea, US Seek to Mend their Strained Ties', *Wall Street Journal*, June 7, 2005; Howard LaFranchi, 'Bush Meets Roh, Untying the Korean Knot', *Christian Science Monitor*, June 9, 2005; David E. Sanger, 'US and Seoul Try to Ease Rift on Talks with the North', *New York Times*, June 11, 2005; and Lee Joo-hee, 'Roh, Bush Put New Pressure on N.K.', *Korea Herald*, June 11, 2005.

66 For coverage of the ways the summit's vague agreements amounted to 'spin', see Paul Richter, 'Bush, Roh Say They Share Goals', *Los Angeles Times*, June 11, 2005; and Jung Sung-ki, 'S. Korea, US Differ on "Strategic Flexibility"', *Korea Times*, June 15, 2005.

very likely to cooperate to help avoid a disaster in North Korea. For the longer run, China also faces an opportunity to facilitate an arrangement where the two Koreas' reconciliation and reunification will occur under Beijing's guidance and where the Korean peninsula's stability will be sanctioned by China. In short, China has a major opportunity to replace the US's central role in Korean affairs since the end of the World War II on an incremental basis as part of the Korean peace process. This would restore a very traditional relationship.

Since the US will not respond to North Korean demands for a type of non-aggression pact that would preempt the Bush Doctrine's preemption strategy, sees progressive economic engagement as appeasement, and is not truly supportive of either the Kim Dae-Jung 'sunshine policy' approach or the Roh Moo-Hyun 'policy of peace and prosperity' successor approach to the inter-Korean dialogue,[67] China is well positioned on all these issues to take advantage of the situation. Beijing can take the lead via diplomatic preemption, carve out a dynamic nuclear role through the UN, undermine what PRC leaders describe as US regional hegemonism, and become a catalyst for the creation of a stable unified Korean nation state – that would owe an enormous moral debt to China.

Although the US might well learn to regret not fulfilling that role were US stature in Korea to be eclipsed by China, the US should not stand in the way if China decides to exert such positive influence at the same time as the US's policy toward Korea leaves much to be desired. On the contrary, in those circumstances China should be encouraged by US policy makers to be innovative regarding Korea. Perhaps China can achieve what the US either cannot or will not accomplish because of flawed policies or lack of resolve – much to the benefit of Korea and Asian regional stability. Since that stability is very important to US–Asian relations, this criteria can be deemed essential.

If events surrounding the Korean peninsula continue to evolve in this manner, the US had better prepare itself to cope with the processes and the results. That challenge is exacerbated by the ways the ROK under President Roh Moo-Hyun is reemphasizing the brand of independent foreign policy that he stressed in his election campaign and subsequent focus on South Korea playing a 'balancer' role in the region. South Korean resistance to harder line US approaches to North Korea is compounded by anxieties about Japanese acquiescence to that approach. The prospects for meaningful US–ROK–Japan trilateral cooperation are not helped by South Korean perceptions of the greater utility of the PRC in the inter-Korean context versus the ambivalent roles of the US and Japan in that context.

The emphasis on South Korean 'independence' and its 'balancer' function is intensified by two factors. Most evident are the tensions stemming from progressive South Koreans' perceptions of the way US armed forces transformation plans will rearrange US military deployments in Korea in a manner that will have a negative impact upon the existing level of inter-Korean strategic stability. These Koreans fear

---

67 Roh's approach is described in detail in ROK Ministry of Unification, *The Policy of Peace and Prosperity* (Seoul: ROK Ministry of Unification, 2003).

US armed forces' shifts could be part of a US effort to set the stage for a preemptive attack on North Korea or some other move aimed at coercive regime change. These fears are behind public opinion polling that indicated more South Koreans think the US poses a serious threat to ROK security than North Korea does by a 39 per cent to 33 per cent ratio.[68] As negative as that is, polls indicate South Koreans think Japan is even more of a threat than either the US or North Korea.[69] These liberal South Koreans, who are President Roh's core political constituency, also resent the level of pressures Washington put on Seoul to commit ROK forces in Iraq. These critics are ambiguous about the US in terms of wanting to be seen as a reliable ally of the US purposes in Iraq in order to assure that the US will remain reliable in support of ROK purposes in the Korean peninsula, but not wanting to be seen as an abjectly obedient ally. This attitude is due to widespread Korean sensitivity to playing an excessively deferential follower's role behind a strong-willed leader – thereby conforming to a *sadaejui* (flunkeyism) paradigm. Both of these factors reinforce rising Korean nationalism and desires for greater South Korean independence from US international guidance.

US Policy Options

Arguably the best way for the US to become more effective in coping with the prospect that responding to North Korea's nuclear brinkmanship could yield this China-focused outcome about which many US analysts would have reservations, complicated by a South Korean 'balancer' role about which such analysts would be equally skeptical, is to pay far more attention than it presently does to South Korean innovative ideas about how to handle North Korea. A solid example of such South Korean innovation was the ROK's successful negotiations that produced a North–South meeting in Pyongyang on the fifth anniversary of Kim Dae-Jung's summit meeting with Kim Jong-Il. The anniversary meeting between Kim Jong-Il and ROK Unification Minister Chung Dong-young, held amidst the ongoing US–DPRK tensions over the nuclear issue, reinforces President Roh Moo-Hyun's overall approach.[70] There are many research centers in South Korea that focus on such aspects of crisis management and confidence-building measures versus North Korea, and China's role as a potential intermediary. The ideas spawned in these South Korean centers could be more thoroughly integrated within US policy if US policy makers paid more attention to them in a systematic institutionalized fashion. One bureaucratic option to accomplish that level of policy coordination would be to

---

68 Choe Song-won, 'S. Koreans: US Bigger Threat than N. Korea', *Pacific Stars and Stripes*, January 16, 2004.

69 'South Korea and Japan, America Loves One of them More', *Economist*, June 11, 2005.

70 Joo Sang-min, 'Unification Minister Meets Kim Jong-Il', *Korea Herald*, June 18, 2005; and Jack Kim, 'Koreas Mark Five Years of Renewed Ties', *Washington Times*, June 16, 2005.

create some kind of joint US–ROK non-governmental research institute tasked with enhancing our shared appreciation for the nuances in peacefully dealing with North Korea and for coping with the results of either success or failure. The more the US does to cooperate with our South Korean counterparts on such an agenda, the more likely it will lead to success – not failure. Clearly this would be a better way to cope with North Korean brinkmanship, deal with China's growing influence, come to terms with Korean nationalism, and avoid the risks of accidentally falling over the brink into a nuclear catastrophe.

As useful as that kind of institution could be, for it to prove to be viable in helping the US and North Korea avoid going over that brink, it is necessary for US officials working on the North Korean nuclear issue and the US public's views of what their government is doing on their behalf to become more familiar with the realities embodied by the DPRK and its policies. To put it mildly, despite decades of US–DPRK adversarial relations, the US's knowledge base regarding North Korea leaves much to be desired. Very few US citizens have been to North Korea. The US's cadre of North Korean expertise is not as substantial as it could be. This is not meant to criticize those US specialists in Korean affairs who do focus on North Korea because they do their best. The point here is that their 'best' would become far better than it is today if the US government would change its policies so that bilateral and multilateral contacts of US and DPRK experts in each other's affairs could be expanded and intensified. This could be done by creating US government-backed financial and institutional support for such regular contacts, reducing the restrictions on North Korean access to the US in ways that would encourage reciprocal opening of North Korea to US citizens, and positioning the US government to make the best of such improved mutual US–DPRK contacts.

Although the immediate objective of such US government policy shifts would legitimately be to create an improved environment for gathering accurate information about North Korea's nuclear weapons and other threatening capabilities and to enable North Korea to fully understand the positive aspects of the US's goals of denuclearizing the Korean peninsula, such shifts also would have broader ramifications. The better informed US experts on Korean affairs are about the realities of North Korea across the board, the more they will be able to provide accurate and valuable analyses to US policy makers who draw on their analytical advice. This level of improved information and assessments would greatly enhance the prospects for US policy toward both Koreas – and eventually toward a unified Korea – on truly diverse political, economic, cultural, and diplomatic issues. Implicit in this would be US recognition and acceptance of the importance for the US to work more closely than we now do with South Korean experts on North Korean affairs and on overall Korean issues so that the US can benefit from such Korean insights. If the US government were to become more open to such interaction with both Koreas' experts on each other's affairs and on the policies of each toward the US on nuclear and other issues, Washington would create incentives for both Seoul and Pyongyang to work more closely with US counterparts. The net result for US policy toward North Korea – nuclear and otherwise – would be greatly enhanced access to information about Korea and insights into what is most likely to be helpful for improving US policy.

Chapter 8

Restraining the Hegemon: North Korea, the US and Asymmetrical Deterrence

Terence Roehrig[1]

On February 10, 2005, the Democratic People's Republic of Korea (DPRK or North Korea) announced that it had 'manufactured nukes for self-defense to cope with the Bush administration's evermore undisguised policy to isolate and stifle the DPRK. Its nuclear weapons will remain [a] nuclear deterrent for self-defense under any circumstances.'[2] While the possibility that Pyongyang possessed nuclear weapons came as no surprise, the formal declaration after years of an ambiguous nuclear program was noteworthy. In this announcement, and others that preceded it, North Korea made reference to the need for its 'own deterrent capability' to protect itself from US aggression.

Since the Korean War, deterrence has been the dominant theoretical framework guiding security relations in Korea as the US and South Korea maintained an alliance with the goal of deterring another attack from the North. Indeed, most of the literature on Korean security focuses on deterrence and US–South Korean security policy. Yet, deterrence has also been a part of North Korean security planning, particularly with the end of the Cold War. In the early 1990s, North Korea saw its security situation gravely shaken as both of its traditional allies, China and Russia, distanced themselves from Pyongyang, qualified their security commitment to the North, and sought a relationship with the economically vibrant South. Not coincidently, this became a time of increased North Korean efforts to acquire a nuclear capability. During the 1990s, the North Korean economy also began its descent with the loss of trading partners and preferential deals from the Communist bloc that made it increasingly difficult to match the defense spending of its adversaries to the south. As a result, North Korea assumed a defense posture that increasingly resembled that of deterrence, a difficult challenge given the asymmetrical power balance between the US and North Korea.

---

1 The views expressed in this article are the author's alone and do not represent the official position of the Department of the Navy, the Department of Defense or the US government.

2 Korean Central News Agency (KCNA), 'DPRK FM on its Stand to Suspend its Participation in Six-party Talks for Indefinite Period', February 11, 2005, available at <http://www.kcna.co.jp>.

The joint statement that emerged from the fourth round of the six-party talks raises some hope for settling the North Korean nuclear issue. Despite this progress, several important issues were postponed for later negotiations and arriving at the more specific measures to implement the agreement will not be easy. Moreover, security relations in Korea will likely retain the characteristics of a deterrence situation for some time, even if there is a finished and functioning deal to denuclearize North Korea. Thus, deterrence will remain an important framework for understanding North Korean actions.

Despite these circumstances, scholars have given little attention to applying deterrence theory to explain North Korean actions. This chapter examines North Korean efforts to implement a deterrence policy in the post-Cold War world and will consist of several parts: a review of deterrence theory, particularly as it relates to an asymmetric relationship; North Korean threat perceptions; and North Korea's implementation of a deterrence policy.

Several important questions are crucial here. How has North Korea sought to deter the combined military might of the US and South Korea? What are the implications for asymmetrical deterrence as smaller states seek to deter larger powers, particularly through the development of nuclear weapons? How does a study of deterrence from the North Korean perspective help to better understand security relations on the Korean Peninsula? Finally, what lessons might be learned for US and South Korean security policy?

Deterrence Theory

The starting point for this study is deterrence theory. Scholars and analysts have devoted great effort to the study of deterrence and a full recounting of this literature is beyond the scope of this article. However, a review of some of the important aspects of the theory is necessary to understand their application to North Korean security policy.

Deterrence is usually defined as using threats to discourage an adversary from taking an unwanted action. The defender's threat must be sufficient to raise the cost of the challenger's action to a level that is unacceptable and will convince the challenger to refrain from the action. If the challenger concludes the costs of the undesirable action outweigh the benefits, the theory maintains deterrence will be successful. Deterrence is distinguished from defense in that it is attempting to prevent an attack from occurring. When deterrence fails, the defender employs its defenses to prevent the challenger from achieving its goal.

Deterrence threats can be divided into two types: deterrence by denial and deterrence by punishment.[3] Throughout history, states have sought to deter foes by possessing sufficient military capability to deny the attacker from obtaining its desired goals. Deterrence by denial meant the defender could either defeat the attack

---

3 Glenn Snyder, *Deterrence and Defense* (Princeton, NJ: Princeton University Press, 1961), pp. 9–16.

or make the assault so costly that the enemy would be dissuaded from attacking in the first place. Beginning with the advent of airpower and conventional bombardment followed by the creation of nuclear weapons, states acquired the capability to bypass the ground forces and defenses of an adversary and strike directly at civilian and industrial targets. As a result, deterrence threats could be made to punish the enemy in ways that did not require defeating an adversary's conventional military forces. Nuclear weapons, in particular, allow a country to threaten devastating retaliatory strikes that drastically raise the costs for an adversary considering a challenge to the status quo. With conventional forces alone, a state could threaten to fight if attacked or exact revenge after defeating the adversary. With nuclear weapons, the defender can assert that regardless of whether it can win or not, punishment will be imposed for attacking.[4]

Implementing deterrence by denial is relative to the military capabilities possessed by the two adversaries; a significant increase to the challenger's military power may erode deterrence to the point that it believes military victory is achievable at an acceptable cost. However, the military balance has little impact on a defender that can issue nuclear threats so long as it possesses even a few survivable nuclear weapons to launch a retaliatory strike against an attacker.[5] Thus, even relatively large differences in nuclear capabilities may not affect one side's ability to punish its attacker.

North Korea Versus the US: What Kind of Deterrence Situation is it?

Over the years, scholars have identified several important refinements to the types of situations where states implement deterrence. Three will be addressed here: immediate versus general deterrence; primary versus extended deterrence; and symmetrical versus asymmetrical deterrence. These distinctions are important because they help determine the specific circumstances of the situation and the appropriate responses necessary for successful deterrence.

Immediate versus general deterrence

Patrick Morgan identified two important differences within which deterrence situations occur: immediate and general deterrence. In an immediate deterrence situation, there is an imminent threat of attack by an opponent that requires specific counterthreats from the defender to deter the aggression. In a timely manner, the defender must make a convincing threat to retaliate in hopes of dissuading the adversary from attacking. In general deterrence, the two states are adversaries with significant hostility and suspicion, and at least one side considering the use of force if

---

4 Patrick M. Morgan, *Deterrence Now* (Cambridge: Cambridge University Press, 2003), pp. 13–14.

5 Robert Jervis, *The Meaning of the Nuclear Revolution: Statecraft and the Prospect of Armageddon* (Ithaca, NY: Cornell University Press, 1989), p. 18.

the proper conditions arose. However, there is no existing crisis or imminent danger of attack. Both sides undertake general defensive preparations that are attentive to the military balance and issue general warnings of its willingness to respond should an adversary assume a more threatening posture. The specific counterthreats under a situation of immediate deterrence are unnecessary, although states may still choose to make them.[6]

It is important to view the distinction between immediate and general deterrence, not as distinct categories but as a continuum whereby situations shift from one to the other and may possess characteristics of each. As a result, deterrence situations may pass through different stages – growing hostility and increasing indications of an attack – as relations escalate from general deterrence to an immediate deterrence crisis and back again.

Primary versus extended deterrence

States face security threats not only to themselves but also to their allies, prompting another important distinction between primary and extended deterrence. Primary deterrence occurs when a state is attempting to prevent an attack on itself, while extended deterrence is an effort to protect an ally. In the case of primary deterrence, a state's most vital interest – its security – may be threatened, and there is little doubt the state will undertake extensive measures to ensure deterrence succeeds. However, when protecting an ally, different factors enter into the defender's calculus including the degree to which the ally is considered an important interest and the level of risk and potential destruction the defender is willing to accept for the ally should deterrence fail. Thus, a defender's willingness to act in an extended deterrence situation is far less certain than when it is defending itself.

Symmetrical versus asymmetrical deterrence

The final aspect of a deterrence situation is the relative military capabilities of the adversaries. Most Cold War analyses of deterrence examined the US–Soviet situation of symmetrical deterrence, where the two opponents had relatively similar military capabilities and could threaten significant destruction on each other. With the end of the Cold War and the super power confrontation, scholars began to look at the idea of asymmetrical deterrence where the power differentials of the opponents are vastly different.

The dynamics in an asymmetrical situation can align in two different directions. In one direction, the defender may be the more powerful state attempting to deter a small, so-called 'rogue state' from taking an unwanted action. Examples of this type of situation include US efforts to deter states like Iraq and North Korea. A lively debate has ensued concerning the difficulties of deterring these states. As noted

---

6 Patrick M. Morgan, *Deterrence: A Conceptual Analysis*, 2nd ed. (Beverly Hills: Sage Publications, 1983), pp. 27–47.

in the 2002 National Security Strategy, the Bush administration remains skeptical because 'deterrence based only upon the threat of retaliation is less likely to work against leaders of rogue states more willing to take risks, gambling with the lives of their people, and the wealth of their nations.'[7] Regarding nuclear weapons and deterrence, 'these weapons may ... allow these states to attempt to blackmail the United States and our allies to prevent us from deterring or repelling the aggressive behavior of rogue states. Such states also see these weapons as their best means of overcoming the conventional superiority of the United States.'[8]

Asymmetrical deterrence can also work in the other direction with relatively small states using their limited resources to hold off larger powers. Prior to the advent of nuclear weapons, there was little a small power could do other than taking the necessary defensive measures to either defeat an attack or make it so costly that the adversary relented. With even a relatively small nuclear arsenal, or biological and chemical (NBC) weapons as well, it may be possible for an otherwise weak conventional state to hold at bay a much more powerful adversary with threats that are far more costly.

Combining these different dimensions of deterrence, North Korea's security situation is largely an example of general, primary, and asymmetrical deterrence. While North Korea might have believed soon after the attack on Iraq that it was next, the situation has been one of general deterrence where hostility and tension dominates the US–DPRK relationship but there is no imminent danger of attack. North Korea sought only to deter an attack on its homeland, a situation of primary deterrence, and the imbalance in military capabilities of the two sides clearly makes this a situation of asymmetrical deterrence.

Rationality

An important assumption often made by deterrence theory is that of rational decision making. In its most simple form, rational decision making occurs when leaders gather a list of possible options along with the attached costs and benefits, weigh the options based on a calculation of costs and benefits, and chose the option that has the greatest benefit for the least cost. While governments and leaders are not capable of 'perfect rationality' and scholars have often criticized the assumption of rationality, it is parsimonious and remains central to the logic of deterrence theory.[9]

---

7   President George W. Bush, 'National Security Strategy of the United States of America', September 17, 2002, 15, available at < http://www.whitehouse.gov/nsc/nss.pdf>.

8   Ibid.

9   For critiques of the rationality assumption, see Patrick Morgan, *Deterrence: A Conceptual Analysis*, 2nd ed. (Beverly Hills, CA: Sage Publications, 1983); Alexander L. George and Richard Smoke, *Deterrence in American Foreign Policy: Theory and Practice* (New York: Columbia University Press, 1974); Robert Jervis, Richard Ned Lebow, and Janice Gross Stein, *Psychology and Deterrence* (Baltimore, MD: Johns Hopkins University Press, 1985).

Concerning North Korea, analysts and US leaders have often questioned the rationality of Kim Il Sung and Kim Jong-Il. A 1977 US Department of Defense report noted, 'our intelligence does not pretend to understand the convolutions of Kim Il Sung's mind.'[10] A 1999 report by the Commander of US Forces Korea (USFK) called North Korea an 'unpredictable regime.'[11] North Korea's brash statements and use of brinkmanship in negotiations further enhance the image of an irrational North Korean regime. Many point to North Korea's economic policy that clings to the self-reliance of *juche* in an increasingly interconnected global economy as another sign of the regime's irrationality. While North Korean actions have done much to create the image of irrationality, South Korea and the US have also helped promote that reputation. Yet it is also possible to argue that North Korean leaders are quite rational in their use of limited resources to pursue their policy goals.

Deterrence theory has usually focused on the rationality of the challenger and its ability to make the necessary cost/benefit calculations for deterrence to be successful. The theory has been less concerned with the rationality of the defender and the impact this has on deterrence. In most studies of Korean security, the focus is on North Korea as the challenger and its ability to make rational calculations. Little analysis is devoted to the question of US and South Korean rationality and most assume implicitly that they possess this quality. However, this chapter examines North Korea as the defender in an asymmetrical relationship where rationality may play a different role, especially as it affects the credibility of North Korea's deterrence policy. Most important are US and ROK perceptions of the North's irrationality that drive fears Pyongyang would be more than willing to use force. According to Denny Roy, 'if states believe a certain government is prone to impulsive violence, they are more likely to behave passively toward that government, in hopes of avoiding provocation.'[12]

Rationality is also tied to North Korea's value system. In a rigid, collectivist culture buttressed by the importance of *juche* and Confucianism, the leadership is able to impose severe suffering on the populace for the greater good. According to one scholar, 'the individualism on which Western rationality is based is especially sensitive to the loss of human life. As such, even if North Korea were to suffer serious damage during a military conflict with the US, the consequent political impact would be less significant for itself than for the US administration.'[13] Thus, the perception of an irrational North Korea plays an important role in its efforts to deter.

---

10 James R. Schlesinger, Secretary of Defense, US Department of Defense, *Annual Report, FY 1977* (Washington, DC: Government Printing Office, 1976): III-11.

11 General John H. Tilelli, Jr., 'Statement before the Senate Armed Services Committee', 106th Congress, 1st Session, March 4, 1999.

12 Denny Roy, 'North Korea and the "Madman" Theory', *Security Dialogue*, vol. 25, no. 3 (September 1994), p. 311.

13 Choi Yonghwan, 'North Korea's Asymmetric Strategy toward the United States', *Korea Focus*, vol. 12, no. 5 (September/October, 2004), p. 74.

Credibility

A successful deterrence policy requires that it be credible. William Kaufmann identified three aspects of a credible deterrence policy: capability, cost, and resolve. First, the defender must convince the challenger that it possesses the necessary military capability to successfully carry out the threats. The defender need not actually have the requisite capability, only that the challenger believes it does. Thus, in the case of Israel and North Korea, though neither has conducted a nuclear test, both possess a sort of 'virtual deterrence' based on the likelihood they possess some level of nuclear arsenal. Second, the defender's military capabilities must be sufficient to impose unacceptable costs on the challenger. Finally, the defender must demonstrate the necessary resolve to convince the challenger it will indeed carry out the threats should deterrence fail.

The application of these criteria to an asymmetrical situation of primary, general deterrence requires further discussion. By definition, asymmetrical deterrence means one side has significantly less military power than the other. If the defender is the weaker of the two states, as is the case with North Korean efforts to deter the US, this makes demonstrating credibility more difficult. Concerning capability, the weaker defender must make threats that are consistent with the military capabilities it possesses. For example, a conventionally armed defender with relatively low level technology could not credibly threaten nuclear retaliation. Many have pursued chemical and biological weapons as a 'poor country's atomic bomb' to provide a capability that exceeds conventional weapons. Likewise, the defender could not threaten to invade a challenger's ally without having the requisite transport capability. The defender need not actually possess the necessary military capability; an ambiguous nuclear capability, as is the case with North Korea may be sufficient to convince the challenger it has the necessary weaponry.

Issuing threats that pose the likelihood of unacceptable costs is a more difficult matter. If the defender must rely on conventional military resources, the options are limited. Utilizing deterrence by denial, the defender can undertake sufficient efforts to make an invasion too costly and discourage the challenger from attacking. The defender might also threaten acts of terrorism or special operations actions that may raise the costs for the challenger. In either case, it may be difficult for the weaker defender to increase the costs sufficiently high to deter the stronger challenger from acting. However, in an asymmetric situation, the interests of a hegemonic challenger in a distant region may be far less valuable than those of the defender. As a result, the defender may need to impose only a modest cost to dissuade the challenger, a goal that could be achieved through a variety of threats.[14]

If the defender possesses nuclear weapons, even a limited arsenal with relatively inaccurate delivery systems, the credibility calculus changes. Nuclear weapons allow a weak state to inflict tremendous loss of life and property. The destructive

---

14 Bruce W. Bennett, Christopher P. Twomey, and Gregory F. Treverton, *What Are Asymmetric Strategies?* (Santa Monica, CA: RAND, 1999), p. 3.

capacity of nuclear weapons greatly simplifies the calculations of the challenger and threatens to impose great suffering. As Kenneth Waltz noted, 'in a conventional world, deterrent threats are ineffective because the damage threatened is distant, limited, and problematic. Nuclear weapons make military miscalculation difficult.'[15] While this was certainly a concern during the Cold War for US and Soviet planners, it still applies in an asymmetrical relationship. As the old anti-nuclear bumper sticker argued, 'one nuclear weapon can spoil your day.'

Finally, the defender must demonstrate to the challenger its resolve to carry out the threat if deterrence fails. In a situation of primary deterrence, there is little doubt that a defender would act to protect its security. However, certainty and credibility are not always clear. If a defender's threat to retaliate was certain, the challenger might still attack believing the costs of retaliation are acceptable. Conversely, an uncertain threat may be sufficient to deter if it poses a dramatic increase in costs, a nuclear detonation for example. Thomas Schelling described this circumstance as the 'threat that leaves something to chance.' Schelling maintained 'a response that carries some risk of war can be plausible, even reasonable, at a time when a final, ultimate decision to have a general war would be implausible or unreasonable. A country can threaten to stumble into a war even if it cannot credibly threaten to invite one.'[16] As a result, resolve does not rest on precise calculations but rather is a shifting balance of the costs and certainty of retaliation.

Despite the likelihood that a state would defend itself if attacked, Patrick Morgan raised some important concerns regarding rationality and the credibility of threats to retaliate in an asymmetric deterrence situation. The challenger must believe the defender would really carry out the threat for deterrence to be successful. However, executing a threat that involves NBC weapons would likely escalate the conflict and provoke an even worse response from the challenger. If the challenger is the stronger state, the result could be the elimination of the defender. As a result, the challenger may not find credible a threat that might lead to the end of the defending state.[17] Thus, there is an inherent contradiction regarding credibility in an asymmetric relationship. The more a defender attempts to display the three traits of a credible deterrence posture, the more the challenger might view that posture as not being credible.

While this is convincing logic, in North Korea's case, it is mitigated by two factors. First, as a situation of primary deterrence, North Korea is likely to view any significant US military action as either the prelude to, or launching of, a full-scale attack on its homeland. The US has not launched an offensive military operation against the North since 1953. Thus, even a limited strike would risk misleading Pyongyang into believing Washington was initiating a full-scale war. In any case,

---

15 Scott D. Sagan and Kenneth N. Waltz, *The Spread of Nuclear Weapons: A Debate Renewed* (New York: W.W. Norton, 2003), p. 9.

16 Thomas C. Schelling, *Arms and Influence* (New Haven, CT: Yale University Press, 1966), pp. 97–98.

17 Morgan, *Deterrence Now*, pp. 270–272.

Pyongyang will see the elimination of the regime as the likely outcome and believe it has little to lose in carrying out a threat to use NBC weapons. Indeed, speculation of a DPRK response to US military action often includes the possibility of Pyongyang lashing out in desperation.

Second, the perception of an irrational North Korean regime aids in deterring a vastly more powerful adversary. In a situation of asymmetrical deterrence, irrationality helps to level the playing field. According to Denny Roy:

> ... with the presumption of irrationality on its side, a weaker player can intimidate a stronger player. In the event of a confrontation, irrationality compensates for a shortfall in military power; the weaker player announces, in effect, 'I am willing to risk my life in an attempt to cut off your arm.' Convinced the weaker player is not bluffing, and unwilling to trade an arm for the opponent's life, the stronger player backs down.[18]

Thus, despite the seeming irrationality of responding, North Korea can make a convincing case that it would carry out its threats should deterrence fail.

The Threat

An important starting point for analyzing a deterrence situation is the threat perception of the defender. This analysis will focus on two dimensions of that threat, the capabilities and intent of the challenger. While analyzing North Korean threat perceptions could begin at its creation in 1948, the chief concern is on more recent events, particularly from the end of the Cold War to the present. It is also important to note that given the closed nature of the North Korean political system, it is difficult to determine the leadership's perceptions on any subject. Finally, over the years, North Korea's security threats have emanated largely from South Korea and the US. In more recent years, with the implementation of the sunshine policy by Presidents Kim Dae-Jung and his successor Roh Moo Hyun, North–South relations have improved significantly. Since 2001 and the inauguration of the Bush administration, DPRK concerns have shifted more towards the US. It is also important to note that North Korea faces serious internal security threats from a deteriorating economy.

Capabilities and the military balance

North Korea confronts a combined US–ROK military that is well trained and technologically advanced. In 2004, South Korea fielded a standing military of 687,700 personnel accompanied by 2,330 tanks, 3,500 towed artillery pieces, 180 multiple rocket launchers, and 468 combat aircraft.[19] US forces on the peninsula augment ROK capabilities with 34,500 military personnel along with 116 tanks

---

18 Roy, 'North Korea and the "Madman" Theory', p. 311.
19 *The Military Balance, 2004–2005* (London: International Institute, 2004), pp. 179–180.

and 84 combat aircraft.[20] In 2004, the US reduced its troop presence in Korea by sending 3,600 soldiers to Iraq. Washington also announced that further reductions of an additional 8,900 troops would occur by 2008 along with the repositioning of the bulk of the remaining soldiers to locations south of Seoul. To address any ill effect of the withdrawals, the US has pledged to spend $11 billion on various force upgrades and new equipment such as Patriot missile batteries and Apache helicopters.

The US presence is also a link to other American forces in the region, including two naval fleets, the Third and Seventh, the III Marine Expeditionary Force, consisting of units in Japan and Hawaii, the Twenty-Fifth Light Infantry Division located in Hawaii, and finally, Air Force units stationed in Japan, Guam, and Hawaii. All of these forces could be brought to bear in a conflict in Korea and pose a serious security threat to North Korea.[21]

North Korea fields a military of 1.1 million people including over 88,000 in special forces units. The DPRK has a tank force that numbers approximately 4,060 but is composed largely of light tanks and old Soviet design T-34, T-54/55, T-59 and T-62s.[22] More menacing are the North's 10,400 artillery pieces and 2,500 multiple rocket launcher systems, many of which are deployed in hardened, underground facilities, or tunnels burrowed into the sides of mountains providing protection and the ability to attack with little warning. The increased artillery capability was part of a major modernization effort undertaken by the DPRK in the early 1990s so that, according to a US Army estimate, 'without moving any artillery pieces, the North could sustain up to 500,000 rounds an hour against [ROK–US] defenses for several hours.'[23] North Korea also has deployed at 24 FROG rockets along with at 30 Scud B/C and 10 to 50 Nodong surface-to-surface missiles.[24] Finally, the North has 584 combat aircraft but only 100 of these are the more advanced MiG-23, MiG-29, and SU-25. The majority are the older Soviet MiG-17s, 19s, and 21s that face US and South Korean F-15s and F-16s.[25] Moreover, DPRK pilots spend limited hours training in their aircraft, possibly only seven to eight hours each year, due to chronic fuel shortages and a lack of spare parts.

Nuclear weapons have long been part of North Korea's threat perceptions. The US threatened the use of nuclear weapons on several occasions in a bid to end the Korean War and, in 1958, deployed its first nuclear weapons to the Korean Peninsula

---

20 Ibid, p. 31.

21 For a more detailed review of US capabilities see Michael O'Hanlon, 'Stopping a North Korean Invasion', *International Security*, vol. 22, no. 4 (Spring 1998), pp. 135–170. David C. Kang, 'International Relations Theory and the Second Korean War', *International Studies Quarterly*, vol. 47, no. 3 (September 2003), pp. 301–324.

22 *Military Balance*, p. 178.

23 US Senate, 'Statement of General Thomas A. Schwartz, Commander in Chief United Nations Command/Combined Forces Command & Commander, United States Forces Korea', testimony before the Senate Armed Services Committee, 106th Congress, 2nd Session, March 7, 2000, p. 5.

24 *Military Balance*, p. 178.

25 *Military Balance*, pp. 178–179.

for use with Honest John missiles and 280-mm cannons.[26] Nuclear weapons remained in South Korea, though not publicly acknowledged by US officials, until 1991 when President Bush removed them as part of an attempt to prod North Korea into giving up its nuclear ambitions and a larger effort to secure tactical nuclear weapons during the breakup of the Soviet Union. President Bush hoped Gorbachev would follow suit, making it less likely that 'stray' weapons would fall into the hands of others.

The US has never given a 'no-first use' declaration and on several occasions, gave indications it would use nuclear weapons in a regional conflict. In one example, in response to the killing of two US soldiers in the Demilitarized Zone (DMZ) in 1976, B-52 bombers, planes the North Koreans knew could carry nuclear weapons, flew from Guam up the Korean Peninsula. At the last second, the planes turned away from the North and according to a US intelligence analyst, the North Koreans 'didn't know what was in them and it blew their ... minds. We scared the living shit out of them.'[27] Pentagon officials announced after the crisis that these flights would continue at a rate of once or twice a month.[28] Later in 1983, the US employed the Airland battle doctrine in Team Spirit exercises that simulated the use of nuclear weapons for strikes deep behind enemy lines.[29] Referring to Team Spirit 1982, North Korea noted 'nobody can guarantee that this unprecedentedly large-scale war exercise staged with many nuclear weapons will not escalate into a full-scale nuclear war against our republic.'[30] A few years later, North Korean statements expressed similar worries, announcing that its forces were going to be placed on full alert during Team Spirit 'in face of the grave situation under which the danger of a new war, a nuclear war, has been created in our country owing to the reckless military provocations of the US imperialist and the South Korean puppet clique.'[31]

There is little doubt that combined US–ROK military power posed a grave threat for North Korean security. US forces could conduct an operation ranging from limited air strikes and cruise missile attacks to a full-scale invasion of the DPRK in an effort to oust the current regime. North Korean forces could certainly exact a high cost for an invasion but US–ROK conventional forces would eventually overwhelm the DPRK's capabilities and resources. Moreover, North Korea was doubtful of any significant support coming from China or Russia. Estimates of Pyongyang's ability

---

26 US Department of State, 'Memorandum From the Deputy Secretary of Defense to the Secretary of the Army', December 24, 1957, *Foreign Relations of the United States, 1955-1957*, vol. 23, pt. 2, pp. 532–533.

27 Peter Hayes, *Pacific Powderkeg: American Nuclear Dilemmas in Korea* (Lexington, MA: Lexington Books, 1991), pp. 60–61.

28 Ibid., p. 61.

29 Ibid., pp. 89–103 and 'Pentagon Draws Up First Strategy for Fighting a Long Nuclear War', *New York Times*, May 30, 1982.

30 Byung Chul Koh, *The Foreign Policy Systems of North and South Korea* (Berkeley, CA: University of California Press, 1984), p. 90.

31 *The Pyongyang Times*, March 3, 1990 as quoted by Tae-hwan Kwak, 'The Reduction of US Forces in Korea in the Inter-Korean Peace Process', *The Korean Journal of Defense Analysis*, vol. 2, no. 2, (Winter 1990), p. 192.

to conduct an invasion of the South often indicate it could sustain such an operation for 30 to 90 days. Though a defensive operation would be less taxing, the North Korean military with scarce resources and a poor infrastructure would be hard-pressed to hold off a US–ROK invasion for much longer. Thus, the military balance sheet points clearly in the direction of an asymmetrical relationship.

Intent

Assessing North Korean perceptions of US intent is a difficult task. North Korean officials and state-controlled media outlets regularly blast the US with inflammatory rhetoric that indicates fear of Washington's intent. This has been particularly so during the past five years of the Bush administration but has also been relatively consistent throughout the history of the DPRK. Yet leaders in all countries often inflate the hostile intent of adversaries to buttress political support at home and it is likely that North Korea is no different in this respect. Nevertheless, North Korean rhetoric and reports from US officials and scholars who have visited North Korea indicate that the DPRK indeed believes that the US is a serious threat to its security. For example, in November 2002, former US ambassador to South Korea, Donald Gregg met with North Korean officials and afterward remarked, 'I strongly felt in the last few days that the North truly fears a possible attack from the United States … I think that they would like the United States to give them some assurances that we don't want to blow them out of the water.'[32] While the US indicated it would provide North Korea with a security guarantee and that it would treat the DPRK as a sovereign state, Bush administration officials also noted at times that 'all options remained on the table.' In an April 2005 press conference, President Bush remarked that Kim Jong-Il is 'a dangerous person' and 'a tyrant,' yet, soon after, he made the symbolic gesture of referring to Kim Jong-Il as 'Mr.' For the North Korean leadership, these were no doubt confusing signals of US intent.

South Korea has become a different matter in the last 7 to 8 years since the implementation of the sunshine policy. Seoul has sought to engage the North in a series of inter-Korean dialogues and has promoted several economic development ventures, most notably the Mt. Geumgang tourism project and the industrial development zone at Gaesung. Though South Korea is still viewed with a wary eye, it has become far less an immediate security threat in recent years, especially when compared to the US. No doubt, Seoul would respond if sufficiently provoked by Pyongyang, but barring any incendiary acts, North Korea sees little likelihood of an offensive strike from the South. Though South Korea has significant military resources, North Korea's chief external security threat is from the US.

Since the North's creation, it has faced a US that has been largely hostile to DPRK interests. After the Korean War, the US maintained a robust deterrence policy

---

32 Seo Hyun-jin, 'Pyongyang Ready to Act in Concert with Washington over Nuke Issue', *Korea Herald*, November 8, 2002.

to protect South Korea from invasion.³³ While largely a defensive effort, in the 1970s, US commander in Korea, James F. Hollingsworth, shifted US war plans, Operational Plan (OPLAN) 5027, to be more offensive minded. This shift required the forward deployment of US forces, indicating that after blunting a North Korean invasion, the US intended to move north, seize the North Korean city of Gaesung, bomb North Korean targets, and eventually capture Pyongyang.³⁴ The US has often pointed to North Korea's forward deployments as an indication of its offensive intent. It is likely North Korea makes the same assumption. In 1994, US authorities altered the OPLAN to include a counteroffensive to remove Kim Jong-Il and his regime. Another planning document written in 1999 noted 'all forces will continue combat operations to unseat current North Korean leadership to reinforce the message that US/South Korea Military forces are prepared to continue decisive combat operations until victory is achieved.'³⁵ In 1994, the Clinton administration designed plans for airstrikes to take out the North's nuclear facilities at Yongbyon, and other revisions to the OPLAN in 1998 included preemptive strikes on North Korea should intelligence provide solid evidence of an impending attack.³⁶

The North Korean reaction to the 1998 OPLAN revisions was outrage, arguing the new plans were the precursor to an invasion of the North. Pyongyang indicated the plan as a sign of an impending US attack raising the tension level with Washington. According to a statement from the general staff of the Korean People's Army, OPLAN 5027 was 'a plan for a second Korean war of aggression allegedly to "retaliate" against the DPRK for the US defeat in the past Korea War.'³⁷ In a reference to US demands to inspect a suspected nuclear site and criticism of the North's August 1998 ballistic missile test, the statement continues:

Nowadays, the US imperialists are loudly crying that 'tensions have been heightened.' ... What they seek in this is to find a pretext to ignite the train of war according to the 'operation plan 5027.' Clear is why the United States has begun executing the 'operation plan 5027,' throwing away the mask of 'appeasement' and 'engagement' which it had once worn for some time. Unable to destroy our socialist system with its isolation and suffocation strategy and 'appeasement strategy' to induce us to 'reform' and 'opening,' the United States has adopted a reckless adventure, losing reason. From the outset, our

---

33 For a detailed treatment of US deterrence policy, see Terence Roehrig, *From Deterrence to Engagement: The US Defense Commitment to South Korea* (Lanham, MD: Lexington Books), forthcoming in 2006.

34 'OPLAN 5027 Major Theater War – West', available at <http://globalsecurity.org/milita-ry/ops/oplan5027.htm>.

35 'CFC (KOREA) OPLAN 9518', 29 December 1999, available at <http://www.global-security.org/military/library/policy/dod/oplan9518/CFCIIOPLN.DOC>.

36 'OPLAN 5029 – Collapse of North Korea', available at <http://www.globalsecurity.org/mil-itary/ops/oplan-5029.htm> (July 2004) and 'OPLAN 5026 – Air Strikes', available at <http://www.globalsecurity.org/military/ops/oplan-5026.htm>.

37 KCNA, 'KPA will Answer US Aggression Forces' Challenge with Annihilating Blow', December 2, 1998, available at <http://www.kcna.co.jp>.

revolutionary armed forces have expected little from the 'appeasement policy' of the United States that seeks to demolish our socialist system.[38]

Though it is unclear the degree to which North Korean leaders truly believe this rhetoric, it is likely there were ever increasing fears for their security.

Threat perceptions decreased dramatically in 2000, beginning with the historic summit meeting between Kim Jong-Il and Kim Dae-Jung in Pyongyang. This event was followed by visits to Washington by senior military official General Jo Myong Rok in October 2000 and Secretary of State Madeline Albright's trip to North Korea in November. Secretary Albright's visit narrowed the gap on a possible deal to address North Korea's ballistic missile program but some important differences remained. A subsequent visit by President Clinton might have finished a deal but he declined to make the trip citing a lack of time as his administration came to a close.[39]

Though initially indicating that it would continue the Clinton administration efforts at engagement, the Bush administration soon opted for a more confrontational approach and often had harsh words for Kim Jong-Il and the North Korean regime. In January of 2002, President Bush included North Korea in the 'axis of evil' and in 2003, the US invasion of Iraq demonstrated that it would remove hostile regimes before they threatened US security with NBC weapons. Most likely, North Korean leaders believed they might be next after the US dispatched Iraq.

As events unfolded following the US invasion of Iraq, North Korea's perception of its security problem with the US shifted. Based on North Korea's demands, it began to see the deterrence situation shift from one of immediate deterrence to a more general deterrence problem. In the early days of the US invasion of Iraq, North Korea feared they might be the next target for regime change. Seeing the US threat as an immediate deterrence situation, Pyongyang called for a security guarantee from Washington to protect it from invasion and issued specific threats to retaliate. Since that time, the US became bogged down in Iraq and gave assurances that it will not invade or attack North Korea. Despite other statements from Washington that 'all options remained on the table,' North Korea began to see the situation more as one of general deterrence where the threat of imminent attack decreased. As a result, the North shifted to calling for a change in the hostile US policy while indicating it would give up its nuclear weapons in return for normal relations. These provisions are part of the recent joint statement that concluded the fourth round of the six-party talks.

North Korea's Deterrence Policy

After the Korean War, the US implemented a deterrence policy that included a formal US–ROK security treaty, declarations of resolve to defend South Korea, the presence

---

38 Ibid.
39 Michael R. Gordon, 'How Politics Sank Accord on Missiles With North Korea', *New York Times*, March 6, 2001.

of ground troops, and placing tactical nuclear weapons in Korea. While designed primarily to be defensive and deter a North Korean invasion, US preparations also appeared menacingly offensive to Pyongyang. For years, North Korean leaders and the state-controlled media spewed out threats of retaliation should the US and its 'puppet state' in the South dare to attack the DPRK. Since the early 1990s, US officials suspected North Korea had nuclear weapons, yet Pyongyang was careful to avoid any overt threats to use them. Prior to the 1994 Agreed Framework (AF), North Korea chose the route of an ambiguous nuclear program where it neither confirmed nor denied with absolute certainty its nuclear weapons status.[40]

In October of 2002 when confronted with the highly enriched uranium (HEU) program, North Korea may have made its first public threat regarding NBC weapons. After US officials presented its evidence, DPRK representatives initially denied the accusation but later recanted and said 'they have more powerful things as well,' a possible reference to either the suspected one or two nuclear weapons or its stockpile of chemical and biological weapons.[41] Subsequently, North Korea denied the existence of the HEU program but not the earlier effort using plutonium. Soon after the AF began to unravel, North Korean statements began to speak directly of deterrence and the development of a nuclear capability, culminating in the formal announcement on February 10, 2005 that it had nuclear weapons to deter potential US aggression. Utilizing Kaufman's criteria – capability, cost, and resolve – for a credible deterrence policy, the remainder of this chapter will assess the various dimensions of North Korea's efforts to deter a possible US use of military force.

Capability and cost

North Korea possesses a sizeable conventional military force that has often been viewed as a threat to invade the South. However, this force is also part of North Korea's strategy of deterrence by denial that would mount a determined defense against a South Korea/US invasion. The DPRK's conventional capabilities would exact a high price for an invasion and though, eventually, it would likely succumb, the costs have been sufficiently high to deter any US–ROK action.

Despite its role as the inferior military power, North Korea does possess some elements of deterrence by punishment with only its conventional military forces. North Korea has close to 500 artillery and multiple rocket launcher (MRL) systems that are forward deployed, within range of Seoul and in underground or hardened sites.[42] Without crossing the border or challenging US–ROK forces directly, North Korea has a credible and survivable threat to punish South Korea by destroying its

---

40 Michael J. Mazarr, 'Going Just a Little Nuclear', *Internatonal Security*, vol. 20, no. 2 (Fall 1995), pp. 92–122.

41 David Sanger, 'North Korea Says It Has a Program on Nuclear Arms', *New York Times*, October 17, 2002.

42 General Thomas A. Schwartz, 'Statement Before the Senate Armed Services Committee', 107th Congress, 2nd Session, March 5, 2002, p. 7.

capital and largest city that is also the financial center of the country. In 1994, in response to US threats to impose economic sanctions, North Korea responded that sanctions would be considered an act of war, and 'Seoul will turn into a sea of fire.'[43] More recently, North Korea indicated that any effort to bring the nuclear weapons issue before the UN Security Council would also be viewed as an act of war. US and ROK planners are well aware of North Korea's ability to carry out such a threat, including the capability to punish another US ally in the region, Japan, with missile strikes using conventional warheads. The DPRK currently has deployed at least 10 to 50 Nodong missiles that are capable of hitting Japan and the US military bases located there.[44] North Korea also likely has artillery munitions and ballistic missile warheads outfitted for chemical weapons.[45]

North Korea's two suspected nuclear weapons programs have added the most recent elements to its deterrence policy. It is believed that North Korea has two programs to develop nuclear weapons, one based on plutonium and the other utilizing HEU. While the plutonium program has yielded material for eight to nine nuclear weapons, the HEU program will take several years before it is operational and even less is known about the exact status of this effort.

Much of the deterrent value of North Korean nuclear weapons has been based on uncertainty and rhetoric. North Korea has yet to conduct a nuclear weapons test, and there is no definitive confirmation that it possesses nuclear weapons. Prior to the November 2004 US presidential election and again in May 2005, reports indicated that the North might be preparing for a nuclear test. In a May 2005 statement to a delegation of Japanese academics in Pyongyang, a North Korean official indicated that a nuclear test was 'indispensable' toward proving its military capabilities, noting a test might be conducted soon. Despite these indications, no test has occurred.[46] Since 1993, the CIA has estimated that the North may possess one to two nuclear devices based on spent fuel it diverted in an earlier effort to develop nuclear weapons prior to the conclusion of the 1994 AF.[47] After the AF unraveled in 2003, the North reprocessed the 8,000 spent fuel rods that had been sealed under the pact, adding an additional five to six nuclear weapons to its arsenal. On several occasions since, North

---

43 Michael R. Gordon, 'US Will Urge UN To Plan Sanctions For North Korea', *New York Times*, March 20, 1994.

44 *The Military Balance*, p. 178, and Robert S. Norris and Hans M. Kristensen, 'North Korea's nuclear program, 2005', *Bulletin of Atomic Scientists* (May/June 2005), p. 66.

45 Joseph S. Bermudez, Jr., *The Armed Forces of North Korea* (London: I.B. Tauris, 2001), pp. 222–231.

46 James Brooke and David E. Sanger, 'North Koreans Say They Hold Nuclear Arms', *New York Times*, February 11, 2005; Anthony Faiola and Sachiko Sakamaki, 'N. Korean Official: Nuclear Test 'Indispensable' Step', *Washington Post*, May 9, 2005, available at <http://www.washingtonpost.com>; and David E. Sanger and William J. Broad, 'US Cites Signs of Korean Preparations for Nuclear Test', *New York Times*, May 6, 2005.

47 Eric Schmitt, 'Koreans May Hold A Nuclear Device', *New York Times*, December 13 1993; Michael R. Gordon, 'US Sees Easing By North Korea On Nuclear Sites', *New York Times*, December 31, 1993.

Korea proclaimed the reprocessing was complete but its most explicit announcement came on February 10, 2005 when it declared:

> The US disclosed its attempt to topple the political system in the DPRK at any cost, threatening it with a nuclear stick. This compels us to take a measure to bolster its nuclear weapons arsenal in order to protect the ideology, system, freedom and democracy chosen by its people.... We had already taken the resolute action of pulling out of the NPT [Non-Proliferation Treaty] and have manufactured nukes for self-defence to cope with the Bush administration's evermore undisguised policy to isolate and stifle the DPRK.[48]

In April 2005, satellite photos indicated that North Korea might have again shut down its reactor, raising fears it was extracting more spent fuel for nuclear weapons. However, intelligence reports were uncertain whether the shutdown was to extract fuel or simply to perform maintenance on the reactor. Other reports suggested the North may have pulled the fuel because of technical problems or fears of a US air strike on the reactor.[49]

The other important component necessary to inflict nuclear punishment is having a means to deliver nuclear weapons. North Korea is well known for its ballistic missile production and has exported domestic versions of Soviet and Egyptian-designed Scud missiles to several countries including Syria, Iran, Yemen, and Pakistan. The DPRK has also manufactured a more advanced medium-range Nodong missile that has been flight-tested on several occasions with sufficient range to reach all of Japan. North Korea has continued work on another missile, the Taepodong, that intelligence estimates maintain may be able to hit parts of the US by 2015.[50] North Korea conducted a flight test of the missile in 1998, ostensibly to launch a satellite. The effort failed to place the satellite in orbit but a portion of the missile traveled over Japanese airspace causing great concern in the region. Development of the Taepodong continues but none have been deployed. Moreover, considerable disagreement remains over the exact progress and capability of the North's efforts with this missile.

While the DPRK has extensive expertise in missile development, it is not clear how far they have progressed in mastering the task of placing a nuclear warhead on a ballistic missile. It is likely that North Korea intends to configure the Nodong and, eventually, the Taepodong to carry a nuclear payload. Yet, there are doubts that North Korea has accomplished this task. In testimony before the Senate Armed Services Committee in April of 2005, Vice Admiral Lowell E. Jacoby of the Defense Intelligence Agency indicated Pyongyang had developed the ability to arm its

---

48 KCNA, 'DPRK FM on Its Stand to Suspend Its Participation in Six-party Talks for Indefinite Period', February 10, 2005, available at <http://www.kcna.co.jp>.

49 James Brooke, 'North Koreans Claim to Extract Fuel for Nuclear Weapons', *New York Times*, May 12, 2005.

50 George J. Tenet, 'Worldwide Threat-Converging Dangers in a Post 9/11 World', Testimony of Director of Central Intelligence before the Senate Armed Services Committee, 107th Congress, 2nd Session, March 19, 2002, p. 13.

missiles with a nuclear payload. Soon after his statement, other officials backed away from that assessment stating North Korea remained several years away from accomplishing the task.[51] Thus, this capability too remains uncertain.

Resolve

The final element of a successful deterrence policy is resolve. As a situation of primary deterrence, resolve is less problematic than in an extended deterrence situation. While a defender may have to go to considerable lengths to show it will fight for an ally should deterrence fail, there is little question the defender will fight to protect itself. In a US–ROK military operation that appears to have regime change as its goal, the North Korean armed forces are sure to respond. This is certainly supported in the rhetoric that is often present in official North Korean statements. In the February 10, 2005 announcement of its nuclear capabilities, officials indicated that US efforts at regime change were the 'far-fetched logic of gangsters ... fully revealing the wicked nature and brazen-faced double-dealing tactics of the US as a master hand at plot-breeding and deception.' In response to a US action to 'topple the political system in the DPRK at any cost,' the government will 'bolster its nuclear weapons arsenal' and the Korean people will resort to 'the use of force in kind.'[52] Later, in April 2005, Vice Marshal of the Korean People's Army, Kim Yong Chun maintained, 'should the US start a war of aggression on the Korean Peninsula despite our repeated warnings, the revolutionary armed forces of the DPRK will mobilize the military deterrent force built up for years and wipe out the invaders to the last man and win a final victory in the stand-off with the US.'[53] Given that the regime's chief goal is survival, the leadership might be willing to sacrifice a lot in people and resources in a fight to the end. However, it is not clear how long the military and the populace would be willing to fight in a losing effort. At least initially, North Korea is likely to put up a vigorous defense if the US and South Korea conducted a major operation that appeared to have regime change as its goal.

The more difficult challenge is demonstrating resolve to respond to a more limited US–ROK strike. North Korea has indicated that it would defend itself, yet in the face of say, a US air strike on North Korean nuclear facilities at Yongbyon, it is unclear how DPRK authorities might respond. In response to US threats of economic sanctions or taking the nuclear issue to the UN Security Council, North Korea has threatened war. While it is unlikely North Korea would respond with a full-scale war against the South, many US officials are concerned the DPRK might lash out in some way, possibly some sort of limited strike against South Korea. Though a North

---

51 Bradley Graham and Glenn Kessler, 'N. Korean Nuclear Advance Is Cited', *Washington Post*, April 29, 2005.

52 KCNA, 'DPRK FM on Its Stand to Suspend Its Participation in Six-party Talks for Indefinite Period', *KCNA*, February 10, 2005, available at <http://www.kcna.co.jp>.

53 KCNA, 'DPRK to Steadily Bolster Its Nuclear Deterrent for Self-Defence', April 25, 2005.

Korean response raises serious questions that events would escalate, an issue that will be addressed in greater detail shortly, US defense planners fear that Kim Jong-Il and the North Korean regime just might be sufficiently impulsive to take such an action. Even though a DPRK response could be the very excuse some US and ROK authorities need to eliminate the regime, this situation is akin to Schelling's 'threat that leaves something to chance.' As Schelling notes, 'to say only that one may carry out the threat, not that one certainly will, is to invite the opponent to guess,' and North Korea may stumble into an inadvertent war 'through somebody's panic, madness, or mischief.'[54] North Korea may be willing to lash out in anger at US–ROK actions, a response leaders in Washington and Seoul believe is plausible.

Role of nuclear weapons

A threat to use nuclear weapons meets the criterion of imposing unacceptable cost; even a few nuclear warheads delivered in an urban area would exact a horrific price. Yet as Morgan noted, if a weaker state in an asymmetrical deterrence relationship decides to use nuclear weapons, it will escalate the conflict and 'risks provoking a furious determination to destroy the offending regime,' since the action 'would breach important political and psychological barriers, invite universal condemnation, and provoke a thorough effort to stamp out the regime.'[55] Even if US and South Korea were the instigators of a limited conventional attack, a nuclear response by North Korea might generate the response suggested by Morgan. While a limited US air strike on the North would have significant but tolerable costs for the DPRK, its use of nuclear weapons would likely trigger a chain of events that would have unacceptable costs, namely the end of the regime. Consequently, one might argue it is not credible for North Korea to threaten an action – nuclear retaliation – that would be irrational to carry out since it would be counter-productive to North Korea's chief goal of regime survival.

As noted earlier, two threat scenarios are likely uppermost in the minds of the DPRK leadership: a US-led, Iraq-like invasion to impose regime change, or a limited strike to take out the North's nuclear facilities. In the case of invasion, North Korea is already confronting an 'escalated' conflict that threatens to impose the ultimate penalty, the end of the regime. North Korean leaders may believe they have little left to lose by using nuclear weapons and, thus, can credibly threaten their use. US authorities believe that North Korea may be sufficiently foolish or desperate to use its NBC weapons to defend itself or simply lash out in anger. Any US invasion plans would likely include efforts to preempt North Korea's use of these weapons, indicating the credibility of the DPRK's threat.[56]

---

54 Thomas C. Schelling, *The Strategy of Conflict* (New York: Oxford University Press, 1960), pp. 187–188.
55 Morgan, *Deterrence Now*, p. 271.
56 Ibid., p. 272.

Threatening to use nuclear weapons in response to a limited strike is a different matter and one more in line with Morgan's argument. If North Korea responded to a US air strike against its nuclear facilities with nuclear retaliation against South Korea, Japan, or US bases in either of these two countries, this would likely provoke a vigorous response from these three countries and signal the end of Kim Jong-Il and the DPRK regime. The international sympathy North Korea might receive as the target of 'US aggression' would be lost after it resorted to the first use of nuclear weapons since World War II. Even if North Korea refrained from using nuclear weapons and confined itself to a conventional military response such as shelling Seoul, the US and South Korea might be tempted to escalate the conflict. In either case, the 'gloves come off' and North Korea loses. Thus, this appears to be a difficult threat for North Korean leaders to make with any degree of credibility. Pyongyang might be inclined to absorb the costs of a destroyed or damaged nuclear capability in the short run rather than risking the more costly possibility of regime change later.

Despite this logic, deterrence with threats that appear incredible may still work for North Korea. First, as Kenneth Waltz argues,[57] if both sides of a conflict possess nuclear weapons, they are apt to move more cautiously. Thus, even the possession of a small nuclear arsenal and the costs it poses for the US and its allies is sufficient to give US leaders pause. Washington may be less likely to push its efforts to challenge the North Korean regime given even the possibility of it incurring such high costs.

Second, North Korea's perceived irrationality overcomes the doubts about resolve. In the minds of US leaders, the DPRK just might be willing to respond to a US–ROK action in a manner that would be considered irrational by any other state. As Morgan notes 'while it is irrational ... to use its ultimate weapons governments cannot guarantee to be completely rational and in control. Thus, a state can threaten nuclear retaliation and be believed enough to make deterrence work.' A state 'with nuclear weapons will be more difficult to confront because even though it would be a terrible mistake ... to use those weapons no one can be certain it would not do so.[58] This is particularly so if the regime believes its survival is at stake. Even in the case of a limited air strike, North Korea might not perceive this to be a limited operation and instead view it as the prelude to a full-scale invasion.

Conclusion

North Korean efforts to implement a deterrence policy point to some important conclusions regarding deterrence and Korean security issues. First, North Korea has implemented a relatively credible deterrence strategy. It possesses the conventional and NBC capability to defend itself and impose a serious level of punishment on US allies and interests in the region. Sometime in the future, North Korea will be able to threaten the US homeland, given continued improvement of its ballistic missile force. With the likelihood that the North Korean regime will perceive a US

---

57 Sagan and Waltz, *The Spread of Nuclear Weapons*.
58 Ibid.

attack as an effort at regime change, a North Korean response is likely. The US perception of an irrational North Korean regime helps to make this a more credible policy, despite the possibility that a DPRK response to a US attack might lead to the end of the Kim Jong-Il regime. The US is not entirely sure how the DPRK would respond and whether it might lash out. Plans to move its troops south of Seoul point to US concerns for this possibility. This has evoked caution and indeed, despite the inclination of some in the Bush administration to use military force in dealing with North Korea, most have come to the conclusion that there are no good military options. The benefit of North Korean irrationality is even greater given this is an asymmetric deterrence situation; it is one of the few strengths it brings to the table. Pyongyang has sufficient military capability to exact costs on important US interests in the region and uncertainty regarding North Korea's intent helps to make it a credible policy.

North Korea's efforts to present credible deterrence threats do raise some important concerns. Threats that are intended to be defensive can also appear to be offensive, raising fears that North Korea might just be crazy enough to initiate an attack. As a result, the tension and hostility of a general deterrence situation is likely to continue with ongoing military preparations and counter threats. It will take the willingness of one side or the other to break out of the deterrence cycle and lessen the perceived security threat to begin a process that reduces the level of tension. Progress in the six-party talks has been positive but much work remains.

Second, North Korea's efforts to acquire nuclear weapons may not have been necessary to implement a credible and effective deterrence policy. North Korea began with a relatively ambiguous nuclear program that became more concrete as the threat increased. Yet, it is not clear nuclear weapons are crucial to the North's threat to retaliate. North Korean conventional forces and the ability to bombard or launch missile strikes on Seoul, parts of Japan, and US bases in the region may already be sufficient to deter the US. The threat in the early 1990s to turn Seoul into a 'sea of flames' may have been partly rhetorical when referring to the imposition of sanctions. However, it was also a threat should the US consider an air strike or military action to remove the North Korean regime. Nuclear weapons may be 'overkill' and may even worsen the North's security situation, especially once the Taepodong missile has been improved to the point it can hit the US with a nuclear payload. Rather than deterring the US, the acquisition of nuclear weapons that can hit the US may actually provoke Washington to be more confrontational and willing to risk military action to eliminate the threat, at least in the early stages of a nuclear program. This is certainly the logic expressed in the Bush Administration National Security Strategy. The lesson here for weaker states attempting to deter stronger ones is that acquiring nuclear weapons may not necessarily enhance their security situation, especially if they are able to establish a deterrence policy without them.

Third, given the threat North Korea faces from what it sees as the global hegemon, it should not be a surprise that Pyongyang seems to have opted for acquiring NBC capability when it has the ability to do so. Moreover, while South Korea remains under the US nuclear umbrella, North Korea has lost any similar assurances from its former allies. The US under the Bush administration has stated its contempt for the Kim Jong-Il regime on numerous occasions, possesses unmatched military capability, and has demonstrated the will to use that power in Iraq. With North Korea's paranoid nature in the best of circumstances, acquiring a nuclear capability is a relatively rational response to its security threats. To lessen North Korea's need for nuclear weapons, the US will have to lower its threatening posture toward North Korea. Indeed, the Bush administration has shown greater flexibility in the recent round of negotiations. Yet, throughout much of the recent crisis, the US has treated North Korean proliferation largely as a legal problem; North Korea broke an agreement and until it is back in compliance, there will be little further discussion. However, for North Korea, the dilemma is a political and security issue. Without recognizing this, the US will likely fail in its efforts to keep North Korea from developing nuclear weapons.

Finally, deterrence either with conventional or NBC weapons has helped North Korea's security interests in the short run. Though some in Washington were tempted to strike North Korea in some fashion, most admit there are no good military options. However, this will be a difficult, long-term strategy for North Korea. On its own, the DPRK lacks the resources and industrial base for a lengthy, general deterrence relationship with the world hegemon. North Korea has shown a remarkable ability to sustain itself through horrendous economic circumstances but the heavy focus on military security will continue to drain precious resources from a struggling economy. Though security is always the top priority for states, North Korea will need to move beyond the constraints of a deterrence relationship to attend to its other needs. North Korea's decision to return to the six-party talks indicates that it sees the level of tension dropping from an immediate deterrence problem to that of general deterrence where the threat of military action is not imminent. Pyongyang will need to make greater efforts to relax tensions in the region so that it can focus more on pressing economic concerns.

Is North Korea willing to give up its nuclear weapons capability? The recent joint statement from the six-party talks indicates Pyongyang may be willing to give up its nuclear weapons ambitions. However, the agreement is only a broad statement of principles. Many issues remain for the next round of talks and the details of future agreements will be complex and difficult to come by. However, North Korea certainly will not relinquish its nuclear weapons if its leadership believes they are necessary to address important security concerns. In the 1990s, there was great speculation whether North Korea was determined to obtain a nuclear capability for security concerns or whether it was simply using the issue to generate attention with a willingness to trade its nuclear weapons for economic and political concessions. Once again, there is hope that the DPRK may indeed be willing to trade the weapons for economic aid and normalized relations with the US. If these security issues can be addressed, there may yet be a way out of this nuclear box.

Chapter 9

Stability with Uncertainties: US–China Relations and the Korean Peninsula

Fei-Ling Wang

Beijing's policy towards the Korean peninsula has always been inseparable from US–China relations and crucially important to peace and stability in Northeast Asia. It now also illuminates the future development of the overall foreign policy of China, a widely expected rising world power.

Currently, Chinese ties with the Koreas appear to be fundamentally conditioned by the Sino-American relationship. As Beijing's conducts and concerns in reference to the ongoing issue of North Korean nuclear program has shown, the PRC pursued a pro-status quo policy in Korea with a clear objective of dealing with the US for its main strategic and geo-political interests in Northeast Asia.[1] In the 2000s, China's Korea policy displays continuity as the US–China relationship continues to be basically stable and Beijing's incentive structure of foreign policy making remains largely unchanged.

Barring any major changes in the Sino-American relationship and any catastrophic development inside the People's Republic of China (PRC), Chinese policy towards the Korean peninsula is expected to be stable and conservative: Beijing prefers the continued survival of the Democratic People's Republic of Korea (DPRK or North Korea) regime for its political and strategic needs while developing ever-closer relations with the Republic of Korea (ROK or South Korea) for important economic interests and geo-political considerations of cultivating counterweight to Japan and the US. Nominally supporting a Korean unification, the PRC seeks to maintain the

---

1   Fei-Ling Wang, 'Changing Views: Chinese Perception of the United States–South Korea Alliance', *Problems of Post-Communism* (formerly *Problems of Communism*), vol. 43, no. 4 (July–August, 1996), pp. 25–34; *Tacit Acceptance and Watchful Eyes: Beijing's Views about the US–ROK Alliance* (Strategic Studies Institute, Carlisle Barracks, PA: The US Army War College, 1997); 'China and Korean Unification: A Policy of Status Quo', *Korea and World Affairs*, vol. 22, no. 2 (Summer, 1998), pp. 177–198; 'Joining the Major Powers for the Status Quo: China's Views and Policy on Korean Reunification', *Pacific Affairs*, vol. 72, no. 2 (Summer, 1999), pp. 167–185. Also Tae-Hwan Kwak and Thomas L. Wilborn, eds, *The US–ROK Alliance in Transition* (Seoul: Kyungnam University Press, 1996) and Tae-Hwan Kwak and Edward A. Olsen, eds, *The Major Powers of Northeast Asia: Seeking Peace and Security* (Boulder, CO: Lynn Rienner Publishers, 1996).

political status quo and a denuclearization on the Korean peninsula. Beijing has shown that it can play a positive and effective role in the six-party talks in 2005. However, the uncertainties and complications of the Sino-American relations, the growing Sino-Japanese discord, and the Taiwan issue likely develop further to profoundly alter China's strategic calculation about the Korean peninsula and hence Beijing's policy about the status quo and denuclearization. China may be ready to accept both a nuclear North Korea and a Seoul-dominated united Korea, stable and friendly to Beijing, in the not too distant future.

To discuss these points, this chapter will first outline the key concerns and constraints of the making of Chinese foreign policy: the peculiar incentives in Beijing and the relations China has with the US. In line with its overall objective in its diplomacy, Beijing is seeking a shared strategic interest with the US and other major external powers on the Korean peninsula yet may make significant changes as the overall US–China relationship evolves amidst profound differences and uncertainties.

A Rising Power with Peculiar Motivations

In the past two decades, the PRC has managed to achieve two seemingly impossible goals: a remarkable socio-political stability and a record-shattering economic growth. After surviving the political scare of 1989, the Chinese Communist Party (CCP) perpetuates a monopoly of political power in China with a still poor, albeit improving, record of social liberty and human rights. The Chinese economy has been experiencing a major boom that promises a rise of China as a world-class power in the foreseeable future.

China's gross domestic product (GDP) has grown at the speed of 8-9 per cent annually for the past 25 years.[2] By purchasing power parity (PPP), in 2005, according to the CIA, the Chinese economy was already the world's second largest, about 62 per cent of the US and over 1.9 times of that of Japan. And China is now considered a middle-income nation with a per capita GDP over $4,500, almost twice as much as that of India.[3]

Foreign investors have shown great interest and confidence in China by investing great sums and making China the world's second largest recipient of foreign direct investment (FDI), after the US. In 2003, China received eight times more FDI than Brazil, seven times more than Mexico, and almost 21 times more than India. China is now the fifth largest trader in the world. As the combined result of the massive inflow of foreign capital and significant trade surplus, China's foreign currency

---

2   Charles Hutzler, 'China May Be on Course To Overtake US Economy', *The Wall Street Journal*, January 24, 2005.
3   CIA, *The World Factbook 2005* (Washington, DC: CIA, 2005).

reserves have ballooned from $10 billion in 1990 to over $700 billion by mid-2005, second only to Japan's.[4]

To be sure, China's rising economic power still has significant problems. About two-thirds of the Chinese population is systematically excluded from the glittering, vibrant urban centers and have the low living standard typical of a developing nation. China is essentially still a giant labor-intensive processing factory. Among the great variety of industrial goods China now produces and exports, few are invented or designed by Chinese. As a result, the Chinese end up earning low wages at great cost to their environment, while foreign patent holders, investors and retailers capture the lion's share of the profit.[5]

Nonetheless, China's economic record in the past two decades has been truly impressive. With that, Beijing has successfully justified its political system to the millions of Chinese, especially the economic, social, and intellectual elite. A new ruling class and a new developmentalist political consensus have emerged and taken strong hold in China to stabilize the CCP's authoritarian one-party regime. 'Under the neo-authoritarianism banner' of the CCP, described a PRC analyst, '[China's] political elite, economic elite, and intellectual elite have all reached a consensus and joined an alliance' to rule China as a new ruling class that monopolizes political power.[6] Many CCP officials and leaders are so pro-business and so devoted to economic growth that they appear to be almost identical to their counterparts in places like Seoul, Taipei, and Singapore. Opinion polls and anecdotal evidence have widely suggested that the CCP's political monopoly is secure, as long as the economy grows and the income of the people (mainly the politically potent urban population) increases. It seems that political legitimacy can indeed be effectively purchased in China, at least for the time being.

More active Chinese participation in the management of international affairs and a more evenly constructed multipolar world seem to highly appeal to a rising China. Many PRC analysts prefer to be first given a great power (*daguo*) responsibility in the Asia-Pacific region to ensure a 'just and rational' new security order in the region. Beyond that, China could take advantage of the differences between the US and its allies in Europe – the so-called strategy of 'utilizing the West–West conflicts' by forging more ties between the 'rising Asia' and the European Union (EU).[7] Or to

---

4   For the achievement and power of the Chinese economy, see the special coverage, 'Great Wall Street: How China Runs the World Economy', *The Economist*, July 30–August 5, 2005 and the special issue on China and India by *BusinessWeek*, August 15, 2005.

5   Fei-Ling Wang, 'Lots of Wealth, Lots of People, Lots of Flaws: China Rising', *International Herald Tribune*, July 21, 2005.

6   Kang Xiaoguang, 'Weilai 3–5 nian zhongguo dalu zhengzhi wendingxing fengxi' (Analysis of the political stability issue in Chinese Mainland in the next 3–5 years), *Zhanlue yu guanli* (Strategy and management), no. 3 (Beijing, 2003), pp. 1–2.

7   The PRC started to actively participate in the Asia-Europe Meeting (ASEM), a dialogue between the EU and East and Southeast Asia nations created in 1996, in the early 2000s. In 2004, China participated in the 39-nation dialogue. Huang Haiming et al. 'ASEM Enhances Overall Asia-Europe Relations', Xinhua News Agency, Beijing, October 6, 2004;

form a China–India–Russia alliance to counter the US–EU–Japan dominance.[8] In 2004–05, Beijing made a somewhat surprising move to support New Delhi's bid for a permanent seat in the UN Security Council while openly and repeatedly stating its objection to Japan's similar aspiration.[9] Eventually, many in Beijing hope that China's rise will make it a new world leader to provide new norms and create a new history for itself and for the world.[10] One analyst put the economic reasons for more Chinese power very bluntly: 'China's sustained development in the future can not be sufficiently supported by [our] domestic resources, we must have the right to share the world's resources and use it to support China's development.'[11]

A new and bigger role by China in international affairs in the near future in Asia and beyond has now become not just a hot topic, but also a widely accepted fact among analysts in and outside the PRC. An apprehension and even fear about the dragon is seen in China's neighboring areas.[12]

Yet, the rising Chinese power has already faced important and rather peculiar concerns and constraints. In the 2000s, Beijing's top concern in foreign policy remains to be the preservation of the one-party political system of the CCP. Short of effective political reforms to produce a better governance, the preservation necessity remains the top objective for Beijing. Tangible and continued economic prosperity has become *the* avenue to reach that goal; international acceptance and approval have become major sources of legitimacy for the CCP at home, while nationalistic demands for more Chinese power and prestige have presented Beijing with an additional opportunity for, and a new challenge to, its political preservation. Together, a peculiar incentive structure of political preservation, economic prosperity, and national power/prestige, fundamentally motivates China's foreign policy.

For the CCP's political survival, China's foreign policy remains basically conservative, pragmatic, pro-status quo, and reactive. External respect itself has

---

and Xiao Chenglin 'Asia, Europe Move Closer in Cooperation', Xinhua News Agency, Beijing, October 5, 2004. In 2005, Beijing's tenacious pursuit of EU arms sales, over the objections of Washington, is a good example of such strategy.

8 Authors' interviews in Beijing, 2004. The Russians, however, seem to deeply doubt this. Russian News and Information Agency, 'Alliance Between Russia, China and India Hardly Possible According to Expert Opinion', Moscow, January 20, 2005.

9 Indo-Asian News Service, 'Shift in China's Foreign Policy under Hu', October 21, 2004. For China's objection to Japan's bid, see, for example, 'Four Barriers on Japan's Way to "Permanent Seat"', *Renmin Ribao* (People's daily), Beijing, September 26, 2004, in FBIS-NES-2004-0927.

10 Zhang Feng, 'Zhongguo fuxin kaiqi xin lishi' (China's rejuvenation creates new history), *Global Times*, Beijing, August 30, 2004.

11 Zhang Wenmu, 'Quanqiuhua jincheng zhong de zhongguo guojia liye' (China's national interest in the process of globalization), *Zhanlue yu guanli* (Strategy and management), no. 1 (Beijing, 2001), p. 63.

12 Jane Perlez, 'China shoring up image as Asian superpower', *International Herald Tribune*, December 2, 2004. 'Fear of the Dragon', *The Economist*, London, November 17, 2004.

become a leading source of political legitimacy, hence Beijing cultivates hard its peaceful and cooperative posture in international relations. But China's conservative foreign policy for political preservation and its drive for economic prosperity have combined to generate fuel for a rising sense of Chinese nationalism. On the one hand, rapid economic growth and technological advances have powered nationalistic sentiments and demands; on the other hand, Beijing's preservation-oriented conservative foreign policy has frustrated many Chinese nationalists. To seek more power in international relations is creeping up inside China as an increasingly strong factor to be reckoned with, although the official line in Beijing remains to be the mild and benign 'peaceful development', after a fling with the new and more majestic idea of 'peaceful rise' during the power transition from Jiang Zemin to Hu Jintao in 2003–2004.[13] The rise of nationalist emotions and demands in the PRC is here to stay, as the massive anti-Japanese demonstrations in China in spring of 2005 vividly illustrated.

Practically, China has developed an unprecedented dependence on international trade. In 2003–2004, 20 to 25 per cent of China's GDP was directly related to foreign trade; and China imports increasingly more oil from the troubled region of the Middle East.[14] Economic globalization, hence, appears to Beijing as a worthwhile gamble. A senior CCP official argues that as long as China seizes the currently available 'development opportunity that presents itself only once in a thousand years so to ride the tide to catch the express train of economic globalization, we will realize our ideals of having a frog-leap development and having a powerful nation and rich people.'[15] For that, China clearly needs to be part of the existing international economic institutions, trade aggressively with everyone, and especially maintain a good relationship with the developed nations. Recently, Beijing is also actively flexing its economic muscles for more gains. A leading example is the idea of constructing a free trade zone that includes basically all of East and Southeast Asia, the so-called 'ten plus three' scheme. In 2004, Beijing joined the meeting of financial ministers and central bank governors of the G-7 countries for the first time.[16] It seems to the CCP that to selectively embrace globalization pays and substantial political legitimacy can be purchased internationally as well.

---

13 Zheng Bijian (former executive vice president of the CCP's Central Party School) first officially proposed the concept in his speech in November of 2003. Hu Jintao (as late as in February of 2004) and Wen Jiabao (as late as in March of 2004) both advocated the new concept of 'peaceful rise' as it was customary in the PRC for a new leadership to come up with a new slogan. See <http://news.xinhuanet.com/zhengfu/2004-03/26/content_1386611.htm>. However, presumably under pressure and after second thoughts, the phrase disappeared from PRC official speeches, statements, and reports by mid-fall of 2004.

14 For China's needs for more energy and oil imports, see Brian Bremner, Dexter Roberts, Adam Aston, Stanley Reed and Jason Bush, 'Asia's Great Oil Hunt', *Business Week*, November 15, 2004.

15 Qiu Yuanping 'Minaxiang shijie de xunyan' (Declaration to the world), *Qiushi*, no. 3 (Beijing, 2003), pp. 27–28.

16 *Financial Times*, September 22, 2004.

Guided by such a 'three-P' incentive structure, Beijing believes that the post-9/11 War on Terrorism and the US invasion and occupation of Iraq have provided a 'period of strategic opportunity' for the CCP to concentrate on its strategy of stability and development in the first two decades of this century.[17] So the CCP hopes for a continuation of the current stability in the US–China relationship and a generally peaceful international environment for China's economic growth.[18] Some insiders in Beijing have leaked in 2005 that PRC President Hu Jintao has personally shown strong support to Pyongyang on the ground of ideological and political similarities, a 'unique socialism.' Days before Hu visited South Korea in November of 2005 to attend the APEC summit meeting in Busan, he paid his first formal visit to Pyongyang in October 28–30.[19] Some Chinese analysts hailed this as a major new Beijing effort for a closer and better relationship with Pyongyang, while others think this is just to comfort the battered DPRK leaders with a $2 billion aid package.

It is worthwhile to note that many Chinese analysts are now increasingly candid about the inadequacy of the Chinese power, primarily defined as China's lack of military capabilities. While the PLA may be capable of safeguarding the PRC political system and the stability of the CCP regime against foreseeable domestic threats, it is clearly under equipped and poorly trained to carry out missions outside of China's borders. The PLA is viewed as increasingly falling behind that of the Western militaries, with perhaps the exception of nuclear capable land- and sea-based ballistic missiles.[20] A possible collision course between Pyongyang and Washington over the North Korean nuclear issue may force Beijing to fight the US forces in Korean War II, with a much slimmer chance of another stalemate. Consequently, increasingly many now in the PRC are calling for a quiet but steady building up and exercising of China's national power, especially military forces, to safeguard its political system and national sovereignty, seek the appropriate Chinese 'sphere of influence', and 'regain' China's rightful but deprived great power status and influence.[21] PLA analysts now openly write that China 'must increase' its military

---

17 Jiang Zemin, Political Report to the 16th CCP National Congress, Beijing, November, 2002. Under Hu Jintao, Beijing kept this estimate but rephrased it as a 'coexistence of opportunity and challenges.' CCP, 'The Communiqué of 4th Plenum of the 16th CCP Central Commission', Beijing, September, 19, 2004.

18 For more discussion of the Chinese foreign policy making in the 2000s especially Beijing's peculiar incentive structure, see Yong Deng and Fei-Ling Wang, eds., *China Rising: Power and Motivation in Chinese Foreign Policy* (Lanham, MD: Rowman & Littlefield, 2005).

19 Jing-dong Yuan, 'Hu goes to the Hermit Kingdom', *Asia Times*, October 27, 2005. Xinhua News Dispatch, 'President Hu's Pyongyang visit successful, fruitful', Pyongyang, October 30, 2005.

20 David Shambaugh, *Modernizing China's Military: Progress, Problems, and Prospects*, (Berkeley, CA: University of California Press, 2003), pp. 330–332.

21 Tang Shiping 'Zailun zhongguo d da zhanlue' (Another threat to China's grand strategy), *Zhanlue yu guanli* (Strategy and management), no. 4, (Beijing, 2001), pp. 29–37. Zhang Wenmu, 'Quanqiuhua jincheng zhong de zhongguo guojia liye' (China's national

spending and keep its military spending growing at the same pace with the economy in the future.[22] Leading Chinese economists also argue for a 'massive increase of military spending' by as much as 50 per cent in the near future as a key to a new grand strategy to make China a world-class power by the mid-21st century.[23] With a fairly complete industrial system, reasonably sophisticated technology, millions of soldiers, and a booming economy, the PLA indeed could resort to a militarization that will make the alleged weapons of mass destruction in the so-called 'Axis of Evil' nations (Iraq, Iran, and North Korea) look like a fairy tale. A fully mobilized military-industry complex in China would likely render futile any US effort for absolute security.[24]

US–China Relations

In the mid-2000s, the basics of Sino-American relations, widely believed to be the most important bilateral relationship to both countries, are expected to remain stable as the second Bush Administrations openly seeks to build 'a candid, cooperative and constructive relationship with China that embraces our common interests.' However, as Secretary of State Condoleezza Rice told the US Senate, there are 'considerable differences about values' between Washington and Beijing.[25] Furthermore, there are several explosive mines that could seriously damage the US–China relationship, among which the Taiwan issue is a major one.[26] Stability with considerable uncertainties that have great consequences seem to be the proper characterization of the current US–PRC relationship, which serves as the most powerful external constraint of the Chinese foreign policy.

For the three-P objectives outlined above, Beijing has been seeking to avoid direct conflicts with the US, at least for now, by pursuing a conservative, pro-status quo, and risk-averse policy that is quite unusual for a rapidly rising power.[27] Beijing appears to be betting its future on its efforts *within* the current international political

---

interest in the process of globalization), *Zhanlue yu guanli* (Strategy and management), no. 1 (Beijing, 2002), pp. 52–64.

22 Lou Yaoliang, *Diyuan zhengzhi yu zhongguo guofang zhanlue* (Geopolitics and China's national defense strategy) (Tianjin: Tianjin Remin Press, 2002), p. 255. Yan Xuetong, 'Zhongguo zonghe guoli shangbu pingheng' (China's comprehensive power is not balanced), *Global Times*, August 24, 2004.

23 Hu Angang and Meng Honghua, 'Zhongmeirieying youxing zhanlue ziyuan bijiao' (A comparison of tangible strategic resources among China, the US, Japan, Russia, and India), *Zhanlue yu guanli* (Strategy and management), no. 2 (Beijing, 2002), pp. 26–41.

24 Geoffrey York and Marcus Gee, 'Flexing its Military Muscle', *Global and Mail*, Toronto, October 23, 2004.

25 Rice's statement at the US Senate's Confirmation Hearing, January 18, 2005.

26 TV interview with Richard Armitage, December 10, 2004. Released by the US Department of State on December 30, 2004.

27 Hu Jintao's speech at the Summit Meeting of the Shanghai Cooperation Organization, Moscow, May 30, 2003.

and economic system and its focused program of economic development by taking advantage of Western capital, technology and markets to make the PRC an equal to the West. In addition, after more than two decades of opening to the outside world (mainly the West) and as a new Chinese elite, which tends to have great vested interest in a good relationship with the US, increases in number, China is now increasingly and genuinely developing some shared values, interests, and even perspectives with reigning Western powers.[28]

The US, as the lone superpower and the leading external players that can realistically undermine or accept, hence legitimize, Beijing's political system and help or hinder Beijing's economic and foreign pursuits, is heavily influential in the PRC.[29] Both finding the status quo in their interest, Washington and Beijing have developed some shared strategic interests in the global war on terrorism and in handling regional or UN-related issues, such as the control of weapons of mass destruction. Nuclear-armed and deemed by many to be condemned into a hopeless course of collision between the reigning power and the rising power, US and China appear to be surprisingly peaceful and cooperative with each other, so far.[30]

Beijing shows great deference to the US power and leadership. A senior 'American Hand' in Beijing wrote in 2002 that 'even if the US economy and the Chinese economy maintain 3 per cent and 8 per cent growth rate respectively, it will take 46 more years for China's GDP to reach the size of that of the United States.'[31] Another analyst estimated that China's GDP, about 10.9 per cent of the US GDP in 2000, will only increase to be about 18.6 per cent of the US GDP by 2015.[32] As a result of the disparity of power and differences, the US is viewed in Beijing as 'the largest external factor affecting China's national reunification and national security.'[33]

Luckily, the current de facto alliance of anti-terrorism has offered the CCP leadership a breathing opportunity. One authoritative analyst wrote to educate PRC

---

28 Yong Deng and Fei-Ling Wang eds, *In the Eyes of the Dragon: China Views the World* (Boulder, CO: Rowman & Littlefield, 1999). Li Shengming and Wang Yizhou, eds, *2003 Nian quanqiu zhengzhi yu anquan baogao* (2003 yellow book of international politics and security) (Beijiing: Shehui Kexue Wenxian Press, 2003), especially pp. 1–15 and pp. 84–105.

29 Ding Gang, 'Tuo meiguohua: buke huibi de wenti' (De-Americanization: an unavoidable question), *Global Times*, Beijing, September 13, 2004.

30 Samuel Kim, ed., *The International Relations of Northeast Asia* (Lanham, MA: Rowman & Littlefield, 2004).

31 Wang Jisi ' Gailun zhongmeiri sanbian guanxi' (On the triangular relationship among China, the US and Japan), in Lin Rong *Xinshiji de sikao* (Thinking in the new century), vol.1 (Beijing: Central Party School Press, 2002), p. 3.

32 Tang Shiping, '2010–2015 nian d zhongguo zhoubian angquan huangjin' (China's neighboring security environment in 2010–2015), *Zhanlue yu guanli* (Strategy and management), no. 5 (Beijing, 2002), p. 40.

33 Zhu Tingchang et al., eds, *Zhongguo zhoubian anquan hunagjin yu anquan zhanlue* (China's security environment and strategy in the neighboring areas) (Beijing: Shishi Press, 2002), p. 5.

officials that, although the US has not changed its policy of concurrently engaging and containing China after 9/11:

> ... right now, the tip of the US spear is not all pointed at China. This brings a rare opportunity for us to concentrate on economic construction and create beneficial international and neighboring environments. We must seize upon this rare opportunity after more than ten years since the end of the Cold War. [We] should not stand out diplomatically so as to avoid drawing fires to ourselves; instead, [we] should concentrate on doing a good job internally, speed up economic construction, accelerate development, to strive for a larger elevation of China's comprehensive national power in the first ten to twenty years of the new century.[34]

Yet, as perhaps a weather balloon or a sign of the changed times, CCP's foreign policy guru Qian Qichen unexpectedly published an article on the eve of the 2004 US presidential election harshly criticizing the foreign policy of the Bush Administration as an attempt to 'rule the whole world' by force; and asserting that the 21st century 'is not the American century.'[35] Whether Qian's article is an opportunistic move, an accidental misspeaking, or a sign of upcoming defiance and confrontation remains to be seen.

There are significant uncertainties between Beijing and Washington that may make the US–China relationship just another repeat of the tragic history of great power politics. While not unavoidable yet, a more confrontational cross-Pacific relationship will necessarily produce profound shocks and costs to the whole world, especially the Korean peninsula.

Cyclical US domestic politics may cause new ups and downs in US–PRC relations. Rhetoric critical of China, especially in the area of Beijing's human rights record is likely to continue and even increase as the second Bush Administration professes to actively promote freedom and democracy, 'seeking an end to tyranny in the world.'[36] To the dismay of Chinese political exiles as well as opposition groups like the Falun Gong, US ideological criticisms of Beijing are mainly for domestic consumption and are unlikely to lead to concrete actions against China beyond words. Given the more urgent, real US need for China's cooperation in fighting international terrorism and working on the North Korean nuclear issue, human rights and ideological differences, perpetuating as they indeed are, will take a back seat.

Out of all the uncertainties between the US and China, the most explosive problem has been the Taiwan issue. It is widely believed that the Taiwan issue is the single issue that could destroy the peace and prosperity of East Asia, and ruin Sino-US relations. Taiwan, a de facto independent entity that seeks a full or *de jure*

---

34 He Dalong, '9.11 hou guoji xingshi d zhongda bianhua' (Major changes in international situations after 9/11), *Shishi ziliao shouce* (Handbook on current affairs) Beijing, no. 4 (October 20, 2002), p. 12 and p. 15.

35 Qian Qichen, 'US Strategy Seriously Flawed', *China Daily*, Beijing, November 1, 2004.

36 George W. Bush, 'State of Union Address', February 5, 2005.

independence, is of core interest to China as it directly affects the CCP's political preservation, China's economic prosperity, national power, and prestige. No Chinese ruler, Communist or not, can afford to 'let Taiwan go' without the collapse of his own regime. Wary of the cost of 'swallowing' a democratic Taiwan, which will pose a great threat to the CCP's one-party political monopoly, Beijing is hence sincerely preferring the status quo to be stabilized with the nominal reunification of 'one country, two systems' for its own domestic consumption. But Beijing is nonetheless also preparing to fight a war with even the US to keep Taiwan within a 'one-China' framework. Regarding Taiwanese independence, one detects very little difference in attitude among the Chinese elite, street people and even political exiles, as they all appear to oppose it on the ground of nationalism, history, fairness or simply Chinese pride.

The US has officially recognized Taiwan as part of China through numerous official statements and three bilateral communiqués with the PRC since 1972. A skillful play of the Taiwan card has very effectively yielded considerable geopolitical benefits for Washington. However, a war between Beijing and Taipei is likely to draw the US into the fray as US law (The Taiwan Relations Act) mandates US action in response to Taiwan's security needs. To have a direct military confrontation between the US and China because of Taiwan would be one of the worst tragedies in modern international relations, with destruction beyond imagination. Mindful and fearful of that, the US has been cautiously walking a tightrope: Washington wants to preserve and utilize Taiwan as a strategic asset and promote it as a worthwhile cause, yet is careful not to end up fighting a Taiwanese independence war against China. And the PRC seems to view the US position well in its 2004 national defense white paper.[37]

Will Beijing trade the DPRK for Taiwan? Chinese officials and analysts seem to see the futility and danger of making such a connection. Nonetheless, from Beijing one frequently hears comments such as: 'Of course, the American strategy towards China (mainly on the Taiwan issue) strongly shapes the Chinese attitude (towards the Korean Peninsula).'[38]

Beijing and the Two Koreas

More than half-century after the Korean War, the major powers in the region, the US, China, Japan, and Russia, continue to hold the key to the political future of the Korean peninsula. Currently, China and the US have demonstrated a view that there is a shared interest in peace and stability in Northeast Asia through maintaining the status quo and pursuing denuclearization on the Korean peninsula. After 'joining the great powers' on how to deal with the nuclear ambition of the DPRK and on the

---

37 PRC State Council, 'Chinese National Defense in 2004', Beijing, December 2004.

38 Wang Yiwei, 'China's Role in Dealing with the North Korean Nuclear Issue', conference paper, July 2005, p. 3.

Korean unification issue in general in the 1990s,[39] the PRC has continued to play its happy role of hosting and participating in the six-party talks that seem to help to stabilize the situation. This position and role fits well Beijing's overall three-P diplomatic objectives as analyzed earlier. An analyst in Beijing gladly and candidly concluded:

> The future new international political order in Northeast Asia depends on the relations among the four major powers: the US, Japan, China, and Russia. The interests of the four major powers will affect the issue of Korean reunification. Korean reunification will be decided by inter-Korean factors under the influence of the political attitudes of the four major powers.[40]

Up to the mid-2000s, Beijing has continued its status quo Korea policy as 'a responsible great power,' in line with its overall foreign policy and reflecting the largely stable US–China relationship. China's views and policies towards Korea, according to foreign policy analysts in Beijing, 'have been nearly unanimous and consistent' for nearly two decades now.

Officially supporting an *independent* and *peaceful* reunification of Korea in principle, but unsure of the consequences of a Korean reunification and apprehensive about the possible negative impact associated with a likely continuation of US military forces in a united Korea, China has continued to advocate a 'balanced' policy that aims at the preservation of the status quo of political division on the Korean peninsula.

Being 'tricked into entering the Korean war' more than 50 years ago, the PRC harbors strong, though well-hidden, resentment and distrust towards Pyongyang. Beijing has felt deep frustration and constant irritation with its Pyongyang comrades, who not only failed to reform the North Korean economy, but have also attacked China's unorthodox reforms.[41] In recent years, the DPRK has created considerable thorny diplomatic problems for the PRC: repeated North Korean defectors seeking protection in Japanese and ROK diplomatic missions in the PRC have continuously put Beijing in an awkward position. There is also the costly problem of how to repatriate the significant number of North Korean refugees in China's Northeast that creates local problems and tensions with the South Koreans. Beijing is especially

---

39 Fei-Ling Wang, 'Joining the Major Powers for the Status Quo: China's Views and Policy on Korean Reunification', *Pacific Affairs*, vol. 72, no. 2 (Summer, 1999), pp. 167–185.

40 Guo Xuetang, 'Chaoxian bandao tongyi: wenti yu qianjing' (The reunification of the Korean peninsula: Issues and prospects), *Guoji guancha* (International observation), no. 5, (Beijing, May, 1996), pp. 26–29.

41 Wang Yiwei, 'China's Role in Dealing with the North Korean Nuclear Issue', conference paper, July, 2005, p. 7. Some senior CCP officials commented in private that the North Koreans are 'really a sham of socialism' because they have failed to pursue a Chinese or Vietnamese style reform, criticized the Chinese as 'revisionists', and become a group of 'socialist paupers.'

unhappy with the DPRK's playing with nuclear fire, since it not only threatens China's preference for peace and stability in Northeast Asia, but also may lead to a possible show-down with the US on the Korean peninsula that will directly affect the core of the PRC foreign policy objectives.

Unable to control or abandon Pyongyang, yet clearly unwilling to fight the US and its allies for the DPRK, Beijing is caught between two tough choices. The best way out is to muddle through by trying to preserve the status quo and prevent a showdown. Hence, Beijing continues its discrete but vital assistance to the DPRK for mainly geo-political reasons coated with humanitarian and ideological rhetoric. Energy and food from China are now literally a lifeline for Pyongyang, with Beijing supplying more than 70 per cent of oil to the starving DPRK. Beijing further insists that it 'has always maintained close contacts and cooperation' with the DPRK in just about every aspect of their relations.[42] When Chinese scholars published an article criticizing the North Koreans for their domestic polices and external adventures in September 2004 in the influential *Zhanlue yu guanli* (Strategy and management), Beijing ordered the issue to be recalled and banned the journal indefinitely. In the multilateral negotiations of the six-party talks, Beijing tries hard to be an honest broker between the US and the DPRK and an inconspicuous but consistent agent and spokesman for its North Korean comrades.

China's economic and cultural ties as well as the overall relationship with the ROK took off shortly after the two swapped full diplomatic recognition in 1992. Trade grew at an astonishing speed of 40 per cent annually in the 1990s.[43] By the mid-2000s, the PRC became the largest trade partner of South Korea. Sino-South Korean exchanges of students and cultural products have grown at a breath-taking pace to make the ROK a major source of education, cultural influence and even culinary fashions to millions of Chinese. Over 30 thousand Chinese students now study in the ROK while a similar number of ROK students are studying in the PRC. At the end of 2004, China opened a cultural center in Seoul, its sixth in the world and first in Asia.[44] Dozens of Korean companies now supply up to 70 per cent of the entire online electronic game market in China. One study reports that a Korean snack food, Chocopie, now takes about 40 per cent of China's pie market. A 'han-ryu' or fever for Korean culture products has been developing extensively in China. ROK-produced TV programs, movies, and music videos have become a cultural phenomenon in the PRC, so much so that Beijing has decided in 2004 to step up its regulation of Korean culture products to protect Chinese 'pride.'[45]

---

42 PRC Ministry of Foreign Affairs, New Release on DPRK, Beijing, October 23, 2004.

43 *Zhongguo Waijiao Gailang* (Survey of Chinese diplomacy) (Beijing: Shijie Zhishi Press, 1990–97).

44 Xinhua News Dispatch, Seoul, December 28, 2004.

45 Mary Han, 'Northeast Asia: A New Center of Culture', unpublished paper, Georgia Tech, Atlanta, December, 2004.

Nonetheless, distrust and undercurrents of problems between the PRC and the ROK exist and develop. Other than the periodical outcry over Beijing's handling of North Korean refugees and defectors that has often led to public burning of the PRC flags in Seoul, South Koreans seem to be developing strong nationalist sentiments against the Chinese. The recent PRC–ROK disputes over Chinese history books are a good illustration of the uncertainties and how Beijing typically reacts. In early 2004, South Koreans, interestingly joined by the North Koreans, protested strongly over a new Chinese textbook interpretation of history that claimed the history of ancient Korean kingdom of Koguryo (37 BC to 668 AD), which existed in part of today's Korean peninsula and part of China's Northeast region, was part of Chinese history.[46] Beijing, in its now familiar pattern of risk-averse and conflict-avoiding foreign policy, strictly controlled the Chinese media reports and public reactions to this inside the PRC and tried to silence the Koreans. A few months later, Beijing managed to reach a five-point agreement with Seoul to effectively shelve the dispute and exclude the Chinese claim from the PRC official teaching materials. This conciliatory act barely quieted the South Koreans,[47] but, very interestingly and simply not known to the Chinese, is very much in line with the PRC policy of keeping factual but sensitive information away from its own people. When two Chinese web sites published a story about the five-point agreement, they were reported to have been ordered to shut down by the PRC police.[48]

In addition to this possible 'turning point for China–Korea relations' that may signal a more competitive and sensitive era for the PRC and ROK,[49] uncertainties and new problems between them seem to have no end. On January 18, 2005, a Korean newspaper angrily called for a 'second look at China' and questioned Beijing's stated policy for peace and friendship.[50] Two days later, Beijing got another taste of Korean nationalism in the ROK. The Mayor of Seoul formally declared that it would change the Chinese name of Seoul city from Han-Cheng to Shou-Er and requested the Chinese to comply, so to erase the old name for the city and avoid confusions about the true nationality of the ROK capital.[51] This has already sparked negative responses from the Chinese, critical of South Koreans for their 'narrow nationalism,'[52]

---

46 Donald Kirk, 'Chinese History – a Cause that Unites the Two Koreas', *South China Morning Post*, February 28, 2004.

47 Seo Hyun-jin, 'Controversy Lingers despite Korea–China Agreement', *Korea Herald*, August 24, 2004. Ryu Jin 'China's no. 4 Man to Visit Seoul Thursday', *Korean Times*, August 25, 2005.

48 'PRC Closes Two Internet Sites Reporting PRC–ROC Agreement on Koguryo History', *China Times*, Taipei. August 30, 2004.

49 Scott Snyder, 'A Turning Point for China–Korea Relations?', *Comparative Connections* (third quarter, 2004).

50 Editorial, 'A Second Look at China', *Korea Herald*, Seoul, January 18, 2005.

51 Xinkuai Bao (News Express), Beijing, January 20, 2005. UPI, Seoul, January 20, 2005.

52 For example, see <http://fjt.todayisp.com:7751/www.xinjunshi.com/Article/wangyou/200501/5315.html>.

although, officially, Beijing has quietly and quickly accepted the change. The long, close and complicated relationship between China and the two Koreas, especially the economically confident South Korea, has always had a mixture of emotions and will continue to offer both great opportunities and consequential uncertainties for the Koreas and for the US in the years ahead.[53]

Chinese Objectives: No Unification and No Nukes

Currently, Beijing's dominant interest is in a peaceful and stable Korean peninsula, divided or unified, preferably divided. It is also strongly interested in seeing the Peninsula free of nuclear weapons.[54] To avoid the entanglement and shocks at a time when Beijing is worrying about its own political stability and desires an avoidance of conflict with the US, China is happy to play a passive, arguably indispensable, role in dealing with the North Korean nuclear program and the process of Korean reunification. While openly professing its preference that the Korean peninsula should remain nuclear-free, Beijing insists that the US should not use that issue to destroy the DPRK or cause a military confrontation in Northeast Asia. 'After all,' a PRC analyst wrote in mid-2005, 'DPRK's nuclear program imposes a threat to the US, not to China.'[55]

The PRC exhibits a clear ambivalence towards the unification of Korea: a unified Korea may create stability and peace on the Peninsula over the long run, and may eliminate the existence of external military and political forces in the region; a united and stronger Korea will likely serve as an important force countering Japan in East Asia – to constitute the new multipolar structure desired by Beijing; Korean reunification also echoes the similar desire China has with regard to Taiwan. However, Beijing has a strong sense of uncertainty and serious reservations about Korean reunification. A military alliance between a united and perhaps nationalistic Korea and the US clearly makes Beijing uncomfortable. Hence the following official statement by the PRC several years ago still holds true today:

> China takes maintaining peace and stability on the peninsula as the fundamental principle in its handling of Peninsula affairs ... China has dedicated itself to maintaining peace and stability there, endorsing the improvement of relations between the North and South of Korea and supporting an independent and peaceful reunification.[56]

---

53 Michael Yoo, 'China Seen from Korea: Four Thousand Years of Close Relationship', RIETI, Tokyo, May 8, 2003.

54 Nina Hachigian, 'China's Stake in a Non-nuclear Korea', *Christian Science Monitor*, February 17, 2005.

55 Wang Yiwei, 'China's Role in Dealing with the North Korean Nuclear Issue', conference paper, July 2005, p. 3.

56 PRF Foreign Ministry announcement, *Xinhua Daily Telegraph*, Beijing, December 9, 1997.

Practically, China is likely to continue its active role as a good host to the six-party talks aiming at control, if not resolution, of the Korean nuclear issue and tries hard to give it a good spin every time, as it did in the summer of 2005. It appears to be in Beijing's interest to exert more pressure on Pyongyang to have a realistic and timely peaceful end to the US–DPRK dispute over the North Korean nuclear ambition and secure the survival of the Pyongyang regime, as some analysts have reported,[57] before the US shifts its full attention to Northeast Asia after pulling out of the quick sand of Iraq. To have the whole weight of a freedom-promoting and tyranny-fighting US concentrate on its border area is not in the CCP's core interests. Thus, instead of just blaming the US for the deadlock of the six-party talks, Beijing now frequently uses 'the mistrust between the DPRK and the United States' as the official explanation.[58] The encouraging agreement reached by the six parties in September 2005 seemed to have a considerable amount to do with Beijing's efforts, even though its implementation is still an unresolved question. No nukes on the Korean peninsula is indeed a shared interest with the US; no unification of the Koreas and no confrontation with the US on the Korean peninsula seem to be Beijing's higher goals, in the name of stability and peace. For that, Beijing is learning from the US what its analysts called a 'dual strategy of coaxing and coercing' in carrying out its Korea policy.[59]

One PRC scholar candidly described the 'dilemma' Beijing now faces in dealing with the North Korean nuclear issue: it has strong concerns over the consequence of a nuclear Korea and beyond: 'China worries about Japan's nuclear capability more than North Korea's;' it also clearly opposes the use of force on the Korean peninsula by the US. Furthermore, Beijing is obviously not very happy with Pyongyang on many issues and acts, as few in China 'have good feelings towards North Korea,' and 'huge distrust exists between China and North Korea ... and North Korea will remain suspicious of China's intentions;' yet it earnestly wants to preserve the DPRK regime. In the final analysis, 'what China worries about the most is that the US will help Japan and Taiwan to build up theater missile defense (TMD) systems using the excuse of the North Korean nuclear threat.' Hence, Beijing worries about being 'used' by the US and seeks low-key effort first to maintain the status quo and then address the DPRK nuclear program peacefully, so as to escape from the dilemma and the 'American trap.'[60]

For its own gains of prestige and influence, Beijing has used the annual China–Japan–ROK summit meetings to create another mechanism to work on the regional issues, without the US and outside the six-party talks. In November, 2004, the

---

57 You Ji, 'Understanding China's North Korea Policy', *China Brief*, vol. 4, no. 5 (March, 2004).

58 Xinhua News Agency, 'Yearender, Mistrust Between DPRK and the US Snags Six-Party Talks', Beijing, December 18, 2004. In FBIS-CHI-2004-1218.

59 She He, 'Coaxing and Coercing in International Politics', *Guangming Ribao* (Guangming daily), Beijing, January 12, 2005.

60 Wang Yiwei, 'China's Role in Dealing with the North Korean Nuclear Issue', conference paper, July 2005, especially pp. 4, 5, 7.

PRC Premier Wen Jiabao met the Japanese Prime Minister Koizumi Junichiro and the ROK President Roh Moo-hyun in Vientiane, the sixth such trilateral summit, and pledged to work on peace and stability in Northeast Asia and on the Korean peninsula in a 'strategy on cooperation.'[61] The three countries also announced that they will join the 10-member Association of Southeast Asian Nations (ASEAN) to hold the first East Asian Summit in 2005.[62] It should be expected that Beijing will pursue further such regional efforts as a way to expand its emerging leadership.

There are obvious limits to how far a trilateral relationship in Northeast Asia can go. Beijing continues to watch attentively the US policy and action in the region, among which a key aspect is the US–ROK military alliance.[63] The recent redeployment of the US Forces in Korea (USFK) has been interpreted by some in Beijing as an innovative use of the US–ROK alliance that may have implications for Taiwan and elsewhere in the region. The popular belief, official announcements and actions in Tokyo treating China and the DPRK as the two major security threats to Japan, may have made Beijing ponder in considerable displeasure, and feel hurt for being viewed as the same as Pyongyang, an international outcast, by the Japanese.[64] The PRC Foreign Ministry Spokeswoman called the Japanese concerns hyped and objectionable, and in turn accused the Japanese of 'affronting China's sovereignty and territory integrity.'[65] In October of 2005, by paying his fifth homage to the controversial Yasukuni Shrine in so many years, Japanese Prime Minister Koizumi once again add ice to the already cold Sino-Nippon political relations.

As China grows stronger and more confident, especially when the need to preserve a CCP one-party regime becomes less pressing, Beijing may conceivably develop different views and policies. In practice, it may worry much less about the possible destablizing effect Korean reunification could produce. The key external factors that may change Beijing's views and policies remain to be the overall Sino-American relations and the status of China's own reunification with Taiwan. If Washington and Beijing are on good terms, China will be making satisfactory progress in its own reunification effort with Taiwan, the US–ROK military alliance will fade and even disappear as the Korean unification proceeds, the unified Korea will at least be neutral in the major power games in East Asia, and Beijing may throw in its weight to facilitate Korean unification. Otherwise, China is expected to simply continue to play a passive role and let the US do the heavy lifting through leading the international effort aimed at maintaining the status quo on the Korean peninsula. Beijing contributes to this effort by supporting the Kim Jong-Il regime in the North, and cultivating a good relationship with the South.

---

61 PRC Ministry of Foreign Affairs, Press Release, Beijing, November, 29, 2004.

62 Xinhua News Dispatch, Vientiane, November 29, 2004.

63 Wang Mian, 'A Reshapiing US–ROK Alliance', Xinhua News Agency, Beijing, December 19, 2004.

64 Xinhua News Agency Commentary, 'Who's Japan's New Defense Program Outline Intended to Defend Against?', Beijing, December 11, 2004.

65 Xinhua News Dispatch, Beijing, November 10, 2004.

The sine qua non seems to be still the US–China relationship that is greatly defined by the Taiwan issue. Other than what will transpire between Washington and Beijing in the various aspects of the bilateral relationship, especially on the handling of the Taiwan issue, a key seems to be what the US will do to the DPRK.[66] So long as Beijing worries about a US threat to its political stability and even its national security, China's support for Korean reunification is likely to be very limited. Beijing is anxious to see the DPRK on its own feet economically through a Chinese-style reform and proactive 'help' from the PRC.[67] Beijing may even militarily intervene (as some ROK analysts have speculated) to prevent a rapid reunification of Korea,[68] especially if the US military presence, as viewed by most observers, is to be continued on the peninsula beyond Korean reunification. It will be difficult for Beijing to accept a united Korea (most likely on the ROK terms) with a fully functioning US–ROK military alliance, while the US is viewed as a political and ideological challenger to Beijing, and an obstacle to China's own unification effort.

Focusing on its core strategic interests, the PRC also appears to be interested in some strategic reciprocation with the US regarding the Korean peninsula. If Washington is willing to help more on the preservation of the status quo in the Taiwan Strait, as it has been signaling since Spring of 2004, then Beijing shows willingness to work more with the US to pressure its comrades in Pyongyang concerning the DPRK nuclear programs, especially when it feels that the 'no nukes' and 'no unification' objectives on the Korean peninsula are in trouble. The trip by the US emissary Michael Green to Beijing in early February 2005 and 'the highly unusual meeting' he had with the PRC President Hu Jintao illustrates the development of a new round of the strategic game.[69] The resumption and the encouraging achievement of the six-party talks by fall of 2005 constituted another round of the continuation of the diplomatic game. The US has demonstrated some flexibility in dealing with the DPRK bilaterally on what really matters in the summer of 2005. And that seems to be in Beijing's interest. The denuclearization objective may indeed be achievable, while preserving the stability of the peninsula, if the six-party agreement of September 2005 can be implemented, a proposition that will certainly require more and continued cooperation from China.

---

66 Victor D. Cha, ' Korea's Place in the Axis', *Foreign Affairs*, vol. 81, no. 3 (May/June, 2002), pp. 79–92.

67 John Park, 'China Takes "Xiaokang" Approach to North Korea', *The Strait Times*, May 5, 2004.

68 For a report on the possible PRC military intervention in the Korean peninsula through 'taking over' North Korea, see Hamish McDonald, 'Beijing considers its Korean options', *The Age*, September 7, 2003.

69 David Sanger and William Broad, 'US Asking China to Press North Korea to End Its Nuclear Program', *The New York Times*, February 9, 2005.

Conclusion

Ever since the late-1990s, the PRC has managed to have a stable working relationship with the US, despite the existence of differences and uncertainties, as the central piece of its foreign policy that is motivated by the pursuit of political preservation, economic prosperity and national power. In Northeast Asia, Beijing has gingerly joined the US and other major powers in forming a 'consensus' to maintain peace and stability through the status quo on the Korean peninsula. This policy has sufficiently enabled the PRC, as analyzed by the Chinese, to keep its long-time official commitment to a Korean reunification while enjoying a stable, manageable, and profitable division of the Korean peninsula. As one senior policy analyst commented in private: with China's political 'skills' (*shouwan*), Beijing has managed to keep the Korean division while, among the four major external powers, enjoying 'the only good relationship' with both Seoul and Pyongyang. The six-party talks are welcome developments to Beijing, promising to further sustain the status quo thorough a protracted dialogue towards a final cross-recognition process and a peace treaty replacing the often shaky armistice agreement, thus institutionalizing stability on the Peninsula. The talks also allow Beijing to prove to Washington that there are real shared strategic interests between them regarding stability and denuclearization of the Korean peninsula.[70] The PRC is only glad to be viewed as a valued help to the US and continues to enjoy the best strategic position on the Korean peninsula among all major powers.

In the near future, in the same style as the overall Chinese foreign policy, Beijing is likely to leave the leadership and initiatives, as well as the burden, to the US, pro tempore. The agreement of principles reached at the six-party talks in September 2005 showed how Beijing can work to help resolving the DPRK nuclear issue. However, that decade-long PRC policy towards Korea could quickly change should the stable US–China relationship sour, become more uncertain or even enter a probable crisis over, chiefly, the dispute over Taiwan, or should Beijing fail in maintaining its domestic political stability.

The Korean peninsula has historically been a major playground and battlefield to the major powers; it now tests the future of China's foreign policy in close association with the all-important US–China relationship.[71] Beijing may conceivably trade the DPRK for Taiwan or for its own political survival; it may also think, as one Chinese posted on the Internet, 'the enemy of your enemy is your friend. Nobody likes North Korea, but we should support everyone who opposes the United States.'[72]

---

70 Doug Bandow, 'Enlisting China: The Battle for Nuclear Free Koreas', *National Review*, April 29, 2003.

71 Phillip C. Saunders and Jing-dong Yuan, 'Korea Crisis will Test Chinese Diplomacy', *The Asian Times*, January 8, 2003. Liu Aicheng, 'US Foreign Policy Tends to Be More Hardline', *Renmin Ribao* (People's daily), Beijing, November 11, 2004.

72 Keith Bradsher and James Brooke, 'Chinese News Media Critical of North Korea', *New York Times*, February 13, 2005.

In short, the key objective of China's policy towards the Korean peninsula appears to be outside the peninsula itself. To stabilize the Sino-American relationship and to avoid a showdown over the Taiwan issue remain to be the key, as that fulfills the peculiar three-P incentives that motivate the Chinese foreign policy today. For that, Beijing is now pursuing a shared interest with the US on the Korean peninsula. The Chinese policy is becoming more important as the latest developments seem to suggest that Beijing may have become the key player in the diplomatic efforts addressing Pyongyang's nuclear program and beyond.[73] To address a feared threat seemingly arising from a 'US–Japan–Taiwan bloc', China's policy for status quo and denuclearization of the Korean peninsula could make drastic changes, soon. Some leading Chinese scholars have already signaled this recently by predicting, 'Like it or not, the world will probably have to accept North Korea's nuclear status.'[74] Others have suggested the forthcoming Chinese acceptance of a South Korea-dominated Korean unification.[75] After all, the ties between the ROK and the PRC now are at their historical best and a nuclear Korea, or a nuclear North Korea, is unlikely to treat China as its main target anyway. In its grand games with Japan and, mainly, the US, Beijing wants to cultivate and could use any help. A friendly and stable Korean peninsula, expected to be increasingly more nationalistic towards Japan and the US, united and armed with nuclear weapons or not, may now increasingly appear to Beijing as a rather desirable future in Northeast Asia.

---

73 Michael Hirsh and Melinda Liu, 'North Korea Hold 'Em: Washington Used to Have Most of the Chips in Six-Party Talks over Pyongyang's Nuclear Program. But Beijing is the Key Player Now – for Better and Worse', *Newsweek*, October 5, 2005.

74 Shen Dingli, 'Accepting a Nuclear North Korea', *Far Eastern Economic Review* (March, 2005), p. 54.

75 Wang Yiwei, 'China's Role in Dealing with the North Korean Nuclear Issue', conference paper, July 2005, especially pp. 6–7.

Index

386-generation, 2, 40, 54, 88

9/11 terrorist attacks, 13, 41, 47, 58, 102, 114, 141, 142, 153, 156, 190, 193
9/19 joint statement of principles, 17, 20, 23, 25, 26, 28, 38, 58

ABM treaty, 142
Agreed Framework (Oct. 1994), 15, 50, 56, 118, 119, 142, 177
Albright, Madeline, 124
Anti-American sentiments, 1, 5, 6, 11, 42, 43, 51, 53–54, 104, 144
Anti-American protests, 54
Annan, Kofi, 35
APEC, 7, 12, 46, 92
Armitage, Richard, 57
ASEAN, 12, 61, 64, 65, 69, 70, 84, 87
ASEAN+4, 90
ASEAN+3, 92
Asian regionalism, 89–98
asymmetrical deterrence, 166
axis of evil, 4, 8, 41, 53, 144, 149, 155, 176, 191

Ban, Gi-moon, 22, 55, 105
Burns, Nicholas, 7
Bush, G. H., 3
Bush, George W., 1, 2–10, 21, 25, 26, 28, 38, 40, 46, 47, 48, 50, 51, 53, 54, 56, 59, 102–103, 112, 115, 116, 123–124, 137, 146, 193
    on HEU, 119–120
    State of the Union address, 3, 4, 8, 9, 41

Campbell, Charles C, 108
CBMs, 37, 108, 109, 111
CFC, 49, 113, 114, 129
Cha, Victor, 137
Chang Sung-taek, 127
Cheney, Richard, 122

China see People's Republic of China
    China, India, Russia alliance, 188
    goals vis-à-vis Korea, 198–201
    on North Korea's nuclear issue, 108
Clinton, Bill, 120, 124, 142, 175, 176
credibility, 169
Cold War, 1, 2, 13, 14, 39, 47, 94, 99, 103, 149
confidence building measures (CBMs), 22
crushing deaths of two Korean girls, 43
Cumings, Bruce, 43
CVID, 10, 13, 122, 136

Daguo, 187
Dallek, Robert, 48
Demilitarized Zone (DMZ), 30, 32, 33, 49
Democratic People's Republic of Korea (DPRK), 1, 3, 4, 6, 7, 9, 10, 13, 15, 17, 21, 22, 23, 26, 27, 36, 39, 40, 42, 50, 57, 125, 129, 139, 141, 144, 148, 160, 163, 172, 177, 179, 182, 201
    brinkmanship, 119, 124, 129, 137, 140, 145, 149, 160
    deterrence policy, 176–182
deterrence theory, 164–167
DeTrani, Joseph, 135
DPRK–Japan abduction issue, 9
DPRK–Soviet alliance (1961), 2

European Union, 17, 65, 188
extended deterrence, 166

FOTA, 100, 104, 110
four-party talks, 15, 17, 19, 20, 28–38
Future of the Alliance Policy Initiative talks, 49

Gaesung industrial complex, 52, 56, 103, 174, 175
Gallucci, Robert L., 120
GATT, 62

general deterrence, 165
Geneva Agreed Framework; *see* Agreed Framework
global posture review (GPR), 48, 49, 100, 103–105, 109, 110, 129
global war on terrorism, 1, 3, 41, 48, 58, 59, 121, 192
Goguryeo, 55
Grand National Party, 124

Harrison, Selig, 119
HEU, 13, 15, 19, 24, 27–28, 42, 56, 57, 114, 116, 118–121, 177–178
Hill, Chris, 7, 22, 23, 25, 53, 135
Hu Jintao, 189, 190, 201

IMF, 61, 76, 91
immediate deterrence, 165
inter-Korean basic agreement, 30–32
inter-Korean relations
　　defense ministers' talks, 30
inter-Korean military balance, 169–174
inter-Korean summit (June 2000), 1, 3, 4, 15, 18, 27, 28, 35, 42, 51, 58, 107, 114
International Atomic Energy Agency (IAEA), 10, 15, 18, 19, 22, 24, 27, 33, 56, 58, 118, 119

Japanese Self Defense Force, 106, 110
Jiang Zemin, 189
juche (self-reliance), 1, 142, 168
June 15 Joint Declaration (2000), 15, 28, 38, 52

Khan, A.Q., 121, 122
Kang sok-ju, 56, 116
Kelly, James, 5, 35, 42, 56, 116, 119–121
Kim Dae-jung, 3, 4, 15, 29, 35, 40–42, 50–52, 56, 107, 117, 146, 158–159, 171, 176
Kim Jong-il, 3, 6, 8, 15, 26, 28, 40, 43, 49, 51–53, 115, 117, 123, 126–129, 133, 140, 142, 150, 159, 168, 174, 175–176, 181, 184, 200
Kim Chong-nam, 127
Kim Kyong-hee, 127
Koizumi, Junichiro, 57, 93, 153, 200

Korean armistice agreement, 11, 15, 16, 17, 20, 31, 34, 37
Korean peace process, 1, 2, 6, 7, 8, 9, 11, 15, 16, 17, 21, 23, 33, 37, 38, 40, 53, 54, 55, 56, 76, 78, 85, 86, 87, 88, 94, 95, 96, 142, 152, 154, 155, 160, 167
Korean peace regime building process, 11, 16
Korean peace regime initiative, 16–20
Korean Peninsula Energy Development Organization (KEDO), 10, 19, 21, 22, 27, 179
Korean War, 2, 3, 13, 36, 37, 39, 45, 49, 50, 101, 135, 139, 141, 142, 147, 157, 163, 172, 174, 190

Lee Hoi-chang, 5, 42
light water reactors (LWR), 18, 21–28, 58

missile defense program, 110, 199
Morgan, Patrick, 170
MRL, 177

National Defense White Paper (2004), 194
National Security Council (ROK), 6, 45, 114
National Security Council, (US), 43, 111.
national security strategy (2002), 4, 12, 41, 48, 109, 114, 167, 183
NBC, 177
neo-conservatives, 2, 40, 47, 143, 144
Nodong missile, 172, 178, 179
Non-Proliferation Treaty (NPT), 10, 13, 15, 17, 19, 22, 23, 24, 27, 28, 33, 42, 56, 58, 179
nordpolitik, 146
North Korea *see* Democratic People's Republic of Korea
North Korean refugees in China, 195, 197
Northern Limit Line (NLL), 108

OPLAN (Operational Plan), 175

Park Chung Hee, 52, 140
People's Republic of China (PRC), 14, 16, 34, 38, 150
PKF, 99
PLA, 191
The Policy for Peace and Prosperity, 50, 56

Powell, Colin, 7, 46
PPP, 186
preemptive war, 1, 4, 16, 41, 42, 47, 49
The Proliferation Security Initiative (PSI), 50, 110, 137

QDR, 103, 107
Quick Reaction Force, 104, 105

rationality, 167
RC, 135, 44
Reagan, R., 3
Republic of Korea, 1, 15, 27, 39, 69, 73, 75, 99, 139, 163, 185
Rice, Condoleezza, 7, 9, 25, 46, 105, 177, 181, 191
RMA, 103
Roh Moo-hyun, 2, 5, 7, 11, 40, 42, 46, 50–51, 56, 124, 125, 130, 140–141, 145–146, 155–156, 158–159, 171, 200
ROK–China history dispute, 197
ROK Defense White Paper 2004, 101
Rumsfeld, Donald, 7, 48, 49, 54, 55
Russia, 14, 16, 17, 21, 25

Schwartz, Thomas A., 107
September 11 attacks, 37, 39, 53, 54, 58, 72, 82, 118, 155
Sherman, Wendy, 117
shouwan, 202
six party talks, 1, 8–13, 15–37, 57, 59, 116, 123, 129, 133–138, 148, 183, 186, 199, 213
    breakthrough, 133–136
smile diplomacy, 3
SOFA, 5, 43, 54
South Korea *see* Republic of Korea

sunshine policy, 50–51, 56, 114, 142, 158, 171, 174
    goals of, 29

Taepodong missile, 79, 83
Taiwan factor, 198–203
Taft-Katsura agreement (1905), 39
TCOG, 152,
TMD, 199

UNC, 33, 49
Ury party, 45
US policy options, 159–161
US–ROK alliance, 1, 2, 6, 11, 12, 39, 44, 48, 49, 55, 59, 99–113, 141, 144, 145, 156, 200
US–ROK frictions, 47–55
US–ROK–Japan trilateral cooperation, 158
US–ROK mutual defense treaty, *See*
US–ROK summit, 6, 7, 46, 157
US troop withdrawal from South Korea, 49
USFK, 1, 2, 33–34, 99–105, 110, 200

Weiji, 157
Wigi, 157
Wolforwitz, Paul, 108,
WMD (Weapons of Mass Destruction), 1, 17, 18–20, 31, 50, 102, 103, 107, 108, 110, 112–114, 117, 122, 134, 137, 147
WTO, 62, 76, 77, 92, 93, 97, 98

Yoon Young-Kwan, 6, 45
Youngsann garrison, 49

Zhao Huji, 126
Zoellick, Bob, 7, 97
Zhu Rongji, 110

For Product Safety Concerns and Information please contact our EU
representative GPSR@taylorandfrancis.com
Taylor & Francis Verlag GmbH, Kaufingerstraße 24, 80331 München, Germany

www.ingramcontent.com/pod-product-compliance
Lightning Source LLC
Chambersburg PA
CBHW071355290426
44108CB00014B/1558